*Education in New France*

# Education
# in New France

ROGER MAGNUSON

McGill-Queen's University Press
Montreal & Kingston • London • Buffalo

© McGill-Queen's University Press 1992
ISBN 0-7735-0907-0

Legal deposit third quarter 1992
Bibliothèque nationale du Québec

Printed in Canada on acid-free paper

This book has been published with the help of a grant
from the Social Science Federation of Canada, using
funds provided by the Social Sciences and Humanities
Research Council of Canada, and with funding from
the Faculty of Education and the Department of
Administration and Policy Studies of McGill University.

Excerpts from Roger Magnuson, "Jesuit Pedagogy and
the Wilderness Classroom in 17th-Century Canada,"
are published by permission of *Canadian Journal of
Native Education* 17, no. 1 (1990): 68–75.

Publication has also been supported by the Canada
Council through its block grant program.

**Canadian Cataloguing in Publication Data**

Magnuson, Roger
    Education in New France
    Includes bibiographical references and index.
    ISBN 0-7735-0907-0
    1. Education – Quebec (Province) – History –
17th century. 2. Education – Quebec (Province) –
History – 18th century. 3. Indians of North America –
Canada – Missions – History – 17th century. 4. Indians
of North America – Canada – Education – History –
17th century. I. Title.

LA418.04M34 1992    370'.971'09032    C92-090210-3

Typeset in Sabon 10.5/13 by
Caractéra production graphique inc., Quebec City

# Contents

# Tables

# *Preface*

No one can accuse historians of neglecting New France. The period has been and continues to be a source of fascination for researchers. Most aspects of New France life, from the political and economic to the social and religious, have been investigated and reported on, often with painstaking detail.

Education has been less well served. The problem is not that historians have ignored learning in seventeenth- and eighteenth-century Canada. In fact, there is a considerable literature on the subject, including articles, chapters, and monographs. What is lacking is a comprehensive treatment of learning in New France in all its forms. The only book-length work on education for the period is Amédée Gosselin's *L'instruction au Canada sous le régime français*, published in 1911. Though the study has much to commend it, Gosselin subscribes to a narrow definition of education, equating it with the activities of the institutional school. As a result, missionary instruction, apprenticeship training, and other forms of informal learning are neglected.

Education in early Canada could benefit from a fresh look and a broader treatment, one that draws on newer research and that subscribes to the view that the formal school was not the only source of teaching and learning. At the same time, such a work cannot be divorced from its cultural context, for education is ultimately a product of the social, political, and economic forces impinging upon it. In this respect, if schooling was a marginal activity in New France, it was because a knowledge of letters was not a condition for living and working in a pre-industrial society.

# *Introduction*

New France existed in the period in the seventeenth and eighteenth
centuries when a vast territory of North America was under French
influence or control. At its height, New France stretched from Acadia in the east to the Mississippi River basin in the west, from Hudson Bay in the north to Louisiana in the south. As a working colony,
the population of New France was concentrated in Canada, in the
area bordering the St Lawrence River between the towns of Quebec
and Montreal. In 1760, the colonial population numbered fewer
than sixty thousand souls.

In spite of its modest population, Canada possessed many of the
institutional trappings of a normal society, including government
offices, courts of law, stores, churches, hospitals, and schools, most
of which were located in the towns. Heading the colonial government was the governor, who was the king's representative in New
France, and the intendant, the colony's chief administrator. An attorney general, councillors, judges, and lesser officers completed the
administrative network. The Roman Catholic clergy, regular and
secular, male and female, were dominant in the social-welfare
domain, as they ran the schools and hospitals. New France also had
a military character, as witnessed by a string of forts strategically
placed between Louisbourg and Detroit. In addition, regular troops
from France were permanently stationed in the colony and were
seconded by the local militia, which included all able-bodied adult
males.

The distinctive feature of learning in New France was not its
modest provision or that it was a church affair; educational patterns
in France and Europe answered to the same general description.

Where New France departed from the mother country was in providing a measure of learning to two culturally disparate peoples: the principal religious communities – the Jesuits, the Sulpicians, the Ursulines, and the Congregation of Notre Dame – numbered both French and Indian children among their pupils. The prosecution of learning on two cultural fronts, however praiseworthy as a goal, put a strain on already thin human and material resources.

Education in New France was less an organized system than a loose collection of schools and other learning arrangements, for the line between formal and informal learning was frequently blurred. What education lacked in size and reach was balanced by diversity. Learning assumed many forms: it was a missionary struggling to explain abstract Christian doctrine in the local dialect to a restless group of Indians in their smoke-filled cabin; it was a colonial officer's son wrestling with Cicero's orations in the original Latin in the Jesuit college at Quebec; it was a rural youngster receiving a smattering of letters from a roving lay schoolmaster; it was a French girl being instructed in the arts of sewing and embroidery and the ways of social behaviour in a convent school; it was an adolescent apprentice acquiring the secrets of a trade at the foot of a master craftsman.

*Education in New France*

### CHAPTER ONE

# The Educational Legacy of France

That learning in New France bore a resemblance to that of the mother country should not surprise us. New France, as its name implies, was a political and cultural appendage of France. The colony looked to France for many of its educational ideas, practices, and resources, both human and material. The educational leadership, including most teachers, comprised religious persons who had been born, reared, and schooled in Europe. Similarly, the schools of New France were largely institutional transplants from abroad. In outlook and character, the Jesuit college at Quebec and the colony's *petites écoles*, or elementary schools, departed little from their European models. As in France, the apprenticeship system came to be the principal method of training skilled workers. And since the colony was without a printing press, teachers and schools were entirely dependent upon the mother country for their school-books and pedagogical guides.

Those who dispensed learning in the New World drew freely and unapologetically upon the educational traditions of France. When the explorer Samuel de Champlain strove to instruct his two adopted Montagnais girls in Christian knowledge and the arts of sewing, he unwittingly paid homage to the reigning notion of female learning in France. And when the Sulpician schoolmaster Antoine Forget arrived in Montreal in 1701, his educational baggage included the new pedagogy of Jean-Baptiste de La Salle, which he had acquired at the Christian Brothers' teacher-training seminary near Paris.

The preceding remarks are not intended to suggest that education in New France was a carbon copy of that in the mother country. It was not, for the exigencies of a frontier society would not allow it.

The existence of an Indian clientele, an inhospitable climate during a good part of the year, and a small and scattered colonial population, among other realities, forced changes in educational strategy and tactics. Still, there were persistent attempts to shape Canadian education in a Gallic mould. Thus, it behooves us to review the state of learning in seventeenth-century France in order to gain an understanding of the ideas and practices that crossed the ocean to serve as foundation blocks for educational developments in early Canada.

The seventeenth century was a period of educational progress in France, marked by the multiplication of schools and increased learning opportunities for children, particularly those from the lower classes. Much of the surge in educational activity throughout Europe had its origins in religious strife. The Protestant Reformation of the sixteenth century had rocked the institutional and doctrinal foundations of the Christian church, leaving in its wake a revolution in learning as well as in religion. When the Protestant leader Martin Luther boldly called on civil authorities to establish schools for the common people, his plea heralded a new era in education.

However, in France as elsewhere in seventeenth-century Europe, the extension of learning to the common folk was more promise than fulfilment. Most children continued to grow up without ever seeing the inside of a school, a situation that remained unchanged until the nineteenth century and the rise of public systems of education. On the other hand, the education reforms of the seventeenth century should not be written off as superficial and temporary. Measured against the context of time and place, they were substantive and permanent. Fundamental to the period was a deepening interest in learning, a growing sentiment in favour of extending the benefits of education to a wider public. The traditional view that education was the birthright of the few began to weaken before a society that had suddenly discovered poor children and girls. The century also witnessed basic changes in what was taught and how it was taught. Of importance is that French gradually dislodged Latin as the language of the lower schools, both as the medium of instruction and as a subject in its own right, with the result that the school ceased to resemble a foreign-language institution. As organized learning became more popular and schools and classes grew in size, there were pressures to reform teaching methods. Thus, the traditional mode of individual instruction began to give way to the class method of teaching. All was made possible by a healthy increase in the number of schools, many of them established by the emerging religious communities, which offered free instruction.

One thing that did not change during this period, and indeed may have been strengthened by events, was church control of education. The Catholic church and its representatives continued to establish, operate, finance, and staff schools. Indeed, until the French Revolution the state or civil authority bowed to the church at almost every educational turn and rarely took initiatives on its own. For the most part the monarchy kept its educational distance, content to issue the occasional directive on learning. For example, a royal proclamation of 1698 enjoined parents, guardians, and others responsible for the care and supervision of children to send them to parish schools until the age of fourteen to learn the principles of religion. This order, however, was directed mainly against those regions of France where Protestantism had gained a foothold.

In the seventeenth century, male and female religious teaching orders sprouted like mushrooms across the educational landscape of France. Among the most active in starting elementary schools were the Ursulines, the Congregation of Notre Dame, the Port-Royalists, the Piarists, and the Institute of the Brothers of the Christian Schools. At the same time, parish schools under the authority of the local clergy enjoyed a revival and supplemented the impressive efforts of the teaching orders. The century also witnessed an entirely new educational institution. Convinced that the key to good schools was competent teachers, Jean-Baptiste de La Salle, founder of the Christian Brothers, established in Rheims in 1685 what is often recognized as the West's first normal school, though the Jesuits and other groups had already made informal moves in that direction. The founding of a training facility for elementary-school teachers represented a disavowal of the prevailing principle that teaching was a haphazard occupation open to all comers, and offered the more reasoned view that those destined to govern the young ought to submit to a period of formal preparation. La Salle's pioneering gesture heralded the dawn of teaching as a profession and challenged the notion that the well-filled head alone was sufficient for good teaching.

Leading the way at the secondary-school level were the powerful Jesuits, who enjoyed a reputation as Catholic Europe's finest schoolmasters and whose graduates could be found in the highest councils of church and state. Joining the Jesuits at this educational level were the Fathers of the Oratory and the Port-Royalists. By 1629, the Oratorians had some 150 colleges across France, and in some towns their schools rivalled those of the Society of Jesus. The Oratorian college at Juilly, which in 1638 became a royal academy under the patronage of Louis XIII, was as highly esteemed as the Jesuit colleges of Clermont and Laflèche. The Port-Royalists maintained "little schools," so named because each one numbered fewer than fifty pupils, a teacher rarely having more than six or seven boys under his care. Sticklers for close supervision, the Port-Royalists believed that small schools were a happy compromise between tutorial instruction, which was socially restricting, and large classes, which were socially overwhelming. The schools of the Port-Royalists, which sprang from the controversial Jansenist movement within the Catholic church, were short-lived. The group was unable to cope with the doctrinal attacks of the powerful Jesuits, and its schools were suppressed by a royal decree in 1661, some fifteen years after their founding. Despite their short tenure, the Port-Royalists exerted a lasting influence on French education, mainly because of the literary outbursts of their followers.

The colleges of the Jesuits and the Oratorians received both day and boarding students, though the latter accounted for only a small proportion of the student population. Most students lived at home or in lodgings close to the school. This is to observe that the boarding school, as we know it, was still an infant institution in seventeenth-century France, not to come into its own until the rise of the *lycée* in the early nineteenth century.

As I mentioned earlier, seventeenth-century France was marked by an enlightened interest in the welfare of poor children. This concern for the lower rungs of society had its origins in the Catholic piety movement, itself an offshoot of the Counter-Reformation. At the centre of the mouvement was a desire to rescue poor children from the ill effects of a depressed and down-trodden existence. Out of this concern was born the *petite école*, the forerunner of the modern elementary school, in which the unfortunates of society were fed a diet of Christian morals, rudimentary letters, and practical instruction. To the modern eye this development may pass almost unnoticed, but it represented a revolutionary step in French education, since it implied that children other than Latin choirboys and those of gentle birth could profit from educational exposure. No less significant in its impact was the accompanying view that the school could play a social function – that there were moral and intellectual benefits to be derived from formal learning, for society as well as for the individual.

The education of poor children found its most devoted advocate in the schools of the Brothers of the Christian Schools, founded by La Salle in 1684. Convinced that ignorance was at the source of much that was evil in the world, La Salle strove to provide learning for poor boys, believing that families were too occupied with earning a living to attend to the learning needs of their children. The schools of the Christian Brothers grew rapidly in the following years, and on the eve of the French Revolution over a hundred were scattered across the land.

Along with poor children, girls were singled out for educational attention in seventeenth-century France. Before this time, girls as a class received no formal instruction. The likes of an Héloïse – a great lady who dazzled society with her high learning – was a brilliant exception and no more. Girls rarely strayed from the home, growing up in the presence of other females, from whom they learned the practical arts of homemaking. It is true that some girls of noble birth were shipped off to convents, but the education they received was moral and religious rather than literary, in keeping with the prescriptions of female learning laid down by St Jerome in the fourth century. Other well-born girls were exposed to a smattering of letters at the hands of governesses, though the results were often less than impressive. A critic of the day lamented, "It is shameful but common to see women of wit and manners unable to pronounce what they read."[1]

If seventeenth-century France came around to the view that females were deserving of educational attention, most authorities drew clear distinctions between the education of boys and that of girls. First, the tradition of educating the sexes separately continued unchanged, though widespread abuse of the principle occurred in some regions of the country – possibly by teachers in search of more pupils.[2] Second, the female mind was judged to be different from and less proficient than that of the male and thus to require a different cultivation. Few educators of the century were prepared to recommend an intellectual education for girls beyond that of simple letters; neither the place of women in society nor the times demanded it. As the principal role of women was in the realms of child-bearing and family management, it followed that a girl's education was of a practical bent, centred around instruction in domestic *savoir-faire* and rounded off by religious knowledge and elementary letters. Generally, the teaching of writing was not accorded the same priority in boys' and girls' schools. Writing was regarded as a manly skill, and not a few girls' schools withheld instruction in the forming of letters in the belief that it was both unnecessary and improper to female learning.

The most influential treatise on female learning for the period came from the pen of a thirty-six-year-old priest. In 1687, Abbé Fénelon wrote his *De l'éducation des filles*. Though the work is crammed with pedagogical suggestions far in advance of their time, it ultimately comes down on the side of the traditionalists in its prescriptions for female education. Highly critical of the woman who adorns herself with the ornaments of learning, Fénelon said that the best education for girls was that which recognized their future station in life – that of wife, mother, and homemaker. Like his contemporaries, he made few concessions to academic instruction for girls, suggesting that if they must learn a foreign language let it be Latin, since it was the language of the church and hence morally safe. Lest one think that Fénelon was alone in his beliefs about an education proper for girls, consider the experience of Madame de Maintenon. In 1686, the second wife of Louis XIV founded a boarding school at Saint Cyr for girls of noble bearing. Like Fénelon, she saw her task as that of preparing girls for the duties of motherhood, though she broached tradition by offering her charges a more academic education which included some classical learning. However, after several years she was to regret this innovation, pronouncing it a grievous mistake; she was moved to agree with others that nothing was as detestable as a learned lady, and retreated to the position that female learning ought not to compete with male learning.

Fénelon's notion of female learning went largely unchallenged before the nineteenth century. In 1728, the former rector of the University of Paris, Charles Rollin, established his reputation as a liberal educational thinker with the publication of *Traité des études*, in which he extolled the virtues of popular education and denounced as sterile the teaching methods then in use. However, he sided with Fénelon and others in maintaining that the female mind ought not to be burdened with the weight of intellectual knowledge, by which he meant humanistic learning. A simple fare of religion, manners, domestic arts, and elementary letters would, he said, suffice. Even Jean-Jacques Rousseau, who stood pedagogical theory on its head later in the eighteenth century, was remarkably conservative in his attitude toward female education. In his educational classic *Émile*, Sophie is destined to learn only those things that will enable her to fulfill her predetermined role in life – that of wife and companion to Émile and mother of his children.

Until the seventeenth century, almost all education was conducted in Latin, the undisputed language of religion and scholarship. The sixteenth-century French nobleman and scholar Montaigne captured the spirit of the age; he read and conversed in Latin before he knew a whit of French, later admitting "To me, Latin is, as it were, natural; I understand it better than French." The first thrusts of popular education provoked demands for a more realistic curriculum, one that was attuned to lay rather than clerical interests. A consequence of this development was the substitution of French for Latin in the lower schools. The schools founded by the rising religious communities, along with the parish schools, increasingly opted for French as the medium of instruction. The Christian Brothers were typical of those who directed their instruction to children of the common people, requiring their pupils to study French first and Latin afterward, rather than the other way around.

Although Latin remained firmly entrenched as the language of secondary and higher education in the seventeenth century, particularly in the Jesuit colleges, the vernacular scored some minor victories. The Oratorians and Port-Royalists made concessions to the national language by starting their students off in French before moving on to Latin. Few educators, however, were as bold in their arguments as Charles Rollin, who played on patriotic sympathies by calling for the teaching of French in the nation's higher schools and universities. He deemed it unbecoming for Frenchmen to abandon their mother tongue as they rose up the educational ladder; he recommended that the works of Pascal, Racine, and others be read and studied, and that Latin and Greek be approached through the medium of French.

The displacement of Latin by French in the lower schools facilitated learning among the ordinary folk, if only because the language of home and school were now one and the same. On the other hand, the transformation of the elementary school from a Latin to a French-language institution was a mixed blessing. Nourished on a diet of vernacular learning, elementary-school leavers were confronted with an educational cul-de-sac, as they were unable to qualify for secondary education, which continued to anchor its instruction in Latin. A social consequence was that the lower schools increasingly came to be identified with the interests of the common people, while secondary and higher education, steeped in classical learning, was regarded as the preserve of the middle and upper classes.

Fueling this social-class differentiation was the belief in ruling circles that the lower classes should not be overeducated, since this would threaten the equilibrium of society. That the masses not be educated beyond their station was a recurring theme in seventeenth- and eighteenth-century France. Despite being separated by a century and by a wide ideological breach, Cardinal Richelieu in the seventeenth century and the anticlerics Voltaire and La Chalotais in the eighteenth century were united in the belief that the extension of learning opportunities to the common people was fraught with danger. Even Rousseau, whose political and educational writings are the stuff of modern thought, remained very much the aristocrat in his social outlook, saying that the poor had no need of education.

While the shift from Latin to French was far and away the most fundamental reform in the elementary schools of seventeenth-century France, it was not the only curricular change. Writing gained recognition as one of the curricular mainstays of the lower schools. Until that time, reading and writing had been treated as discrete subjects; indeed, they were sometimes delegated to separate schools. Reading had the reputation of a literary subject, while writing was associated with a commercial tradition. When taught in the same school, writing often took a back seat to reading. In some instances it was not taught at all, owing to the incapacity of the teacher or the scarcity of paper and ink. It must be remembered that writing was taught less as a symbolic expression of thought than as a technical skill – the development of a fine hand. Since the Middle Ages, writing schools had existed to prepare scribes and clerks to keep accounts and records and to copy manuscripts. The neglect of the teaching of writing in the regular schools, whether as a technical skill or as a literary device, meant that pupils sometimes left school in a semi-literate condition, able to read but unable to express themselves in writing. The schools of the Christian Brothers did much to reduce the gap between reading and writing by according the latter full membership in the elementary-school curriculum. La Salle ordered his teachers to make sure that their pupils were as proficient in the forming of letters as in reading them.

By the end of the seventeenth century, the curriculum of the elementary school had settled into a more or less uniform pattern. French was the medium of instruction, and the basic course of study included reading, writing, arithmetic, and religion. Occasionally, some instruction in Latin was added in boys' schools. Sometimes instruction in the manual trades or domestic arts was thrown in to ensure that departing youngsters were not a burden on society – that they would not fall into habits of idleness and immorality. Then, as now, schools were expected to perform social and economic functions as well as intellectual and religious ones.

Unlike the lower schools, those at the secondary and higher level experienced no wholesale changes in curricular orientation, for society continued to believe in classical learning as the badge of the educated man. The Jesuits were the staunchest defenders of this tradition. They were the ultimate Latinists, and held no brief for the teaching of French. To the schoolmen of Loyola, Latin was a living language, and their colleges spared no effort in ensuring that students left with a spoken and written mastery of the ancient tongue. Their teaching was in Latin, and not even extra-curricular activities, for which the Jesuits had a flair, were exempted from the rule. Indeed, student debates and theatrical performances were normally presented in the language of Virgil. On the other hand, the Oratorians and Port-Royalists were more sympathetic to the vernacular. While their schools did not throw off the yoke of Latin, they did reduce its importance in the curriculum by elevating the place of French. Strongly influenced by Descartes, who wrote in French, they elected not to teach Latin straight off, as had been the tradition, but rather through the medium of French. Not until a student had achieved oral and written competence in his mother tongue was he permitted to tackle Latin and Greek. The eminent physicist and Port-Royalist Blaise Pascal facilitated the task of teachers by developing a phonetic method of teaching French.

While French secondary and higher education was firmly anchored in classical learning and was by instinct wary of modern knowledge, here and there new subject matter penetrated the school door. Not surprisingly, the Oratorians, as opposed to the more tradition-bound Jesuits, were more favourably disposed to modern studies. Their interest in the national language was matched and reinforced by a decision to include French history and geography in their teaching. They were also more receptive to the findings of the scientific revolution, which began in earnest in the seventeenth century, led by the work of Galileo in astronomy, Harvey in medicine, Descartes and Leibnitz in mathematics, and Newton in the physical sciences. Until then Aristotle had been the reigning authority in science in Christian Europe – a science centred in logic and reason and neglectful of experimentalism. The shift from thinking about science to investigating it was at the heart of the scientific revolution, a movement grounded in the techniques of the experimental method and the growing use of scientific apparatus. If traditional science had operated from the armchair rather than from the field or laboratory, one reason was that researchers had lacked the tools to carry out major experiments. The development of special instruments in the seventeenth century was one of the driving forces in the rise of modern science. Had Galileo not possessed the telescope, it is unlikely that he could have confirmed the theories of Copernicus.

On the whole, secondary and higher education in France was slow to respond to the awakening discoveries in science. The attachment to ancient learning was of such intensity as to insulate the schools against the curricular thrusts of the parvenu sciences. Though a number of Jesuit scholars distinguished themselves in various fields of scientific endeavour, in the final analysis, they made few curricular adjustments in their colleges, seeing in the new knowledge a threat to the supremacy of Aristotelian learning. Their suspicion of emerging knowledge included harsh attacks on the philosophy of Descartes, who, ironically, had been Jesuit educated. But because Descartes's philosophical and scientific ideas were couched in doubt and scepticism rather than in authority and tradition, they smacked of intellectual and spiritual heresy in the eyes of his former teachers. As a matter of fact, in 1670 the general of the Society of Jesus issued a condemnation of Cartesian philosophy, a position with which the University of Paris sided. The Fathers of the Oratory, on the other hand, were more sympathetic to the evolving sciences, finding curricular accommodation for the teaching of chemistry, physics, and anatomy in their colleges, as well as establishing well-equipped laboratories.

It is somewhat ironic that the Jesuits, the most tenacious opponents of new learning, should lead the way in the promotion of physical and aesthetic education. But there is no contradiction here: the Jesuits were simply reviving a tradition of physical culture which had flourished in ancient times, only to die out in the Middle Ages because of the Christian church's distaste for the body. In the manner of the ancients, the followers of Loyola never forgot that the ideal man was a man of action. Anticipating the British public schools of the nineteenth century, the Jesuit colleges saw educational value in extra-curricular activities, believing that competitive games, swimming, riding, fencing, and even dancing developed poise, discipline, and maturity in learners. The Jesuits even composed works – in Latin, of course – on gymnastics.

No one would hold up the seventeenth century as a golden age of pedagogy. While new instructional methods and approaches were not unknown, few of them found a permanent place in the schools. The true revolution in pedagogy had to await a later period, dating from the appearance of such influential figures as Rousseau, Froebel, and Pestalozzi. The absence of the recognition of childhood before the eighteenth century did much to prevent the emergence of a more enlightened approach to instruction. Children were generally regarded as miniature adults, and little thought was given to educating them as children. It rarely occurred to anyone that children had different learning needs, interests, and capacities. At the same time, the century favoured content over method; what was taught took precedence over how it was taught. Teaching methods were frequently crude and unimaginative, and children were called upon to absorb large amounts of information, as though their minds were bottomless receptacles. Despite the condemnations of Montaigne, Comenius, and other reformers, the schools steadfastly maintained their bookish character, and schoolmasters continued to rely on the pedagogical warhorses of drill and rote learning. Children who failed to respond properly were routinely subjected to blows, beatings, and other forms of physical punishment.

Still, the seventeenth century was not entirely lacking in pedagogical progress, as reflected in the rising popularity of the class method of teaching. Ever since the Renaissance, individualized instruction had been the preferred mode of teaching, from the highly personalized tutorial method favoured by Montaigne to the practice of individual recitation in the schools. But as schools and classes grew there was pressure to come up with a more efficient scheme of instruction. As a result, the time-consuming and extravagant method of individual instruction began to give way to the modern class approach, then known as simultaneous instruction, in which the teacher became less the hearer of individual lessons than the organizer of learning activities for the whole class. La Salle's schools did much to popularize simultaneous instruction. However, not all individual instruction went the way of the dinosaur. Tutorial instruction continued to enjoy a solid reputation long after, particularly among those in the higher classes, who regularly engaged tutors and governesses to instruct their children. But even in better homes tutorial arrangements usually stopped before the age of ten for boys, who were sent off to regular schools. Apparently, tutorial instruction was alive and well on the eve of the French Revolution, since Rousseau based his *Émile* on the principle in 1762.

The short-lived Port-Royalists were among the century's few schoolmen to introduce into their classes what might pass as modern teaching techniques. Belying their stern Jansenism, which was rooted in original sin and man's depravity, the Port-Royalists manifested a care and respect for children that was carried over to the classroom. Like Montaigne, they inveighed against the sterile bookishness of traditional learning and strove to adapt their instruction to coincide with the interests and abilities of the child. In the spirit of Comenius, they grounded their instruction in "sense learning," holding that meaningful learning begins with things and moves to words. Their schools also showed a nationalistic bent in preferring Descartes to Aristotle, drawing the wrath of the Jesuits along the way. In Cartesian fashion, they laid great stress on clarity, exactness, and understanding in their teaching. Unfortunately, the short life span of the schools of the Port-Royalists condemned some of their classroom techniques to oblivion.

The schools of the Christian Brothers, by dint of their number, reach, and appeal, set the tone and pattern of elementary-school instruction in France from the late seventeenth century. Aside from popularizing the class method of teaching and grouping children according to their abilities, La Salle's schools were not renowned for their enlightened pedagogy. If anything, their schools were depressing in atmosphere. La Salle himself possessed an almost morbid fear of noise, and insisted that instruction be conducted in near silence.

He also judged play, movement, and fun to be the work of the devil. Thus, his schools featured little of the happy chatter and commotion associated with the modern classroom, to the extent that communication between teachers and pupils was maintained with the aid of hand signals and whispers.

Plato's reference to Athenian schoolboys being "straightened with threats and beatings like a warped and twisted plank" is as valid a description of disciplinary practices in seventeenth-century Europe as in ancient Greece. The grim connection between instruction and chastisement persisted over the centuries because physical punishment was thought to motivate learners and to discourage misbehaviour. It also may be traced to poor learning conditions: ill-equipped classrooms, untrained teachers, and stilted curricula. While seventeenth-century France did not witness the disappearance of severe punishment in the schools, it did see its decline as educators went in search of more humane methods of correction. Few schoolmen went as far as to call for the outright abolition of corporal punishment, but an increasing number denounced its widespread and arbitrary use. La Salle, for example, did not ban physical punishment in his schools, but neither did he recommend it, describing beating as a humiliating act which tends to degrade the soul. Similarly, the Jesuits retained the use of corporal punishment, though they altered the procedures governing its employment. Not wishing to undermine teacher-student rapport, they chose to leave the administration of punishment to a corrector who was not a member of the order. As in other aspects of teaching and learning, the Port-Royalists were in advance of their contemporaries. In keeping with their indulgence toward children and their more relaxed pedagogy, they banned corporal punishment in their schools.

### CHAPTER TWO

# The Jesuits and
# the Wilderness School

In 1615, Samuel de Champlain, the acknowledged father of New France and an advocate of the policy of Frenchification of native peoples, brought four Recollet friars with him to Quebec. One of the four, Father Le Caron, promptly set off into the trackless Canadian wilderness in pursuit of Indian souls, thus setting in motion a pattern of missionary activity that would be replayed over and over in the years ahead. From that time forward, France's policy in the New World was based on religious as well as economic and territorial motives. The explorer and trader were joined by the missionary as agents of French imperialism.

Up to 1625, the Recollets had a monopoly on missionary activity in Canada. Their members worked the areas around Quebec, Trois-Rivières, and Tadoussac, while some lived among the Hurons to the west for a spell. Although the Recollets were, on the whole, sympathetically received by the native populations – perhaps because the Franciscans had no designs on their land – the fact remains that few Indians were converted to Christianity. The paucity of spiritual conquests may have been due to the Recollets themselves, who lacked the numbers and, it is sometimes alleged, did not possess the force of character to get the job done. A more likely explanation is that the Montagnais, Algonkins, Hurons, and others were not attracted to the white man's religion.

At any rate, by 1624 the Recollet mission was near collapse. Its source of funding had dried up and its numbers – never more than eight – were in decline. In an attempt to rescue the faltering enterprise, a call was sent to France for help. The appeal was answered by the formidable Society of Jesus, six of whose members sailed for

Canada in 1625. Among the six were Énemond Massé, who was returning to the New World, and Jean de Brébeuf, who became a heroic figure in Canadian missionary history. Clearly, things were looking up for the fledgling mission. The number of participants had doubled, and its work was shortly to receive the government's blessing. In 1627, Cardinal Richelieu awarded a commercial monopoly to the newly created Company of Hundred Associates. The company's charter stipulated that one of its goals was to instruct and civilize the Indians so that they might be converted to Christianity. Thus, the way seemed clear for a renewed missionary campaign. But it was not to be, at least for the moment. The year 1629 saw the English capture of Quebec and the expulsion of the Jesuits and Recollets from the continent. For the Jesuits, the return to France proved to be a blessing in disguise. The return of Quebec to France in 1632 raised the sticky question of which religious body would be awarded the Canadian plum. Both the Recollets and the Jesuits were keen to return to Canada, though the Capuchins were Richelieu's first choice. When they refused, he offered the assignment to the Jesuits. While no admirer of the followers of Loyola, the cardinal preferred them to the Recollets because of their stronger financial position and greater success in dealing with the Indians. As a result, the Jesuits returned to Canada in 1632 with a greatly strengthened hand and a monopoly in the missionary field.

One may wonder whether Richelieu acted wisely in granting the Jesuits exclusive missionary rights in the New World. To answer the question, it behooves us to ask what the requirements of the job were and whether the Society of Jesus was the appropriate choice. Were the *annonces classées* of a Parisian newspaper of the day to have advertised openings for missionary duty in Canada, it might have read something like this: "Male missionaries wanted to preach gospel to savages in exotic land with inhospitable climate. Candidates should have teaching experience and a gift for learning new languages. Those who fear for their personal safety need not apply."

If the Jesuits answered this fictitious announcement, it was because they believed themselves qualified for the task. After all, their missionary experience was extensive and impressive. No religious order had accumulated as many travel miles as the Society of Jesus. In 1541, scarcely a year after the order had won papal recognition,

Francis Xavier established a Christian mission in southern India, followed by another in Japan in 1549. Other members founded missions in Africa and South America later in the century. Long before their short-lived mission in Acadia in 1611, the Jesuits had laboured and died at the hands of the Indian. In 1565, three Spanish Jesuits endeavoured to convert the tribes of Florida, only to see one of their members killed. Their efforts to establish a mission in Virginia in 1570 ended in disaster when six of their number were killed by the Indians. As missionaries, the Jesuits had paid their dues.

Because the task of introducing Christianity to the Indians was ultimately an instructional activity, the choice of the Jesuits was an apt one. As we saw earlier, the order had been actively involved in education in Europe, operating as the intellectual shock troops of the Counter-Reformation. By the seventeenth century, the Jesuits were regarded as the premier schoolmasters of Catholic Europe, thanks to their excellence in the classroom and their administrative skills in founding and running schools. The Jesuit census of 1749 lists 845 schools under their authority, of which more than six hundred were secondary and higher schools. In 1599, the Society of Jesus published its famous *Ratio Studiorum*, or plan of studies. Designed as a pedagogical guide for teachers, it drew upon proven curricular and instructional practices. At first glance, the *Ratio* seems to have had little relevance to instructional activities in a wilderness empire, where the usual conditions of learning were nowhere to be seen. But the genius of the plan was not its rather formalistic framework and dry rules, it was its underlying spirit, which urged teachers to adapt their instruction to the character of the clientele and the demands of time and place. The ability of the Jesuits to modify their teaching to account for new circumstances proved to be one of their enduring strengths.

What distinguished the Society of Jesus from other religious orders, and what permitted it to build a network of schools in Europe and develop a far-flung missionary empire, was perhaps the quality and training of its members. The order's founder, Ignatius Loyola, initiated a tradition of recruiting persons of ability irrespective of class, subjecting them to a long and rigorous education and assigning them to different roles; hence, it is incorrect to speak of the prototype Jesuit, as critics have been wont to do. Rather, there were many types of Jesuits: the confessor to the high and well born; the hair-splitting logician satirized by Pascal in *The Provincial*

*Papers*; the Latin scholar teaching rhetoric in a boys' college somewhere in France; the missionary preaching the faith to native peoples in a distant land. The glue that bonded this diverse group was a blend of zeal and single-mindedness in striving to win souls for Roman Catholicism. It was probably this clarity of purpose, coupled with a militant determination – the Society of Jesus was founded by an ex-soldier and organized along military lines – to get the job done that best qualified the Jesuits for the Canadian campaign.

The replacement of the Recollets by the Jesuits in 1632 signalled a change in missionary policy. Like Champlain, the Recollets had been culturally aggressive, believing that the Indians should be civilized as well as Christianized.[1] The strategy of making Frenchmen of Indians as a prelude to conversion was not without logic, for the Recollets maintained that the cultural gap between Europeans and Indians was too wide to effect evangelization straight away. The basic problem was that the Indian value system, grounded in notions of freedom, egalitarianism, and government by consensus, was too far removed from European values. The Recollets reasoned that if the Indian could be induced to discard his own values in exchange for those underlying French language and custom, he would be more capable of grasping and accepting the arguments of Christianity.[2]

For their part, the Jesuits rejected the Recollet policy of cultural imposition, subscribing to the alternative view that the Indian could be turned into a Christian without the necessity of first turning him into a Frenchman.[3] The Jesuits were fond of saying that they had come to the New World to make Christians, not Europeans. Although they admitted that the Indians' beliefs and customs posed certain problems to their proselytizing efforts, they felt these were not insurmountable. In fact, the Jesuit strategy to pursue the evangelization campaign through the indigenous culture implied a margin of respect for Indian ways. Still, the Jesuit tolerance for aboriginal customs had its limits. The missionaries were uncompromising in their opposition to Indian religious beliefs, which they routinely dismissed as lies and superstitions.

If the Recollets and the Jesuits differed as to the role of the French language and conventions in the evangelization process, they also differed as to educational tactics, though both orders attached great importance to the part played by instruction in turning Indian hearts and minds toward Christianity. The Recollets endorsed an élitist and assimilative theory of instruction, as witnessed by the practice of singling out Indian boys for education in French language and culture. Some of the boys were sent to France to receive a thoroughly Gallic education. Others were placed in the Indian seminary near Quebec, which the Recollets opened in 1620, where boys were taught French letters along with Christian knowledge. Neither of the schemes produced lasting results. The seminary was abandoned after a year or so, and the Indian returnees from France invariably reverted to tribal ways.

The Jesuits advanced along a different educational path. Instead of attempting to divorce learners from their own culture, the Jesuits carried the educational attack to the Indians. Thus, the principal educational thrust was played out not in Quebec or Paris but in the hinterland, in the villages of the Indians. In deference to the aboriginal culture and committed to the strategy of instructing those earmarked for baptism and conversion, the Jesuits disregarded the teaching of French language and manners, and concentrated their efforts on instructing all comers in Christian doctrine and ritual through the medium of the local dialect. Indeed, not even the Indian seminary in Quebec, which the Jesuits reopened in 1636 on the same site as the Recollet school of the previous decade, subjected its pupils to French-language learning.

In the early years of the missionary campaign, the blackrobes, as the Jesuits were called by the Indians, devoted their attention to the principal tribes of the St Lawrence Valley – the Abenakis, the Algonkins, and the Montagnais in the east, and the Hurons in the west. By 1640, the Jesuit superior at Quebec had reason to be proud. Missions were in place in Huronia at the base of Georgian Bay, at Tadoussac where the Saguenay River empties into the St Lawrence, on Île Royale, and around the French outposts of Quebec and Trois-Rivières. However, a decade later Jesuit hopes were dealt a serious setback. The Huron mission, which represented the order's largest and most ambitious undertaking, had collapsed, a casualty of the Iroquois military victory over the Hurons. So complete was the Iroquois triumph that the Huron nation ceased to exist; its surviving members were forced to flee their homeland and to seek refuge among other tribes and the French.

In the wake of the demise of the Huron mission, Jesuit interest in the victorious Iroquois was revived. The Iroquois confederacy, then composed of five nations, occupied the territories south of Lake Ontario. The situation, however, did not bode well for an effective missionary campaign among the Iroquois. For one thing, a state of war had long existed between the Iroquois and the French, and attempts to mediate a lasting peace had proven futile; for another, the few missionary incursions into Iroquois country had ended in tragic fashion. The first Jesuit to enter Iroquois country was Isaac Jogues, who came not of his own accord but as a captured prisoner of the Mohawks in 1642, later to be released to the Dutch. In 1646, Jogues returned to the area with the intention of establishing a mission, only to be tortured and killed by the Mohawks.

Improved political conditions in 1653 led to the signing of a peace treaty between the French and the Iroquois confederacy, which opened the door to the establishment of field missions in the territories of the French's traditional enemy. While the Jesuits established five missions in the succeeding years, few converts were won. It would be easy to blame this poor showing on the volatile political situation, broken treaties, and periodic outbreaks of hostilities between the French and the Iroquois, but it is doubtful whether a more peaceful climate would have yielded a different result. The main obstruction to the spread of Christianity among the Iroquois, as among other tribes, was not political and military but cultural and spiritual. The Christian religion, with its sophisticated doctrines and rituals, held little attraction for those whose beliefs and traditions were rooted in simpler truths.

The period also witnessed missionary expansion beyond Huron country. In 1641, an Ottawa mission was established at Sault Ste Marie, which served as the gateway to the western tribes around Lake Michigan and Lake Superior. From the Sault mission and, later, the St Ignace mission to the south, missionary-explorers the likes of Marquette, Allouez, and Ménard branched out in southerly and westerly directions. However, by the late seventeenth century missionary activity in New France began to decline owing to changing political and religious conditions. Fewer missions were established, and existing ones struggled to maintain themselves. The affairs of New France were increasingly directed toward secular matters, with the result that spiritual concerns were assigned a lower priority in the scheme of things. At the same time, the religious fervour generated by the Catholic Reformation lost its momentum, resulting in diminished moral and financial support for the Canadian missions.

In addition, the successors to Brébeuf, Jogues, and others were not only fewer in number but diminished in zeal. Yet even in its reduced state missionary activity continued unabated throughout the eighteenth century with the unwavering goal of winning souls for Christianity.

Viewed overall, the missionary campaign waged by the Jesuits in seventeenth- and eighteenth-century New France enjoyed only limited success. The mass conversions anticipated by Brébeuf and others were never realized. Furthermore, the converted often numbered marginal persons of the tribe, for the count of Indian baptisms reported annually by the Jesuits in their *Relations* included a high percentage of children, the sick, and the dying. The number of healthy adult members who accepted Christianity after a period of instruction was disappointingly small, and even here there are grounds for suspicion. The Recollet Hennepin said that some Indians agreed to instruction and baptism not out of conviction, but to curry favour with the missionaries in the hope of receiving gifts from them.[4]

There is no lack of reasons purporting to explain the spotty religious record of the missionaries. The historian Parkman suggested that Iroquois arms rather than Jesuit methods were responsible for the modest success of the missionaries among the Hurons.[5] Others have suggested that the spiritual efforts of the Jesuits were compromised by the epidemics that ravaged the Indian villages. Since smallpox, measles, and other contagious diseases were unknown among the Indians before the coming of the Europeans, it is believed that they were part of the social baggage of the white man. The Indians were defenceless against the dreaded infections, and quite naturally came to associate the spread of disease with Christianity. It is estimated that one-half of the Huron population was carried off by a contagious disease just after a permanent Jesuit mission was established in Huronia.[6] Still others attributed the spiritual setbacks to the flourishing liquor trade. A missionary at Tadoussac expressed a widespread belief when he declared, "All who know the savages admit that an Angel can be made from a Barbarian, if intoxicating liquor can be kept from him."[7] The Recollet missionary Chrestien Le Clercq, who laboured among the Micmacs from 1675, claimed that drunkenness was one of the most powerful obstacles to the conversion of the Indians. Despite persistent attempts by religious leaders to curtail trafficking in liquor, brandy remained a staple of trade between Indians and Europeans throughout the French period in Canada.[8]

Although war, disease, and drink made the task of the Jesuits and others more difficult, they were irritants rather than determining factors in the missionary campaign. It was the tenacious attitude of the native populations, more than any other factor, that compromised the efforts of the missionaries. The Indians were prepared to accept the methods and articles of European technology, but were far less ready to embrace European ideas and conventions. They were strongly attached to their own values and social arrangements, and the principles of civilized life held little attraction or meaning for them, living as they were in a wilderness environment. Still, the missionaries were not deterred in their quest for Indian souls, though they were aware of the challenge posed by a radically different culture and the aboriginal peoples' natural antipathy to the white man's religion. They could not forget that the Indian, even in his barbaric state, was a human being in possession of a soul and thus deserving of God's grace.

The vast differences separating European and Indian culture were not easily bridged. The Indians had no written language, and their spoken language had little in common with European tongues; their religion was indistinct and lacked the formal and structured trappings of Christianity; their notion of child rearing, anchored in parental indulgence and permissiveness, stood in sharp contrast to the hard regime of the French child; and their concept of learning made no provision for instruction in a formal institution. In an attempt to close the gap between the two cultures, the Jesuits apprised themselves of the tribal dialects and customs, for they realized that unless they could gain insight into the Indian pattern of thought, evangelization attempts were unlikely to succeed.

It was clear to the missionaries that the successful prosecution of the religious campaign required a knowledge of the Indian tongues, without which no effective communication was possible. Since the Indians were without a written language, the spoken word counted for much in their way of life. Paul Le Jeune, the first Jesuit superior at Quebec, observed, "There is no place in the world where Rhetoric is more powerful than in Canada."[9] As in ancient Rome, the person who spoke well was as highly esteemed as the warrior, and exercised a strong influence on tribal policy. Major tribal decisions touching on war or trade were taken only after much public debate and speechmaking. The importance of being able to speak the Indian dialects was not lost on Le Jeune, who said, "If we could make speeches as they do, and if we were present in their assemblies, I believe we could accomplish much there."[10] He was convinced that language acquisition was the key to the evangelization campaign, noting that the Indians were not averse to new ideas if they were soundly argued and simply put. Rare, however, was the missionary who achieved a level of fluency in one of the dialects sufficient to allow him to participate in tribal affairs.[11] For most, a working knowledge of the language was the best that could be hoped for, which explains the appeals from Canadian missionaries to their provincial in France for religious workers with a gift for languages.

The critical importance of language in the missionary campaign imposed a routine on the newly arrived religious to Canada assigned to work among the Indians. He began by immersing himself in one of the local tongues, usually Huron, Algonkin, or Montagnais. Ironically, the Jesuit came to the New World as a seasoned teacher and scholar, only to begin as a language student.

Until such time as the missionary was able to function in the Indian dialect, he had to rely on the services of interpreters or fall back on sign language. The interpreters were either lay Frenchmen who had lived among the Indians or Indians who had spent some time in France. Though interpreters were essential in the early years of the missionary campaign, they had trouble attempting to bridge the language gap between missionaries and Indians. They frequently struggled to find the appropriate word or expression in an impoverished Indian dialect to match the richness of the French vocabulary. The Jesuit Biard tells of the interpreter Monsieur de Biancourt who, "as soon as we begin to talk about God ... feels as Moses did – his mind is bewildered, his throat dry, his tongue tied."[12] Moreover, sign language and gesticulations had their limitations; they sufficed in meeting daily situations, but they were of little use in communicating the abstracts truths of Christianity.

The business of learning an Indian dialect was a time-consuming, frustrating, and humbling experience. Jesuit missionaries, who in their own land had won praise and respect for their learning, were reduced to stuttering pupils before the elusive aboriginal tongues. Brébeuf, who was known for his remarkable command of the Huron language, admitted, "You will have accomplished much, if, at the end of a considerable time, you begin to stammer a little."[13] No one knew this better than Noël Chabanel, who came to Canada in 1643 after having been a successful teacher of rhetoric in France. His inability to grasp the Huron language, combined with his repulsion for Indian ways, left him a broken figure. In 1650, he died at the hands of an Indian. If Chabanel's fate was not representative of the missionaries, his linguistic problems were. Le Jeune, who spent a difficult and sickly winter travelling with the Montagnais in 1634 in order to learn their language, wrote his provincial in France that the Indian dialect had eluded him because of a "defective memory" and the machinations of the tribal sorcerer.[14] The missionaries' struggle to learn the Indian languages was not made any easier by their hosts, who were reluctant to offer themselves as tutors and sometimes made sport of the Europeans' efforts to master their dialects. The Jesuits reported being ridiculed into silence when they could not express themselves clearly in the native tongue. Nor were the Indians above substituting indecent phrases for pious ones and then having a good laugh at the expense of the unsuspecting missionary who used them in his preaching.

Viewed from a different angle, the task of learning the Indian language should have been old hat to the Jesuits, what with their experience with multilingual education. As products of the European school they had learned to read, write, speak, and pray in a language that was not their mother tongue. Besides knowing French and Latin, they often had a facility in Greek and Hebrew as well. On the other hand, the Indian dialects presented problems of a different order and magnitude. Not only did the missionaries have to deal with languages that departed radically from their own in structure, grammar, and vocabulary, they had to effect a radical adjustment in their manner of speaking. Living among the Montagnais in 1625, Brébeuf noticed that in speaking the Indians did not use their lips or mouths as did the French. Rather, they spoke in a guttural fashion, giving the impression that their words originated in the stomach.[15] Another problem was that the Indian dialects could not be acquired through the written form, as was the case with Latin and Greek. When Brébeuf first settled among the Hurons, in 1626, his only written source of their language was a small dictionary prepared by two Recollets several years earlier. To assist others in the formidable task of learning the aboriginal tongue, Brébeuf spent long hours composing grammars and dictionaries in the Huron language. Perhaps his finest achievement was that of translating Ledesma's catechism from Latin into Huron, which served as a standard text for future missionaries.

The missionary who, after a considerable length of time, achieved a working knowledge of the native dialect was confronted by yet another linguistic obstacle – the impoverished character of his adopted language. It is sometimes said that language is a symbolic representation of a people's notion of reality. For the tribes of early Canada, reality had what might be described as a Lockeian base, since it was fixed on the sights and sounds of everyday life. The Indian vocabulary was essentially limited to words and expressions denoting material or physical reality and contained few words that expressed ideas or concepts, which means that it was a flawed instrument for communicating the abstract notions of Christianity. The missionaries labouring among the Hurons were stopped in their spiritual tracks by a dialect that had no meaningful word for god or supreme being.

Another stumbling block in the missionary campaign was the Indians' own set of religious beliefs. Although the missionaries acknowledged that the native peoples practised a religion of sorts, they were quick to condemn it as superficial and embedded in falsehoods. The Jesuits, at least initially, misjudged the importance of religion in Huron life, wrongly assuming that since tribal beliefs were not grounded in formal theology they did not penetrate deeply into the culture. The eventual realization that the indigenous religion reached into every facet of tribal life served only to complicate the efforts of the missionaires. What had first been perceived as solely a spiritual problem was later recognized as a cultural one. Thus, because they attempted to discredit tribal religious beliefs, missionary actions were often interpreted by the Hurons as attacks on their way of life.

Since tribal religions lacked an explicit theology, it is perhaps easier to say what they were not than what they were. The Huron religion, for example, had no institutional church or priesthood, though shamans and others performed religion-like functions. However, these medicine men were pale images of Christian priests, since their pronouncements carried little authority. Indeed, even tribal chiefs tended to rule by consensus and persuasion rather than by coercion; in the spiritual domain as in other areas of Huron life, a fierce tradition of freedom operated. Le Jeune noted, "There is nothing so difficult as to control as the tribes of America ... they are

born, live, and die in a liberty without restraint."[16] The Indian love
of freedom posed a serious problem for the missionaries since it
clashed with the Christian concept of obedience, which presumed a
hierarchical society in which the individual bowed to a higher
authority, including God, his priestly representatives on earth, king,
and family.[17]

Befitting a primitive people, the Indians practised a nature worship that recalls the religion of ancient Japan. Reverence was paid to
those forces or spirits in nature which evoked awe and wonder, such
as sky, water, and trees. The principal doctrines of Roman Catholicism – grace, baptism, and salvation – had no equivalents in the
aboriginal belief systems. On the other hand, while tribal religious
beliefs were more general than specific, more natural than super-
natural, there were some parallels with Christianity. The Jesuits were
encouraged to discover that some tribes believed in the immortality
of souls, worshipped spirits, and participated in prayer. The central
issue was whether the missionaries, armed with imperfect linguistic
weapons, could implant in the incurious mind of the Indian the
abstract tenets of Christianity. At the same time, they wondered
whether the Indian's language and turn of mind were such as to
enable him to grasp the sophisticated notions of the European religion. If the tribal peoples expressed bewilderment with and indifference to Christian doctrine, they could be excused. The mysteries
of the faith were sometimes inscrutable to Christian minds as well.
It cannot be forgotten that it had taken centuries and the church's
best minds to settle on official doctrine.

The missionaries also had to compete against Indian dreams,
which one Jesuit labelled "the God of the country" and which he
said could "undo more in one night than you will have accomplished
in thirty days."[18] Both the Hurons and the Iroquois put great stock
in dreams, interpreting them as messages from the spirits to take a
particular course of action. The missionaries were not distrustful of
dreams as such, for they were also a part of the Christian experience.
Rather, they condemned the Indians' uncritical acceptance of
dreams, their failure to subject them to rigorous evaluation.

Indian child-rearing practices, anchored in parental indulgence,
little punishment, and much freedom, also caused problems for the
missionaries, if only because they stood in stark contrast to the European notion of childhood and upbringing. Le Jeune wrote, "Savages
love their children above all things. They are like Monkeys – they

choke them by embracing them too closely."[19] From the time they were weaned, noted the historian Charlevoix, Indian children grew up in complete liberty, free of all parental restraint.[20] Indians held that nature and experience were life's greatest teachers, that children could best grow and develop if left to their own devices – a view which, incidentally, became the linchpin of Jean-Jacques Rousseau's educational philosophy. Thus, Indian children were free to go naked if that suited them, to wallow in mud and dirt, to run and jump to their heart's content, all of which prepared them for the rigours of life in a wilderness environment.

This permissive regime clashed with the European notion of upbringing, which saw the man in the child and which regarded childhood as a period of preparation, obedience, and discipline, often of a harsh character. Indian indulgence toward children both puzzled and surprised the missionaries. The same Indian who visited unspeakable torture on a captured prisoner could not bring himself to lay a hand on a misbehaving child, and, what is more, was reproachful of anyone who did. Charlevoix admitted that he never saw an Indian parent so much as threaten his child, adding that the severest form of punishment he witnessed was the splashing of a little water in a child's face.[21] The Jesuit explorer and missionary Joseph-François Lafitau explained that if gentleness and indulgence were preferred to scoldings and beatings it was because the Indians believed that children were lacking in reason and judgment and thus could not be blamed for their wrongdoings.[22]

The Indian notion of upbringing also collided with the European approach to learning, which held that the schoolmaster who taught without severity was failing in his responsibility. In defence of the Jesuits, it must be pointed out that they did not fully subscribe to this tradition, maintaining that harsh punishment was detrimental to effective instruction. The Indian conception of child rearing frustrated the efforts of the missionaries, who presumed disciplined and docile learners. But the Jesuits were to discover that learning and coercion did not mix in the wilderness classroom – Indian children subjected to European methods of correction, however mild, often rebelled. At the same time, Indian parents, because of their love for their children coupled with the fear that they would be maltreated by the French, were sometimes reluctant to release them to the missionaries for care and instruction.

The foregoing is not intended to suggest that all deliberate instruction was absent among the tribes of early Canada. To be sure, there were no schools as we understand the term. The European idea of a formal institution designed to transmit discrete subject matter to a group of children had no parallel in a society without a written tradition and which did not distinguish between living and learning. On the other hand, an attempt was made to instill in children a knowledge of the customs and ways of the tribe, though the approaches used were informal and rooted in example and experience. Among the Hurons, as in other tribal societies, a differentiation of sex roles was respected, which meant that boys and girls learned different skills. As future providers and warriors, Huron boys were taught the skills of hunting, trapping, fishing, and fighting. As future wives and mothers, girls learned how to cook, make and mend clothes, gather firewood, and care for children. Since women were also the farmers of the tribe, Huron girls learned to plant and harvest crops. The sexes were also taught acceptable patterns of behaviour and morality. Boys were brought up to show courage in the face of danger, to tolerate extreme privation, and to endure pain and hardship without complaint. Girls were reared to be modest, taciturn, and reserved, especially in the presence of males, and to be gentle and loving toward children. Mental learning was not neglected. In a culture in which the spoken word was paramount and memories constituted the chief repository of knowledge, speech and memory training was stressed. Both sexes were put to work reciting and memorizing the stories and legends of the tribe so that they might be preserved for posterity. As public life in Huron society was predominantly a male domain, boys were encouraged to imitate the mannerisms of the tribe's best orators.[23]

Of all field missions in seventeenth-century Canada, that of Huronia was by far the largest, to judge by the number of personnel committed and the resources poured into it. In 1634, Fathers Brébeuf, Daniel, and Davost set out from Quebec to Huron country, a collection of twenty or more villages at the base of Georgian Bay. The three missionaries represented the advance guard of a Jesuit contingent whose objective was to put the Huron mission on a permanent footing. For Brébeuf, it was a return voyage and a renewal of acquaintances. Between 1626 and 1629 he had lived among the Hurons, during which time he had acquired a fluency in the local dialect and gained an appreciation of Indian ways. The Huron mission was to become in the years ahead, until its collapse at mid-century, the jewel of the Jesuit missionary campaign in Canada. As it was centrally located, it also served as the gateway to the western missions. At its height, in 1649, the Huron mission engaged the services of twenty-two Jesuits and forty-two support personnel for an estimated Huron population of between ten and fifteen thousand.[24]

The decision of the Jesuits to centre their evangelization campaign in Huronia was dictated by several factors. Of all the native peoples in the St Lawrence Valley, the Hurons seemed to offer the best hope for conversion. They were the least nomadic, owing to their agricultural tendencies, generally friendly, and economically linked with the French in the fur trade. Thus, it was in the Huron mission that the missionary campaign found its fullest expression, for which there is much documentary evidence. The various superiors of the mission, from Jean de Brébeuf in 1635 to Paul Ragueneau in 1650, contributed annual reports to the society's *Relations*. Though the reports were edited to satisfy the order's propaganda efforts in France, they remain a vivid record of missionary life in seventeenth-century Canada.

The reports of Jérôme Lalemant from Huronia around 1640 constitute a personal, though not unrepresentative, account of the missionaries at work, their teaching and preaching activities, and the trials of living among the Indians.[25] Like his fellow Jesuits, Lalemant was French born and educated and had held various teaching and administrative positions in France prior to coming to the New World. Arriving in Canada in 1638 at the age of forty-five, he promptly set off for Huronia, where he was to succeed the celebrated Brébeuf as superior of the western missions. Lalemant is closely identified with the construction of Sainte-Marie-among-the-Hurons, the central mission and headquarters of the Jesuits in Huronia, which included residences, chapels, and even a blacksmith's shop. When he assumed his administrative duties in the summer of 1638, Lalemant joined seven other missionaries and a handful of lay workers. As was the practice in Huron country, he was given an Indian name, since his hosts claimed they could not pronounce French names.

Lalemant was surprised to discover that in most respects the missionaries had adopted the Huron way of life. They ate and slept in the Indian manner, survived on a bland diet of corn and fish, and their beds were no more than a mat or piece of bark on the floor of a draughty cabin. On the other hand, the missionaries insisted on living in their own cabins and on wearing the cassock. The decision to live apart from the Indians was not peculiar to the Jesuits. The Recollet Le Caron, who founded the first Huron mission in 1615, had declined the tribe's offer to share its cabins, finding the wails of children and the immoral behaviour of adults too much to bear. Similarly, the Jesuit habit of taking separate living quarters, which some members of the tribe interpreted as a social snub, was rooted in the missionaries' repulsion by what they regarded as lewd behaviour by the Indians. The Jesuit sense of propriety, nurtured by the moral strictures of the Catholic Reformation, was offended by the sight of near-naked women and children and by promiscuous behaviour by young adults before marriage. Indeed, some missionaries could not bring themselves to undress in the presence of Huron men. François du Peron wrote to his brother from Huronia in 1639, "Since I left France I have not taken off my gown, except to change my linen."[26]

In reading Lalemant's reports from Huronia, it is difficult to imagine a more stressful occupation than that of teaching and preaching among the Indians. Not even a carefully edited *Relation* can disguise the psychological traumas suffered by Lalemant and his fellow missionaries in coping with the pressures of labouring among the Indians for a sustained period of time.[27] Lalemant's testimony is not that of a saint or visionary, but that of a man of flesh and blood who is quick to admit that fear and frustration are constant companions. He writes of a hostile land and climate, of a people unresponsive to the arguments of the missionaries, and of the ever present danger of an attack by the feared Iroquois. He describes a society in which life is cheap, in which the sick are neglected and sometimes abandoned, and in which food, when available, is monotonous and hard on the digestive system. Lalemant adds that the missionary must be prepared to suffer every sort of personal indignity, that it is not unusual to see snowballs, cornstalks and other missiles flying over one's head when one is preaching the word of God. He says also that the missionaries are frequently blamed for the misfortunes of the tribe, from a poor crop to an infectious disease. At one point Lalemant offers that a hatchet blow upon the head would be preferable to the life one must endure day after day in striving to win souls for Christianity.[28]

Lalemant's blunt assessment of the trials of living and labouring among the Hurons should not, however, be construed as a weakening of the Jesuit will, nor as an indictment of the missionary campaign. As an obedient soldier in the Company of Jesus, it would never have crossed his mind to question the purpose or commands of his order. He was firmly committed, as were his companions, to the goal of converting the Indians to Christianity. At the same time, like soldiers everywhere, Lalemant was exercising his inalienable right to complain about the conditions of duty.

There is irony in the fact that the Jesuits, who were highly educated and frequently experienced teachers at the secondary and higher-education levels, should in their new surroundings be little more than elementary-school teachers, and with no school to boot. The school or classroom in the field missions was not a building or a fixed place. It was everywhere and nowhere, wherever missionary teachers and Indian learners assembled: a clearing in the forest; a campfire setting; a shady spot beneath a tree; a smoke-filled cabin.

The job description for teaching in the wilderness classroom called for the giving of an introductory course in catechism in the local dialect to a mixed clientele who were without formal learning experience. A question was whether the Jesuits could make the adjustment from college teachers to simple instructors. After all, teaching an uncivilized people the rudiments of religion through the medium of an exotic tongue in an alien and often hostile environment was a far cry from pronouncing on Cicero's speeches or reworking Aristotle's syllogisms in the serene and untroubled atmosphere of a European college. Another problem was that the Jesuits had traditionally centred their educational attention on bright boys, leaving to others the duty of caring for girls and less able boys. But in the Huron habitations there was no luxury of choice; the Jesuits were committed to instructing all comers, irrespective of age, sex, and learning potential. To their credit, the missionaries adjusted remarkably well to their new responsibilities; they pursued their instructional and evangelizing tasks in a spirit of pedagogical flexibility, adapting their teaching to a new group of learners, which included children and adults, males and females, and the converted as well as the unconverted.

The making of a Christian – even in the bush – was not a chance affair; the organizational bent of the Jesuit would not allow it. In the battle for Indian souls the missionaries mapped out a campaign strategy which included the subject matter to be taught and the means by which it was to be transmitted. The curriculum of the wilderness classroom comprised prayers, hymn singing, devotions, and doctrine. The missionary teachers subscribed to the technique of sequential learning: instruction should begin with simple truths and proceed to more complex ones, and ritual should be taught before doctrine.

But before adding knowledge the missionaries worked at subtracting it – at rooting out tribal beliefs which they regarded as repugnant and as inhibiting to Christian truths. To this end, the Jesuits preached against the Indians' wars of vengeance and against the cruelties they inflicted upon captured prisoners. They also exhorted their hosts to renounce polygamy, promiscuity, divorce, and drink.

On the principle that faith precedes and underscores comprehension of Christian doctrine, the missionaries focused on prayers as the opening thrust in the conversion process. It was not lost on the Jesuits that prayers were a fixture in the Indian belief system, which allowed the Hurons to grasp the significance of Christian prayer. In his winter travels with the Montagnais in 1634, Le Jeune noticed that the tribal members prayed to the Manitou for a successful hunt and for protection against their enemies. From a Christian perspective, prayer acted as a bond between the communicant and the Creator. Indians were taught the principal Christian prayers – the Pater, the Credo, and the Ave – along with the sign of the cross and the recitation of the rosary. Once initiated into the rituals of the religion, including prayers, hymns, and the like, the neophyte was ready to move on to the next and higher level, that of catechism, or the learning of Christian doctrine.

Although an enormous gulf separated the Indian and Christian religions, the missionaries attempted, as much as possible, to bridge the differences by drawing on comparable elements. Thus, the concept of a Christian God who is neither flesh nor blood but pure spirit was eased into the native mind by relating it to the soul, for which there was tribal belief. Moreover, the fact that most tribes subscribed to the idea of a future life made easier the explanation of the Christian notion of immortality and salvation. Since the concept of the immortal soul was firmly embedded in the Huron religion, Brébeuf recommended that all catechizing begin with the elemental truth that souls are destined for heaven or hell, saying that when the Indians grasped this fact, many conversions would follow. On the other hand, other Christian beliefs, such as divine grace, baptism, penance, and the Trinity, had almost no reference points and proved difficult to communicate.

At the outset, the Jesuits believed, as had the Recollets, that the best hope for spreading Christianity among the Hurons and other native peoples was through education of their children.[29] The adults of the tribe were judged too set in their ways, too attached to their "superstitions and evil customs," to benefit from instruction. Brébeuf said that while the old men of the tribe admitted to the logic of the Jesuits' arguments, they were unable to rid themselves of their traditional beliefs because that was where their hearts were.[30] For the Jesuits, who were uncompromising in religious matters, this was not good enough. Increasingly they maintained that renunciation of tribal beliefs was the necessary first step on the road to embracing Christianity. Children, on the other hand, were found to be more receptive to Christian teachings, since their minds were not locked into tribal beliefs. A second assumption was that the learning acquired by the children through their missionary teachers would be passed on to their parents, who loved them so much.

Although they were not comfortable in the role, the missionaries included girls in their instruction, for they could not ignore the fact that females had souls worth saving. The Jesuits also feared the consequence of ignoring girls' education that Christian boys, upon marrying, would be led back into a state of barbarism by heathen wives. Still, the missionaries looked to the day when France would send an order of nuns to Canada to relieve them of the responsibility of girls' instruction, which was alien to their tradition.

By 1640, the original policy of favouring children over adults in the instructional process had been discarded as a tactical error. The sheer number of children involved had proven to be a problem, and, more significantly, many had shown themselves unreceptive to or incapable of grasping Christian ideas and practices. The Jesuits also realized that they had erred in assuming that adults learned through their children. While it was true that Indian parents loved and pampered their children, it was equally true that they were little influenced by them. In the realization that adult males were the real power brokers in Huron society, the Jesuits redirected their evangelizing efforts at the leaders and potential leaders of the tribe, confident that if respected adults were won over to Christianity, the rest of the population could not remain indifferent.[31] It was always a cause for joy and excitement among the missionaries when a leading tribesman declared in favour of Christianity, for a ripple effect was anticipated.

Initially in Huronia, the missionaries attempted to instruct the Indians *en masse*. Lalemant said that in his village, one day of the week was given over to community instruction. Accordingly, at high noon of the appointed day the village crier announced by voice or bell the convening of a public assembly to hear a Christian lesson. The assembly was held outdoors, since there was no chapel or cabin large enough to house the audience. Having assembled the villagers, the missionaries began by leading the audience in the chanting of prayers and the singing of hymns, following which a lesson or lecture was presented. To make the prayers and hymns more appealing, they were intoned in the Indian manner. The lesson was usually on a specific topic; a favourite one described the fires of hell awaiting non-believers. The lesson was sometimes interrupted or cut short by disapproving members of the tribe. Frequently the tribal shamans led the protests, for they regarded the missionaries as competitors for the hearts and minds of the villagers. The assembly was concluded by the singing of more hymns and prayers, some of which the audience knew by heart.[32]

The community approach to the teaching of religion had its drawbacks. The missionaries discovered that it was no easy task to bring together the inhabitants of an entire village, what with the tribe's nomadic ways and its general indifference to the Christian religion. For sustained periods of time, particularly during the summer months, most of the tribe was off hunting, fishing, and trading. Only in the winter months did the Hurons remain more or less permanently in their villages. Even then there were problems in assembling them for instruction. Brébeuf complained that attempts to bring the men of the tribe together for Christian learning were frequently sabotaged or undermined by the holding of councils, feasts, and games.[33] Finding that the community approach to disseminating Christian learning was not a viable method, the missionaries increasingly turned their attention to working with small groups.

Accordingly, in the Huron villages the Jesuits rose at four each morning and said masses and performed other religious devotions until eight o'clock, when the doors of their cabins were thrown open to the village population. The arriving villagers were of all ages and categories, including adults and children, baptized Christians, catechumens, language teachers, and the curious. For their part, the missionaries were both teachers and students. They instructed catechumens, most of whom were children, in Christian knowledge and ministered to the spiritual needs of the converted, and were taught by local teachers to master the intricacies of the elusive Huron dialect. Lalemant reported that the work of the missionaries suffered because of the Indians' habit of coming and going as they pleased, saying that any attempt to deny them entrance to one's cabin or to force them out before they were ready to leave produced bad feelings. Brébeuf had expressed the same complaint, saying that his cabin was always so full of Hurons that he rarely had time for himself.[34] At fault were conflicting values. The proverbial relative who overstays his welcome had no parallel in Huron society, where one's cabin was always open to visitors.

A division of labour among the missionaries meant that while some received the Indians in their own cabins, others sought out the villagers in theirs. The latter group, in the fashion of itinerant preachers or schoolmasters, daily visited upward of forty cabins, each of which housed several families. Not limiting their visits to spiritual matters, they lent care and assistance to the sick and dying, prescribing the appropriate remedies and bleedings. Yet they never lost sight of the fact that care of the body was secondary to that of the soul, and thus every effort was made to ensure that no person died without the benefit of baptism. The Jesuits' enthusiasm for baptizing the sick and dying is understandable. In the first place, it was relatively easy to achieve, since the patient was physically and morally vulnerable. In 1640, the Huron mission boasted of more than a thousand baptisms, though most of these conquests were in fact children on the brink of death.[35] Second, the large number of baptisms reaped propaganda dividends in France, justifying the work of the Canadian missions and attracting financial support. On the other hand, the phenomenon of "easy baptisms" was a shaky and dubious foundation on which to build a permanent church in the New World. Moreover, sometimes the missionaries' rush to baptize backfired, sowing in the Indian mind the belief that it caused or hurried death.

Instructing the Indians in their cabins tried the patience of the most dedicated missionary. To enter an Indian lodge, reported Lalemant, was to witness a "miniature picture of Hell." Smoke, dust, and dirt were everywhere, offending the nostrils and causing the eyes to smart. In these cloudy surroundings, added Lalemant, were "naked bodies, black and half roasted, mingled pellmell with the dogs, which are held as dear as the children."[36] Sometimes the visiting missionary was greeted with taunts and insults from the adults, who ascribed to him and his religion all the troubles of the tribe. Were the missionary to endure these harassments and to await patiently the opportunity to speak, he might succeed in saying a few words in defence of his cause.


If the missionaries often found the Indians to be indifferent learners and slaves to their "superstitions and prejudices," they attributed this condition more to ignorance than to an inability to learn. "Mind is not lacking among the Savages of Canada, [only] education and instruction" was Le Jeune's assessment at the end of his first year in Canada.[37] In addition to acknowledging the basic intelligence of the Indians, the Jesuits, like the Recollets before them, expressed surprise at the natives' ability to reason so well. Coming from trained logicians, this was high praise indeed. The missionaries were also struck by the Indians' capacity to retain what they learned, perhaps explained by the fact that in an oral culture memories must do the work of books and libraries. In referring to the tenacious memory of his Iroquois captors, the Jesuit Bressani said that they were able to recall events and things easily without the aid of writings.

Although the Jesuits resorted to teaching methods that had served them well in their European schools, they wisely modified them to meet the conditions of a radically different environment and clientele. Repetition, review, question and answer, rewards, and emulation were among the pedagogical techniques used in the wilderness classroom. Prelection, or lecturing, was played down because it had limited application before restless learners and because few missionaries had sufficient command of the local dialect to sway the audience.

As was noted earlier, learning was directed for the most part at small groups in an informal setting. Ideally, each lesson began with a review of previously learned knowledge, following which new material was introduced and explained. Then the missionary questioned his pupils to determine whether they had understood the material. A variation of this procedure had the pupils questioning each other on some point of the lesson.

A system of rewards or prizes was part of the Jesuits' instructional package. Long before it was codified by a twentieth-century psychologist, the principle that rewards facilitate learning was being employed in the bush school. Brébeuf said that a "little bead of glass or porcelain" was given to children who answered correctly.[38] Le Jeune, for his part, said that he would give his Montagnais language teacher some tobacco in order to make him more attentive. The presentation of prizes for correct responses was seen as serving a double purpose: it motivated the children to learn and it attracted adults, who agreed to instruction in the hope of being given cakes or tobacco. Still, it may be wondered whether the missionaries did not depend too much on the practice, and in doing so abuse the principle. In such a technique there is always the danger that the prize will take precedence over that which is to be learned. But faced with a clientele that was often incurious and sometimes openly hostile to their instruction, the missionaries may be forgiven if they erred on the side of the carrot. Nor should it be forgotten that gift giving was a firmly established tradition in French-Indian relations, so that the missionaries were merely following an accepted practice.

Emulation was a pedagogical staple of Jesuit classrooms in Europe, and it found good use in Canada as a means of familiarizing Indian boys and girls with Christian ritual and ceremony. In the knowledge that children are given naturally to imitating others, the missionaries activated the technique by repeatedly making the sign of the cross and kneeling for prayers in the presence of their pupils.[39] To reinforce these gestures, children were placed at the head of religious processions and given the cross to carry. On Sunday mornings, children assisted at mass and at the offertory. The Jesuits hoped that the example of some children performing religious acts would encourage others to follow suit. On the other hand, the fact that some children went overboard in performing religious gestures (one Huron girl reportedly said her Pater and Ave fifty times a day) raises the question of how much was effective learning and how much was mechanical repetition.

It is often said that the mark of a good teacher is one who adapts instruction and materials to fit the needs and abilities of the learner. Conscious of the fact that the Indians were without the trappings of civilization and consequently not drawn naturally to Christian learning, the missionaries strove to make their lessons simple but interesting. Like effective teachers everywhere, they varied their modes of instruction to attract and motivate learners. Indeed, some of the pedagogical techniques employed have a modern ring to them. For example, a simulated-games approach was used by a missionary working among the Iroquois to sustain interest. Seizing on the competitive instincts of his learners, he developed a game called "from point to point," which was played with emblems and cartouches on which were depicted the principal beliefs of Christianity.[40]

Music was a frequently used device for communicating the Christian religion, perhaps because the melodic form was common to both cultures. The Indians loved singing and sang well; of course, hymns, chants, and prayers were an integral part of the Christian liturgy. The missionaries exploited the Indians' fascination for music by composing hymns in their own dialect. Father Louis André, labouring among the Menominees in what is now northeastern Wisconsin, turned to song writing as an instructional mode. Appalled by what he described as rampant vice and superstition among the local tribes, he composed songs attacking tribal beliefs. The songs were taught to children, who sang them to the accompaniment of a flute as they went from village to village. André said that the elders of the tribe tolerated this melodic assault on their beliefs because it came from the mouths of their children, who in their eyes could do no wrong.[41]

Various artistic devices were used by other missionaries to get their message across. Jean Pierron put his drawing and painting skills to good use among the Mohawks. Pierron was upset by the fact that some tribal members placed their hands over their ears when he began to preach. To overcome this problem, he produced a number of paintings which illustrated with frightening reality the agonies awaiting those who rejected God and were living in Hell. The paintings included surrealistic portraits of demons, devils, and others who had been damned, including Indians with hands over their ears. The Ursuline nun Marie de l'Incarnation said that the illustrations were so horrible as to make one shudder.[42] At any rate, the pictures made a profound impression on the Iroquois, perhaps because of their highly developed visual sense, and presumably resulted in a rash of conversions. Some of the drawings were bound in small "books" so that they could be carried around by their owners for frequent reference. The use of pictures as an instructional tool was innovative, even by European standards. It is generally acknowledged that the West's first illustrated school manual was *Orbis Pictus*, published in 1658 by the Bohemian educator Jan Comenius.

Chrestien Le Clercq, Recollet missionary and historian, developed a system of hieroglyphic writing to teach religion to the Micmacs of the Gaspé Peninsula in the 1670s. He admitted that the idea came to him from watching the Indians make charcoal marks on birch bark to record the meaning of words and events. The use of charcoal as pen and bark as paper was not unique to the Micmacs; there are references in the *Relations* to this practice among the Montagnais and Abenakis. At any rate, the essence of Le Clercq's system was the drawing of characters on cards which represented one or several words, usually of a religious significance. The Recollet said that the device enabled the Indians to learn Christian prayers and beliefs more rapidly, since it eliminated the need for oral repetition and memorization. He also claimed that his system facilitated the spread of learning, saying, "Indians instruct one another in whatsoever place they may happen to be. Thus the son teaches his father, the mother her children, the wife her husband, and the children the old men."[43] Though Le Clercq returned to France in 1686, his hieroglyphic system did not die out. The missionary Pierre Antoine Maillard found traces of Le Clercq's characters among the Micmacs of Cape Breton Island in the 1730s, which he used to design his own system of writing.[44]

A pedagogical problem of a different order was how to ensure that Christian beliefs and practices remained fresh in the minds of the Indians when they were away on their prolonged food-seeking expeditions. A missionary at the Tadoussac mission came up with a scheme for keeping Christian learning alive among the tribal members when he was no longer with them. He issued his learners sticks of different colours, each of which represented a different piece of knowledge. A black stick was a reminder of the spiritual perils of returning to their tribal superstitions. A white one called attention to their Christian devotions, which they must practise daily. A red stick was a reminder of religious celebrations for Sundays and feast days.[45] A variation on this theme was the issuance of a calendar to a Montagnais tribe on the point of leaving Quebec to hunt elk. The object was to encourage the members of the tribe to carry out their Christian duties as if the missionaries were with them. Since the Indians could not read, the days and months of the calendar year were indicated by different marks. Apparently these marks or symbols were understood by the Montagnais, since on their return to Quebec they knew what day it was, reporting to the missionaries that "on the Feast days, we assembled and prayed to God in one cabin, and sang what we knew. On the other days, each prayed to God by himself."[46]

### CHAPTER THREE

# *Indian Seminaries*

The history of the missionary campaign in New France is less a story of ends than one of means. When the first missionary set foot on Canadian soil, he harboured not the slightest doubt as to his purpose there. A vast wilderness offered an abundance of souls to save. It only remained to be determined how best to harvest these souls. As we have seen, one method was to attack, as it were, the Indians on their own territory. Living and labouring among the various tribes in their villages and habitations, the missionaries preached the gospel, instructed the population in Christian knowledge, ministered to the sick and needy, and baptized those whom they judged ready. At the same time, interest in a second approach grew.

At the heart of the problem were the nomadic ways of the Indians. Hunters, fishermen, and traders more than farmers and settlers, the natives were frequently on the move, which made them elusive targets for religious conversion. Father Le Jeune expanded on the problem: "It seems to me that not much ought to be hoped for from the Savages as long as they are wanderers; you will instruct them today, tomorrow hunger snatches your hearers away, forcing them to go and seek their food in the rivers and woods."[1]

It will be recalled that in Huronia the missionaries' instructional efforts were largely restricted to the winter months, since adult males were away on fishing and hunting expeditions from spring to late fall. Attempts by some missionaries to accompany the Indians on their food-gathering trips proved not only spiritually unproductive but physically draining. Thus, the missionaries concluded that one way to facilitate the evangelization of the Indian was to bring him under control, to make him sedentary. As Le Jeune explained, "One of the most efficient means we can use to bring them to Jesus Christ is to organize them in a sort of Village – in a word, to help them to clear and cultivate the land, and to build homes for themselves."[2]

The model for this scheme was the *reducciones* of South America. Earlier, the Spanish Jesuits had been successful in rendering sedentary wandering tribes in the southern continent by assembling them in reductions, or reserves. By this means the Indians were more easily subjected to Christian influences, and the chronic problem of religious defections was reduced. The missionaries had learned early that it was far easier to acquire converts than to keep them.

The Jesuits in Canada were convinced that if the Indians could be broken of their roving habits, much progress could be made. The grand strategy called for weaning them from their villages and hunting grounds, and resettling them in permanent habitations near French outposts. The plan was touted as the best means of Christianizing the native peoples, since it would keep them in constant contact with the missionaries, who would be able to carry out their spiritual duties in more or less uninterrupted fashion in a calm and stable environment. The Jesuits also counted on the fact that the Hurons, the Montagnais, and other tribes would be drawn to the habitations for other than spiritual reasons: they would be protected from their enemies and assured of sufficient food for a good part of the year, thus reducing their need to be on the move for extended periods of time.

An important feature of the Jesuit plan was that while the proposed reserves were to be established in proximity to French settlements, they were not intended as culturally assimilative institutions. Rather, the reserve was designed to isolate the Indians both from their own people and from the Europeans, excepting, of course, the missionaries, who were directly responsible for their spiritual and economic welfare. The Jesuits reasoned that if the Indians were insulated against the immoralities of both races, they could be more effectively controlled. Jesuit reluctance to work toward the fusion of the two peoples was later to draw the wrath of the Crown, which accused the religious order of neglecting to teach the Indians the French language and ways.

Because resources were initially lacking, it was not until 1637 that the first Indian reserve was established, thanks to a generous endowment from Noël Brulard de Sillery, a French nobleman and priest. In that year, workers arrived from France and constructed the Sillery habitation, near Quebec; it consisted of a chapel, a hospital, a Jesuit residence, and Indian cabins. Almost immediately the new installation became a habitation for wandering Montagnais. In 1645, more than 150 Christian Indians were living on the Sillery reserve in spite of the ravages of a recent outbreak of smallpox.

In addition to spawning other reserves, the Sillery mission saw its own character change over the years. What began as a habitation for the Montagnais later became a refuge for the Abenakis of New England. By 1688, however, the Sillery reserve was all but abandoned, since the land was no longer productive for the cultivation of corn, and its remaining occupants were transferred to reserves at Bécancourt and St-François de Sales, on the Chaudière River. In 1674, the Jesuits founded a Huron reserve at Lorette, north of Quebec. Since their destruction as a nation by the Iroquois at mid-century, many Hurons had the status of displaced persons. Thanks to improved relations between the French and the Iroquois during the second half of the century, the Jesuits were able to establish in 1667 an Iroquois reserve at La Prairie, across the river from Montreal, though in succeeding years it would be populated by Indians from several tribes. In 1676, the Sulpicians, of whom more will be said later, founded an Indian settlement in Montreal, which from the outset attracted Indians from various tribes, including Hurons, Montagnais, and Iroquois. Later the reserve was moved to Sault-au-Récollet, then to Baie d'Urfé, and finally to Lake of Two Mountains.[3]

Instruction given in the reserve was of a practical as well as a religious character. Since one of the principal objectives of the reserve system was to encourage footloose tribes to accept the sedentary life of the European, the missionaries, in the manner of vocational educators, taught the principles and techniques of agriculture, including the use of farm implements and carpentry tools, so that the Indians might clear the land, till the soil, and build and repair their own cabins. The missionaries believed, perhaps naïvely, that if the Indians could be transformed into productive and self-sufficient farmers they would lose their taste for the wandering life.

Since the reserve was conceived as a Christian community for Indians, spiritual instruction and activities were integral elements in its operation. Much as they did in their field missions, the missionaries combined teaching and preaching, sometimes working with the inhabitants *en masse*, at other times in small groups. The whole of the reserve was regularly brought together to worship in the chapel, to hear sermons, and to participate in prayers and singing. While the reserves, much like the field missions, did not have schools as such, they were not without informal classrooms. Missionary teachers, sometimes assisted by Indian converts, went from cabin to cabin, instructing the occupants in the rituals and doctrines of Christianity.

The reserves were imperfect institutions. If they enjoyed a measure of success in winning and holding converts, they were less successful in inducing Indians to adopt French ways. Because the sedentary policy flew in the face of the aboriginal tradition of movement and because it emphasized the agricultural arts, the Indians did not take naturally to the reserve system. They were not intrinsically interested in clearing the land or planting crops, with the possible exception of corn, which did not require much care. These activities demanded manual labour, which many male Indians balked at. Farming on the reserves was sometimes done by the resident missionaries or neighbouring French colonists, for hunting and fishing were more the Indians' style. In the winter of 1649, the Sillery reserve numbered only two Frenchmen, the resident Algonkins having gone off to hunt.[4]

The reserves were also plagued by social and economic problems. As they were situated in the heart of French territory, so to speak – in the environs of Quebec and Montreal – their inhabitants were exposed to some of the worst features of civilization. At the head of the list was liquor. The records and reports of New France are replete with references to the devastating effects of drink on the Indian. His weakness for liquor, in conjunction with obliging traders anxious for profits, made for a sorry situation. Religious authorities repeatedly denounced the liquor trade as an abomination, and petitioned government officials for corrective action. In 1660, Bishop Laval threatened a decree of excommunication on those who trafficked in liquor with the native peoples; the declaration had little effect, as commerce proved a stronger force than the denial of the sacraments. The problem of drunkenness reached such serious proportions at the La Prairie reserve that the Jesuits were forced to move the settlement to the more remote area of Sault St-Louis, away from the clutches of the brandy dealers, in 1676. Nor was the situation much different in other settlements. François Dollier de Casson, superior of the Sulpician seminary in Montreal, admitted, "In my twenty-six years in this country I have seen our numerous and flourishing Algonquin missions entirely destroyed by drunkenness."[5] And if reserve Indians were especially vulnerable to the white man's drink, they were no less susceptible to his diseases. Smallpox, measles, and other contagious diseases could work havoc on an Indian population in no time at all. In 1685, there were 488 Indians living on the Sillery reserve; within two years about 150 of them had perished from an infectious malady.[6]

We sometimes overlook the critical importance of money and materials to the success of the missionary campaign, forgetting that vows of poverty and spiritual zeal were no substitutes for full coffers. It will be recalled that the Recollet missionary enterprise almost collapsed in the 1620s owing to insufficient funds. This is to emphasize that the construction and maintenance of Indian reserves did not come cheaply. The missionaries had to bear the cost of food, housing, tools, and sometimes clothes for the inhabitants. While many Frenchmen, including noblemen, merchants, and clerics, generously contributed monies and gifts, often in the form of land tracts, the fact is that such donations were not sufficient to keep the reserves on a sound financial footing.

Like other missionary undertakings in the seventeenth century, the reserve system was launched on a wave of optimism that was fueled by early success. However, after an initial period of often spectacular growth, most reserves experienced a decline in population; some, like Sillery, disappeared entirely. Other reserves continued and became the founding models for their present-day counterparts. On balance, of all missionary projects in New France the reserve was perhaps the most successful in Christianizing the native peoples. On the other hand, the reserve system failed, as did other schemes, in Frenchifying the aboriginal population. Even the Recollets, whose enthusiasm for acculturation was unmatched among missionary groups, failed to induce the Indians to embrace French ways. Returning to Canada in 1670, after an absence of more than forty years, the Franciscan order founded a reserve near Fort Frontenac for the Cayugas, one of the Iroquois nations. The Recollets' persistent attempts to teach them the French language ended in failure.

Preceding the Sillery reserve by several years was an Indian seminary, established by the Jesuits at Quebec. Neither the institution nor the idea of it was an entirely new one; the Recollets, it will be recalled, had maintained an Indian seminary on the same site in 1620. Conditioned by their affinity for élitist learning and believing that one of the keys to successful evangelization was the care and education of Indian boys who would someday hold leadership roles in the tribe, the Jesuits put great stock in the institution. The seminary idea was reinforced by the fact that other approaches taken to effect the conversion of Huron boys had not proven particularly successful. As things stood, results in the field missions had been mixed, and the practice of sending the occasional Indian boy off to France was judged to be time-consuming and impracticable. The attractive feature of the seminary was that it would give the Jesuits complete control over their pupils, free from the meddling ways of Indian parents. Initially, the Jesuits had toyed with the idea of setting up formal schools or seminaries in the Indian villages, but they rejected the plan in the belief that they would get no peace from interfering parents, who abhorred French methods of discipline and who, according to Le Jeune, would on the slightest pretext remove their sons from the school before their instruction was finished.[7] The educating of Indian boys at Quebec was also advanced on security grounds; the prospective seminarists were described as "hostages" whose stationing at Quebec would serve to protect French traders operating in Indian country against abuse.[8]

The Indian seminary, established as a boarding school, opened at Notre-Dame-des-Anges, near Quebec, in the summer of 1636. The first pupils came from Huronia, though in succeeding years Algonkin and Montagnais boys joined them.[9] Recruiting boys for the seminary was more than a matter of arranging their transportation over the long water route between Huronia and Quebec. The missionaries had to overcome the anxieties of Indian parents, who were so attached to their children that they could scarcely bear to part with them, and worried that their sons would be subjected to French discipline, which they always regarded as severe. As a result, it took a good deal of negotiating, coaxing, and gift-giving on the part of the Jesuits before the Hurons agreed to allow some of the children to be taken to Quebec. Bishop Laval, New France's first prelate and an enthusiastic supporter of missionary education, later reasoned that the Indians' real fear was that their children, upon whom they depended in their old age, would not return to care for them.[10] The high churchman based his conclusion on the small size of the Indian family, saying that while French families in Canada had an average of ten children, Indian families had only two or three.[11] Thus, with fewer children Indian parents had paradoxically more to lose.

Although the Jesuits had been promised a dozen or so boys by the Hurons, only six arrived from Huronia in the first year, accompanied by Fathers Daniel and Davost, who were being recalled to instruct and care for the boys. Things did not go well that year: two of the boys fell ill and died, while a third was let go because he could not adapt to the organized life of the school.

Like the reserve, the Indian seminary proved to be a costly undertaking. Le Jeune complained, "When the Savages give you their children, they give them as naked as the hand," implying that the Jesuits were saddled not only with feeding and lodging their charges, but with clothing them as well.[12] Nor did the expenses stop there. Upon their departure from the seminary – after a day or a year – Indian boys demanded and normally received alms from their hosts. In addition, the Jesuits often had to compensate Indian parents in the form of presents for the privilege of caring for and instructing their children. Depending on one's point of view, the Indian seminarists were either the first bursary students or the first social-welfare recipients in North America. In any case, the heavy expenses involved in running the seminary were doubtless a factor in limiting the school's development, and may have contributed to its eventual demise.

The establishment of an Indian seminary symbolized, as it were, a hardening of the cultural arteries. Now that the Indian boys were installed in a French institution on "French territory," the Jesuits assumed a more culturally aggressive posture as the seminarists underwent the experience of living in the French manner. To be sure, the Frenchifying impact came less from the curriculum than from the fact of living the disciplined life of a pupil in a French boarding school for, while the Indian pupils were served up a richer and more varied educational fare by their Jesuit teachers, they were not routinely taught French language and customs.

"Indian seminary" was a misnomer, since the school included French boys as well. At first the two races were taught separately to protect the Indians against being "morally contaminated" by the French boys. Later, however, the Jesuits had a change of mind, believing that there were pedagogical benefits to be derived from instructing the two groups together. With the French boys serving as learning models, it was thought, the Indian boys would progress at a faster rate. Still, the Indian seminary was no French college; it was essentially an elementary school, and its curriculum was rudimentary. On the other hand, the spirit, if not the letter, of the *Ratio Studiorum* was present in the seminary, since all youngsters were subjected to the organized regimen of a boarding school. Moreover, like their French counterparts Indian boys memorized, recited, and were examined in what they had learned. Those who excelled in their studies were awarded prizes.

The Jesuits spoke in glowing terms of their Indian pupils, describing them as intelligent, industrious, well behaved, and docile (a favourite expression of the missionaries to indicate that those under their care were eminently teachable). Not only did the Indian boys willingly do what was asked of them, they surprised and delighted their instructors by being the first to arrive at scheduled classes and religious ceremonies. Their exemplary behaviour may be attributed in part to the missionaries themselves, whose experience in the field missions had given them valuable insights into the native temperament. The Jesuits realized that the business of supervising Indian boys called for tact, patience, gentleness, and flexibility. Hence, the Jesuit tradition of shutting pupils off from the world and watching over them closely during their waking hours was relaxed in deference to the Indians' life of unrestrained freedom. Moreover, recognizing that the rich and varied diet of the French table did not suit the more sensitive aboriginal stomach, the Jesuits modified the school menu to include traditional Indian dishes such as *sagamité*. Again, in the knowledge that even the mildest form of punishment could trigger rebellion in their pupils, they were careful not to chastise them in the French manner. Instead, as Le Jeune advised, "one must seize the occasion to subdue them by love."[13]

A day at the seminary began with prayers, after which the pupils attended mass "as far as the offertory only."[14] From after breakfast to lunch, the boys were formally instructed in both sacred and profane knowledge – a departure from the practices in the field missions, where secular learning was ignored. Thus, in addition to religious instruction, the Indians were taught reading and writing in their own language with the help of dictionaries and grammars which had been composed by the missionaries. In recognition of the Indian boys' free spirit, the authorities scheduled the afternoons as leisure time. The period was spent in hunting, fishing, and making bows and arrows, though at appropriate times of the year some time was devoted to agricultural tasks. Since one purpose of the seminary, as of the reserve, was to encourage the native peoples to accept a more settled way of life, the Jesuit teachers strove to instill in their pupils a taste for agriculture. This they did by practical rather than theoretical instruction. Each boy was given a piece of land near the school which he cleared and readied for planting. He planted corn seed in the spring, nursed its development during the growing season, and harvested the crop in the fall.

In 1640, after five years of operation, the Indian seminary at Notre-Dame-des-Anges closed. Several factors contributed to the demise of the institution, among them a lack of pupils caused, in part, by the reluctance of Indian parents to release their sons to the Jesuits; the inability of some boys to adjust to the regulated life of the school; and the heavy costs of maintaining it. Father Vimont, who succeeded Le Jeune as superior of the Canadian missions in 1639, reported that the Indian seminary failed because "no notable fruit was seem among the Savages"[15] – that is, those who had received instruction had failed to transmit their religious fervour to their own people. The fault, however, did not rest with the Indian graduates themselves, whose zealousness in the Christian religion surprised even their Jesuit mentors; rather, it was tied to the inferior status of the young in Indian society. The truth of this condition surfaced in the comment of an elderly Huron who had been refused admission to the seminary by reason of his advanced age and dull intellect. In appealing the decision, the old Huron told the Jesuits that he would be a better choice to carry the Christian message to his people, since "young people are not listened to in our country."[16]

This and other reminders of the marginal status of children in Indian society caused the missionaries to rethink the policy of concentrating their educational efforts on boys between the ages of twelve and fifteen. A Jesuit report of 1642 speaks of plans to establish an Indian seminary for young men between the ages of twenty and twenty-five.[17] Although no institution was ever established, the Jesuits for a time brought young Huron men to Quebec for "short courses" in religion, which had the advantage of not requiring great expenditures. In 1642, four Huron men spent the winter in Quebec, during which time they received instruction in the Christian religion. After being baptized, they were returned to their people.

The education of Indian girls posed a problem for the missionaries. While acknowledging that girls had souls worth saving and that Christian husbands required Christian wives, the Jesuits were nevertheless reluctant to assume direct responsibility for their instruction. The Jesuit schools of Europe, in the tradition of the day, were male institutions, and this tradition was not easily set aside, even in a wilderness land. To Le Jeune the solution had always been to import female teachers. In his second year in Canada, the Jesuit superior asked, rhetorically, "Is there not some Lady in France who has enough courage to found a Seminary for girls?"[18] Later he added a caveat, advising interested parties not to come unless they have "a good House, some cleared land, and a good income upon which to live."[19] Until such time as the Jesuit superior's appeal was answered, the instruction of Indian girls around Quebec remained the preoccupation of a handful of French families, a tradition spawned by the explorer Champlain and his young wife.

In 1620, Champlain had brought his twenty-two-year-old wife, Hélène, with him to Canada. It was not in the nature of the high-spirited and childless Hélène to sit idly by in Quebec while her husband roamed the wilderness. During her four-year stay in New France she devoted herself to good works among the Indians, visiting them in their cabins near the outpost, teaching the catechism to native girls, caring for the sick, distributing alms, and, in the process, acquiring a facility in the Indian dialects. There is justification for calling Hélène de Champlain the first female educator of Canada.

Champlain himself had observed that Indian parents were reluctant to entrust their children to the French because they were so attached to them. But in 1628 the Montagnais, as a gesture of good will, gave the explorer three girls, whom he named Faith, Hope, and Charity, for care and instruction. One of the three became homesick and returned to her people; the other two remained at Fort St-Louis, where Champlain personally instructed them in Christian knowledge, sewing, and embroidery. He intended to take them to France for formal schooling, but the English capture of Quebec in 1629 upset his plans.

Continuing the tradition of the Champlains, the Jesuits placed Indian girls in the homes of French families in Quebec, some as domestics, where they received a French Christian upbringing, being taught religion and trained in household duties. Finding the scheme less than effective, the Jesuits selected some of the brighter girls and shipped them to France for a thoroughly Gallic education, in the hope that on their return they would stand as shining examples to others of their race. But the small number of girls involved plus the great expenditure in time and money convinced the Jesuits more than ever that a woman's touch was needed in Canada.

The arrival in Canada of a ship from across the ocean in the seventeenth century was always an occasion for excitement. The only tangible link between a small French population and the mother country, ships brought letters and other written materials to a news-starved population, much-needed tools and supplies, and, not least, a human cargo of settlers, artisans, clerics, and soldiers. Of the three vessels that docked in Quebec in 1639, that which arrived on the first of August was clearly the most historically significant because of its interesting passenger list. Father Le Jeune must have welcomed the new arrivals with mixed emotions. Here were those teaching nuns he had wished for; here also was Barthélemy Vimont, his successor. Chief among the female arrivals were Madame La Peltrie, lay foundress and benefactor of the Ursuline order in Canada; several Ursulines, including Marie de l'Incarnation, who would be the order's first and most celebrated Canadian superior; and three Hospital Nuns.

No sooner had the sisters set foot on Canadian soil than they were seen gathering Indian girls about them, leading them in prayers and songs, and instructing them in religion with the help of sign language. The Ursulines had brought a violin with them and used it to good effect in attracting native girls, for they had known from their reading of the *Relations* that the Indians had an ear for music. When Marie de l'Incarnation and her companions heard for the first time Christian Indians singing the praises of God in their own dialect, they were moved to tears.

The Ursulines had come to New France for the express purpose of instructing Indian girls, in response to the appeal of the Jesuits. But almost from the beginning their instructional work included French girls as well, and like the Jesuits, they were forced by circumstances to defy pedagogical tradition by teaching youngsters of the opposite sex. It is reported that the Ursulines taught Indian men living at the nearby Sillery reserve.[20]

The Ursulines brought to teaching a quality of love and patience; no parent was more caring or attentive in governing the young. Still, they were far more than pedagogues or surrogate parents. In a sense, they were the country's first social-welfare authority, for the female community fed, housed, and clothed Indian girls, who, in the words of Marie de l'Incarnation, come to them as "naked as a worm."[21] The nuns also provided dowries for Indian girls marrying Christian men. In addition, social assistance was extended to Indian adults who frequented the Quebec area, and refuge and protection were given to widows and elders of the tribe who were too old to go on the hunting expeditions. When a contagious disease such as smallpox struck the area, as it did in 1640, the Ursulines' quarters were transformed into a makeshift hospital, the nuns caring for the afflicted as best they could. Thus, a good part of the Ursulines' time, energy, and budget went not for education but for charity and social welfare, which provoked one financial crisis after another. Of Marie de l'Incarnation's many letters to France, not a few were appeals for money. For her part, La Peltrie complained that the lack of funds prevented the order from instructing more Indians, saying that "the expense of one ball in Paris, one soirée, would procure the means of opening heaven to these unfortunates."[22]

Like the Recollets and Jesuits before them, the Ursulines realized that the serious business of winning Indian hearts and souls could not proceed until some mastery of the native languages had been attained. But, unlike their male predecessors, they did not have to undertake the arduous task from scratch, thanks to the Jesuits and others who offered themselves as language tutors and the availability of Indian dictionaries and grammars prepared by the missionaries. Still, the complexities of the aboriginal dialects, far removed from the European languages in syntax, grammar, and pronunciation, almost proved too much for some nuns. Marie de l'Incarnation doubted that she could learn the barbaric tongues, and complained that studying them left her with a splitting headache. But she persevered, as did her companions, eventually achieving a facility in the Algonkin and Montagnais dialects, though not before several years of painstaking work. In 1650, the then fifty-year-old Sister Marie wrote her son that she had been studying the Huron language since the previous winter because of an influx of Hurons to the region. She joked that fifty was not the best age for tackling a new language, but quickly added that the conversion of pagan souls demanded no less.[23] In her declining years, she taught the Indian languages to new arrivals in Canada.

Having obtained their own building in 1642 and armed with a working knowledge of the Indian dialects, the Ursulines were ready to begin their educational work in earnest. Finding the cultural differences between the two races too deep and the purposes for which they were being instructed too varied, the nuns initially chose to educate Indian and French girls apart. But around 1668, the Ursulines were commanded to instruct the two races together as part of Crown policy to effect the cultural assimilation of the Indians. The experiment proved unworkable, as the Ursulines had suspected it would, and eventually there was a return to separate classes.

Using written materials prepared by the male missionaries, the Ursulines taught their Indian girls reading and writing in their own language. The Ursuline seminary, or school, was thus for a time a multilingual institution, providing instruction in the Algonkin, Montagnais, Huron, and French languages. To be sure, reading and writing were not taught for their own sake; rather, they were vehicles through which the paramount subject of catechism was taught, for the making of pious Christians, not the preparation of literate persons, was the avowed purpose of the Ursuline school. While the nuns saw in their Indian girls potential converts, they also saw future wives and mothers, and in that respect gave them some practical education. Usually this took the form of instruction in the household arts – the needlework and embroidery for which the Ursulines were known. Occasionally, however, a talented girl was singled out for a more advanced education. The nuns delighted in showcasing such girls to skeptical Indians as a means of encouraging them to place their daughters in the school. In 1655, a delegation of visiting Iroquois chiefs was introduced to eleven-year-old Marie Arinadsit, who dazzled them with her ability to read, write and sing in Huron, French, and Latin.

Still, like the Jesuits, the Ursulines applied the civilizing arts with a measure of restraint. The nuns coaxed rather than coerced, and bowed to Indian habits in several respects. They prepared Indian-style meals for their girls and tolerated their love of dancing. The task of initiating them into the ways of convent school life fell to La Peltrie, who brought joy and parental devotion to her duties. In the belief that cleanliness is next to godliness, the lay foundress gave every new pupil a thorough scrubbing from head to foot, wiping away from her body the coating of animal grease that served as protection against the elements and biting insects. Putting soap and water aside, she then attacked the uncut and matted hair of the neophyte with comb and scissors. After bathing and coiffing the girl and fitting her with a French dress, La Peltrie pronounced her subject ready for instruction.

Like the missionaries, the Ursulines experienced problems with attracting and holding Indian children. Marie de l'Incarnation said that the first seminary pupil was "so used to running in the woods" that it took some doing to get her adjusted to the settled life of the school.[24] Many Indian girls left the seminary before completing their instruction. Some quit the school after several hours; others after several days or weeks. Some succumbed to homesickness; others were fetched by a lonesome parent or suitor. But those girls who were able to adapt to life in a French institution underwent a transformation in attitude and behaviour that both astonished and pleased their hosts. Over time, the heretofore undisciplined, freedom-loving Indians became docile, affectionate, and pious. Marie de l'Incarnation likened them to "petits agneaux" since they were so easily led.[25] One nun asserted that Indian girls were better behaved than French girls, saying of the former that "they assist at Mass every day and with such attention that we are amazed – neither fooling nor talking the way the children do in France."[26]

The number of Indian girls in attendance at the seminary, as day or boarding pupils, fluctuated with changing social conditions. War, famine, pestilence, and other upheavals did their part in curbing or interrupting enrolments. Inclement weather and seasonal planting also played a part. Marie de l'Incarnation said that the best time for undisturbed learning was in the winter months when the Indians went off to hunt, leaving their daughters in the care of the Ursulines. In the summer months, Indian mothers were reluctant to part with their daughters; moreover, it was a time when mothers and daughters had to work in the fields.[27]

The Ursuline seminary made few distinctions with regard to the pupils' ages. In one of her letters, Marie de l'Incarnation refers to an Indian girl of five, another who is seven, and another who is seventeen, and notes at one point, "in the case of Savage girls, we take them at all ages."[28] The seminary charged neither tuition nor maintenance fees, and boasted an "open admissions" policy. Until 1668, the Ursulines claimed that they had never refused an Indian girl to the seminary. In that year seven Algonkin girls were turned away because of a shortage of food, the Ursulines' rations having been allocated to the king's troops.

How many Indian girls were in attendance at the seminary? Enrolment data are unavailable because fires destroyed some of the early records, but some evidence suggests that the number of girls in attendance was substantial. In attempting to determine enrolment figures, a distinction must be made between boarders and day pupils. The latter were from nearby reserves and always outnumbered residential students by a healthy margin. In 1663, the Ursulines announced a daily attendance of "sixty or eighty" Indian girls as day, or external, pupils. The instruction given to day pupils rarely went beyond religious knowledge, but was confined to prayers, hymn singing, and an explanation of Christian doctrine. Indian girls in residence sometimes assisted the nuns in the teaching of day pupils, performing an early form of the monitorial instruction that became the pedagogical rage in early-nineteenth-century Europe and America. Often the day school's activities were capped by the distribution of food, which the Indians greatly welcomed; for their part, the Ursulines discovered that Christian dogma was more appetizing to those with full stomachs.

As for boarding pupils, the scattered bits of evidence suggest that they were far less numerous and that their numbers showed a gradual decline over the years. In 1641, Marie de l'Incarnation informed her superior in Tours that the seminary had forty-eight pupils, but failed to distinguish between day and boarding pupils.[29] In 1668, more than a quarter of a century later, she said that the boarding school numbered nineteen girls, of whom only three were Indians.[30] According to Intendant Duchesneau's census of 1681, nine Indian girls were in residence at the Ursuline convent.[31] At any rate, as the years passed and the colonial population grew, the Ursulines, much like the other orders, devoted less and less time to Indian children. The last class of Indian girls at the Quebec school dates from 1725.

Despite hard work and the best of intentions, it appears that the Ursulines were not successful in winning many permanent converts among the female native population. The documents of the period, particularly the correspondence of Marie de l'Incarnation and the Jesuits' *Relations*, tell of Indian girls caught in a cultural tug-of-war between Franco-Christian ideals and tribal values. In almost every instance, the latter proved to be the stronger force. As far as can be determined, no Indian girl ever took the veil with the Ursulines, and those who returned to their own people following instruction often lost their ardour for Christian beliefs and practices. Some colonial authorities said that fault for the lack of solid converts lay with the Ursulines themselves, whom it was charged were not cut out to oversee the education of native girls. In 1682, the intendant Jacques de Meulles told the minister in France that the austere and cloistered character of the Ursuline order was too far removed from the Indians' unrestrained life style to succeed. He complained, "They learn only how to pray and to speak French, all of which they soon forget, and when they have once been married to some Indian they hardly ever pray and never speak French."[32] The colonial administrator's words found a sympathethic ear in Paris, for the Crown was later to advise that Montreal-area Indian girls not be sent to the Quebec Ursulines for care and instruction.

Upriver from Quebec in the town of Montreal, which had been founded in 1642, two religious communities were making educational gestures. The Sulpicians, a community of secular priests who had come to the town in 1657 to launch a seminary and who later won seigneurial control over the area, established in 1677 a Mountain Mission on the slope of Mount Royal. The Sulpicians assumed responsibility for the instruction of Indian boys, leaving the education of native girls to the sisters of the Congregation of Notre Dame. Interpreting its mandate as that of Gallicizing and Christianizing the aborigines, the male community proceeded to instruct its charges in catechism, French letters, and the agricultural arts.

For the Congregation of Notre Dame the task of instructing Indian girls was not entirely new. The order's Canadian foundress, Marguerite Bourgeoys, had opened a school in a stable given to her by Maisonneuve, founder and first governor of Montreal. The Notre Dame Sisters, much like the Ursulines, had come to New France to assist in the care and education of Indian girls, and welcomed the opportunity presented by the Sulpicians, since it assured them of a regular clientele. With the aid of a royal subsidy a building was erected in 1679, large enough to lodge two teachers and a handful of boarders. Marguerite Bourgeoys agreed with the Ursulines and the Jesuits that the boarding school offered the best hope for the evangelization of Indian children.

The nominal purpose of the female section of Mountain Mission was to prepare native girls for Christian motherhood. Owing to an emerging state policy of Frenchification, however, the aims and activities of Marguerite Bourgeoys's school went beyond spiritual enlightenment. Besides being inculcated in the mysteries and rites of Christianity, initially in their own dialect, Indian girls were instructed in French letters and the household arts. Like French girls, they were taught to sew, spin, and knit, practising on wood and thread that had been purchased with the aid of a royal grant. They were also attired in French dress.[33] Gallic attitudes toward work were emphasized, as were habits of politeness and cheerfulness, which were Sister Marguerite's personal contribution. Laval's successor, Bishop Saint-Vallier, who visited Montreal in 1685, came away deeply impressed with the educational work of the female community, saying that at the "Mission of the Mountain some forty Indian girls are being reared in the French manner, instructing them at the same in the mysteries of the faith ... and not only in their language, but also in ours, to make of them little by little like us."[34]

As was noted earlier, some colonial authorities believed that the Congregation of Notre Dame was better suited than the Ursulines to educate Indian girls. Suggesting that the less severe regimen of the Congregation of Notre Dame better fitted the Indian life style, Intendant de Meulles requested financial support for Marguerite Bourgeoys's school at Mountain Mission. France responded by contributing funds to the enterprise. The Crown must also have had commercial motives in mind, since the minister promised to send additional teachers to Montreal to teach Indian girls "to knit ... to spin and to make lace, so as to be able to introduce these manufactures into the country."[35]

In spite of government aid and backing for the female community, the evidence does not show that the Notre Dame Sisters were any more successful than the Ursulines in converting large numbers of Indian girls. At most, the Congregation of Notre Dame effected several individual triumphs: two girls, an Iroquois and an Algonkin, became members of the order and went on to become teachers.

The seminary, whether Jesuit or Ursuline, was not the only French institution designed to aid in the evangelization of Indian boys and girls. Father Le Jeune longed for the day when an order of nuns would come to Canada to establish a hospital. He predicted no lack of patients, citing the Indians' vulnerability to the white man's diseases and the neglect of their own illnesses. He reasoned that the native peoples would be so taken with the quality of care in a French hospital that their hostility to Christian beliefs and practices would evaporate, and they would be more agreeable to releasing their children to the missionaries for instruction. As for those Indians who died in the hospital, Le Jeune said that their children would fall naturally into the hands of the Jesuits, who would take responsibility for their education and upbringing.[36] Seen in a broader perspective, a hospital would reinforce the sedentary policy underlying the reserve system, for it would make the Indians more dependent on the French and their institutions. Thus, the establishment of Hôtel-Dieu at Quebec in 1639 under the direction of the Hospitalières de la Miséricorde de Jésus, or Hospital Nuns, and a similar establishment under Jeanne Mance in Montreal in 1642 were salutary developments from several points of view.

From its modest beginnings Hôtel-Dieu in Quebec was always more than a hospital for the sick. It was also a social-welfare centre that catered to the needy, the abandoned, and the elderly, and doubled as a school for French and Indian girls. From time to time the Hospital Nuns took in Indian orphans and reared and instructed them, as was the case for Marie Thérèse, a Huron girl, who was later sent to Brittany for further schooling.[37] Lacking sufficient staff and always financially hard pressed, Hôtel-Dieu recruited Indian women to act as orderlies and interpreters in the sick wards. One such female helper was the Huron Agnes Skannudharoi, who had learned French at the Ursuline seminary.[38]

In the early years of the Quebec hospital, the Jesuits performed educational work at the institution, teaching Indian patients Christian doctrine, leading them in prayers and songs, and saying mass for those already baptized. The Hospital Nuns later replaced the Jesuits as instructors. All in all, the Ursulines and the Hospital Nuns gave direction and character to the early Canadian church, making it an institution rooted in good works, social welfare, and female education.

The making of New France a royal province, or colony, in 1663 produced in its wake a closer scrutiny of colonial affairs by the home government. One example was France's growing determination "to extend the blessings of civilization to the Indians," to make them French in language, behaviour, and outlook. The principal architect of the Frenchification policy was the king's minister of marine, Jean-Baptiste Colbert, who saw in assimilation of Indians the means by which Christianity might be expanded and the fragile population of the colony increased, given that massive immigration was an unworkable option. In 1666, Colbert directed Intendant Jean Talon to encourage Christian Indians to come and live among the French so that they and their children might adopt civilized ways.[39] In a later dispatch, the minister commanded the intendant to encourage

the clergy to educate the Indians in the French manner. An outgrowth of the acculturation policy was the insistence that marriage
between the two races favour the Gallic cause. In 1673, permission
was granted to Nicolas Pelletier to marry a widow of the Montagnais
tribe, on the condition that the couple live among the French and
that their children be brought up to speak French.[40]

In 1667, Colbert reproached the Canadian clergy, and in particular the Jesuits, for failing to instruct the Indians along French lines,
charging, "Little effort has been made to detach them from their
savage customs and to oblige them to adopt ours, especially to teach
them our language."[41] While the minister was correct in asserting
that the Jesuits had failed to educate the aboriginal population in
the French language, he was wrong in implying that Frenchification
had not been attempted. Had he reviewed contemporary history
more closely, he would have learned that civilizing efforts had been
attempted and found wanting. Ever since the days of the Recollets
and Champlain, efforts had been made to form the Indian in the
French mould, with little to show in the way of concrete results. If
the Indian had shown himself to be little attracted to the white man's
religion, he was drawn even less to his language and customs.[42]

Colbert's apparent ignorance of events in the colony may be attributed to the fact that he was an ocean away from it and was being
advised by officials in New France who held little affection for the
Jesuits. No sooner had Count Frontenac arrived in Quebec as the
new governor, in 1672, than he wrote to Colbert expressing surprise
and indignation over the fact that the Indians living near the town
neither spoke French nor behaved like Frenchmen, which he blamed
on the Jesuits.[43] Both Talon and Frontenac laid the floundering
Frenchification policy at the feet of the Society of Jesus, accusing the
male order of not participating in civilizing attempts out of fear that
it would lose influence among the Indians. In their own defence, the
Jesuits reminded their critics that they had come to Canada to convert the Indians to Christianity, not to effect the mingling of the two
races. They also defended their policy of isolating the Indian from
the Frenchman as a sound one, claiming that it worked to protect
the natives against French vice and immorality, and citing the tragic
consequences of liquor to illustrate what could happen when the
two races were brought together. In addition, the many years of
living and working among the Indians in their villages, the sobering

experience of the Indian seminary at Notre-Dame-des-Anges, and the more recent collapse of the Sillery reserve had convinced the Jesuits of the futility of acculturation schemes. The Ursulines added their voice to the debate, coming down on the side of the Jesuits. Marie de l'Incarnation said that during the thirty years her order had been in Canada, only seven or eight Indian girls had been successfully Frenchified, a result which she ascribed to the tenacity of the indigenous culture.[44]

Finding that the acculturation campaign was languishing because of the opposition of the Jesuits and others in the colony, Colbert appealed to the secular clergy to assert itself. He wrote to Bishop Laval, asking him to set an example for the rest of the church by organizing the education of Indian boys along French lines, which he suggested could be accomplished by rearing French and Indian boys together. The churchman was quick to act, opening his Petit Séminaire in the fall of 1668, with an initial contingent of eight French and six Huron boys. The "little seminary" offered no formal instruction as such, its residents being sent to the nearby Jesuit school for French instruction. In spite of the bishop's attentiveness toward his Indian boys and the moral and financial support of the Crown, the experiment ultimately suffered the same fate as others involving attempted acculturation of native peoples. On his return to New France in 1670, after an absence of almost two years, Talon noted that the number of Indian boys recruited by the bishop had "strongly diminished."[45] In 1673, Joseph, the last of the original group of Huron boys at the Petit Séminaire, quit the institution at the request of his parents. From that date forward, no Indian name appears on the registration list of the seminary.[46]

Governor Frontenac was personally active in the Frenchification campaign. In 1674, he wrote to Colbert as someone who had just pulled off a master stroke, announcing that he had requested and received from the Iroquois four of their boys for keeping and instruction. He said that the two youngest boys were being kept at his home at his expense, though all were being sent to the Jesuit school for French-language instruction.[47] The records do not reveal how well the governor fared in the social experiment, but it is unlikely that he succeeded where others had failed. The intendant Duchesneau also got into the act, adopting three Indian boys whom he intended to rear along with his own sons. When the Indian youngsters fled his home shortly after having been fitted with French clothes, the colonial administrator grumbled at having "incurred considerable expense on them."[48]

The civil leadership of the colony was learning firsthand what the religious communities had long known, that good intentions and persistence were not sufficient in bringing about the cultural transformation of the Indians. As a matter of fact, not only had the mixing of the two races failed to produce the desired results, it appears to have backfired, as evidenced by an increasing tendency among Europeans to adopt the Indian way of life. Marie de l'Incarnation put it best: "A Frenchman becomes a Savage sooner than a Savage becomes French."[49] Indeed, the large number of Frenchmen – an estimated six hundred in 1685 – who had taken to living in the forest and who went by the name of *coureurs de bois* – had become a problem and an embarrassment to officialdom. Their carefree attitude and disregard for moral conventions outraged many in the colony and brought demands for a curtailment of their activities. And while the missionaries sometimes used their offices in arranging contacts with the Indians, the Jesuits found on the whole that they did more harm than good in the evangelization campaign. In short, the vices and debaucheries of the *coureurs* were to some a living contradiction to the message of beauty, restraint, and purity as represented by the missionaries.

With the arrival in the colony of Denonville as governor of New France, in 1685, came the first official challenge to the Frenchification policy, even though the new colonial head was ordered by the king to encourage marriage between Frenchmen and Indian girls.[50] Shortly after his arrival, Denonville informed the minister that not only was acculturation not working, but the very opposite had happened, for the Indians "have communicated to us very much everything they have which is most wicked and have acquired only that which is evil and vicious in us."[51] Convinced that the missionaries were right after all, that the isolation of the Indians in reserves offered the best chance for turning them into Christians and Frenchmen, Denonville called on the Crown to alter its policy. To that end, he recommended an expansion of the reserve system so that Indians might be properly supervised by the Jesuits and others, and protected from the pernicious influences of the fur and brandy traders.

By the end of the seventeenth century, the French government had grudgingly accepted the fact that the Indian could not be transformed into a Frenchman, whether by education, marriage, or other social means. Thus the Crown showed little enthusiasm for Cadillac's petition of 1703, in which the founder of Detroit requested funds "to set up a seminary here for instructing the children of the savages with those of the French in piety, and for teaching them our language by the same means."[52]

By the end of the century few Indian children were attending French schools. The educational and religious idealism that had triggered the creation of Indian seminaries earlier in the century had given way to hard realism. At the same time, the male and female teaching communities increasingly saw their principal educational clientele as colonial, not Indian, children.

### CHAPTER FOUR

# An Outline of Colonial Education

In 1961, a Quebec historian wrote an important article on nine-teenth-century Quebec education, asking whether it was the respon-sibility of the church or the state.[1] Such a piece could not have been written on seventeenth- and eighteenth-century education, since the period allowed no dispute over the control of learning. Indeed, until the French Revolution the Roman Catholic church was the unchal-lenged authority in education in France, a tradition that reached back to the early Middle Ages and that, if anything, grew stronger during the Catholic Counter-Reformation of the sixteenth century. In education, as in other areas of social welfare, the state or national government remained in the wings, content to leave the organization and administration of learning in private hands. Nor should we expect it to have been otherwise. The time had not yet arrived when education, in the manner of war, trade, and foreign affairs, was an instrument of national policy. It should be remembered that until the nineteenth century and the rise of the modern state, the notion of learning as a public enterprise was little accepted in most lands. The modern view that the social and economic health of a nation is inextricably linked to education was an alien concept during the age of New France.

The foregoing remarks ought not to convey the impression that the civil authority of earlier times was indifferent to learning and always the spectator in its diffusion. The documentary evidence of the day demonstrates clearly that government authorities, from the king and his ministers in France to the governor and the intendant in New France, were involved in education. To be sure, their partic-ipation was irregular and indirect, since the Crown deferred to others in the founding and running of schools. Generally, government intervention took the form of a directive encouraging the adoption of a particular policy or the funding of educational projects. For example, in 1722 the king reminded the Charon Brothers of Montreal that his subsidy of three thousand *livres* was given to the teaching community on the condition that the brothers provide free education in the rural districts.[2] In 1729, the king advised civil authorities in New France that one way of increasing the number of schoolmasters in the rural parts of the colony was to practise a tactic used in France – namely, to have in "each parish some persons who know how to read and write who in time can be enlisted to teach their neighbours' children for a fee."[3] These and other pieces of evidence contradict François-Xavier Garneau's harsh indictment that the French court regarded popular education in the colony as "dangerous and destructive" to the tranquillity of the state.[4]

It was in the financial domain that the Crown played its most active role in education, though its support tended to be selective rather than general and comprehensive. Statutory funding of education was not a characteristic of seventeenth- and eighteenth-century Canada, nor, for that matter, of Europe. Still, religious authorities could normally count on state subsidies for their operations, part of which they used for education. In addition, the Crown periodically provided money grants for specific educational projects that it judged worthy of support. Thus, a subsidy might be earmarked for paying the salaries of schoolmasters, for building a school, or for the purchase of educational supplies. Such payments were often based upon requests submitted by colonial officials to Paris. In the preceding chapter we learned that Marguerite Bourgeoys's order received a royal award of one thousand *livres* for the purchase of wool and other materials, with which her Indian girls practised sewing and knitting. In 1686 the king contributed a sum of four hundred *livres* to pay the salary of a royal hydrographer at Quebec, later increasing the amount so the Jesuits could teach the navigational arts at their college. Sometimes educational aid came in the form of a land grant. A contract dated 1688 and signed by the governor, the intendant, and the bishop authorized the transfer of Crown land in Trois-Rivières to the latter, upon which he could build a girls' school to be turned over to the Congregation of Notre Dame. The colonial government's action was prompted by the belief that "there are a good number of girls to instruct" in the town.[5]

Those in charge of education and welfare in the colony were heavily dependent on royal subsidies and private donations for their operations. Some religious groups were more dependent on external support than others, for while all were rich in zeal and devotion, some were poor in material wealth. The Ursulines, the Congregation of Notre Dame, the Recollets, and the Charon Brothers were paupers alongside the affluent Jesuits and Sulpicians, who enjoyed strong private backing in France and held large seigneurial holdings in New France from which they drew rents and dues. The Gentlemen of St Sulpice, whose members did not take vows of poverty, were seigneurs and administrators of Montreal. Some of their members possessed considerable wealth, which they put at the disposal of the religious community. François Vachon de Belmont, Sulpician superior of New France between 1701 and 1732, was an aristocrat by birth and heir to a large family fortune. Thanks to the private generosity of Belmont and others, the Sulpicians were able to finance not only their own educational activities but those of others as well. Both the Congregation of Notre Dame and the Rouillé Brothers, a seventeenth-century lay teaching community, were recipients of Sulpician largess.

In a constant struggle to make ends meet, the religious orders engaged in a number of schemes to bring in money or to help reduce expenses. The Notre Dame Sisters periodically turned to making and mending clothes, and the Ursulines to farming, to sustain themselves. The female communities also relied on dowries for badly needed income. Girls entering religious life were expected to contribute a sum of money, goods, or land. Still, the fact remains that no religious community in New France was sufficiently well-off to pronounce itself free of all debts. In the manner of today's governments all practised deficit spending, as expenses usually outstripped revenues. Though the Jesuits were financially better off than most, they too were incapable of meeting all their educational obligations without the help of outside funding. The Jesuit plan for a college in eighteenth-century Montreal failed when the Crown refused to release funds for the project. For the Charon Brothers, the annual royal subsidy constituted the financial lifeblood of the teaching order. When, in 1731, the king determined that the brothers were failing in their social and educational responsibilities, he cancelled their subsidy. The Montreal community never fully recovered from the loss of funds.

There is another side to state participation in New France education. While the Crown promoted learning through the power of the purse, its policy of regulating and limiting religious expansion in the colony, through withholding or delaying legal recognition of new religious orders, sometimes produced the opposite effect. Thus, the Congregation of Notre Dame and the Charon Brothers, both of which were active in education, were slowed in their institutional development by a hesitant Crown. There are other examples. When in the last decade of the seventeenth century the Ursulines of Trois-Rivières were founded to provide learning and health care in the town, Bishop Saint-Vallier was criticized by the minister Pontchartrain for having agreed to the establishment of a new order, saying that the bishop's funds and efforts should have been applied for founding new parishes.[6] The Crown's containment policy with respect to religious communities was sometimes expressed by a limitation on the number of their members. In 1701, royal consent was given to the Hospital Nuns of Quebec to found a general hospital, with the proviso that the number of member sisters be restricted to eight.[7] In other words, royal reluctance to extend recognition to new religious communities, coupled with restrictions on existing ones, worked to impede learning by depriving the colony of the very elements to which education was entrusted.

Although the church was the initiating force in colonial education, it does not necessarily follow that the citizenry was a silent and passive majority. The population of New France, particularly in the urban centres of Quebec, Montreal, and Trois-Rivières, was not bashful about voicing its educational concerns, by demanding more and better schools. In some cases, public opinion was instrumental in leading to educational action. In the late seventeenth century, the inhabitants of Quebec's lower town complained of not having a girls' school, and the Congregation of Notre Dame responded by opening a school and staffing it with schoolmistresses. Pressed by the townspeople of Trois-Rivières to provide learning facilities for girls, Bishop Saint-Vallier financed the construction of a school in 1697 and put the Ursulines in charge of it. Sometimes, however, public demands went unanswered. In the eighteenth century, a group of Montreal citizens unsuccessfully petitioned the Crown for a boys' college in the town. Moreover, in the 1750s the parishioners of Detroit wrote to the governor at Quebec, asking for several Notre Dame Sisters to come and set up a school. The inhabitants said they were prepared to finance the operation, since it would free them of the necessity of sending their daughters to Montreal, Quebec, or elsewhere, at a prohibitive cost. The outbreak of the war compromised the scheme.

The local population also exercised influence on education through the parish organization known as the *fabrique* (church council), composed of *marguilliers* (churchwardens) elected by the parishioners. The role of the *fabrique* was essentially economic, as it was responsible for administration of the material affairs of the parish. Using revenues from voluntary contributions and pew rentals, the church council managed the upkeep of the church, the rectory, and the cemetery. There is evidence to indicate that it was sometimes involved in engaging a teacher or providing funds for the construction of a school. In a notarized contract of 1651, the *curé* and the churchwardens of the parish of Quebec agree to engage and maintain Martin Boutet as boys' singing teacher and precentor for the church.[8] Similarly, in 1686 Jean-Baptiste Pottier was engaged by the *fabrique* of Lachine to serve jointly as schoolmaster, precentor, and parish secretary for the sum of fifty *livres* a year.[9]

Inasmuch as formal learning in early Canada was principally a product of private initiative and not widely diffused outside the towns, the period showed few of the structural and organizational trappings of contemporary education. In short, the schools did not come together to form a coherent system. There was no ministry of education or similar administrative body to oversee learning at the central level, nor was there anything approaching school boards at the local level. Moreover, there was no one person in whom the overall direction of education was entrusted, though the higher clergy sometimes performed leadership and administrative functions at the central level and the parish clergy did so at the local level.

A case can be made that the bishop of New France, by dint of his position and power, served unofficially as education minister, since he authorized the founding of schools, contributed financially to their upkeep, and drew up regulations governing their operations. Notwithstanding Bishop Laval's considerable contributions to educational progress in the colony, it was his successor, Jean-Baptiste de Saint-Vallier, who most closely approached the spirit of the modern-day minister of education. Arriving in the colony in 1685 at the age of thirty-two, the young prelate spent the first eighteen months of his office travelling the length and breadth of his large diocese, a trip which, while undertaken to inform him of the state of the church in New France, served also as an educational junket. In the report that followed, Saint-Vallier wrote glowingly of the educational work of the Jesuits at their college in Quebec, noting that if the students were less numerous than in previous years they still compared favourably in quality with the best that France had to offer. He also had kind words for the Sulpicians and the Congregation of Notre Dame, praising their zeal in teaching Christian knowledge, French letters, and the practical arts to French and Indian children.[10]

During his long and often stormy reign as bishop – spanning forty-two years – which was punctuated by bitter battles with the Seminary of Quebec and the Jesuits, and which elicited requests from the king for him to resign, Saint-Vallier's interest in and support for education never flagged. As a product of the Counter-Reformation, he was deeply committed to the spiritual and social benefits of learning.[11] Through the vehicle of the pastoral letter, he lectured the clergy and the people on their responsibilities and duties toward education, with promises of financial assistance to those who responded to his words. In his *Rituel* of 1701, the bishop exhorted parish priests to ensure that their flocks were regularly and properly instructed in religion.[12] He advised his priests to make sure that schoolmasters and schoolmistresses were of good morals, that boys and girls did not attend class together, and that undesirable books did not fall into the hands of children. As did other officials in the colony, he saw in the dearth of parish priests in the country districts a cause of widespread ignorance, for without sufficient clergy there was no one in the rural parishes to provide educational leadership.

Ironically, the spiritual and educational condition of the colony suffered because of the long absences of some bishops. As a matter of fact, Saint-Vallier was gone from New France during seventeen years of his reign, and Laval was absent for twelve years of his. Bishop Lauberivière spent but one year in Canada, and Bishop Mornay never set foot in New France during his six-year espiscopate. Indeed, from the time of Laval's appointment, in the middle of the seventeenth century, to the end of the French regime in Canada, there were no less than forty years during which the colony was without a resident bishop. Without the physical presence of a bishop in the colony, much of the normal work of the diocese was neglected or delayed. Learning was a casualty of these absences, since they meant a leadership vacuum in education.

The attempt to liken the bishop to an education minister must not be carried too far, since the Canadian church was not the monolithic structure that its apologists and critics would have us believe it was.

It will be recalled that Louis XIV allowed the Recollets back into Canada in 1670 to counter the power of the Jesuits, who were cool to the Crown's policy of the acculturation of the Indians. Then, as now, the Roman Catholic church more closely resembled a grouping of self-contained bodies within an umbrella organization than a single, all-embracing entity. The compartmentalization of the church was reflected in its principal dualism: regular and secular clergy, higher and lower clergy, and male and female orders. These divisions contributed to autonomy, competition, and specialization among the various parts, thus denying the bishop absolute authority in education and other social domains. In effect, some clergy, particularly the Jesuits and Sulpicians, enjoyed a margin of spiritual and fiscal independence which afforded them the luxury of charting their own educational course. What is more, the teaching communities had tradition on their side, having staked educational claims in the New World prior to the coming of the secular clergy and the establishment of parishes. On the other hand, if the various religious groupings of New France were of different minds regarding the organization and administration of learning, on the fundamental purpose of education there was little disagreement. Prelate, parish priest, and peripatetic missionary were one in holding that the development of the Christian personality was central to all purposeful learning.

Viewed in institutional terms, New France consisted of a loose collection of schools, mostly of the elementary-school variety that went by the name of *petites écoles*, concentrated in and around the towns of Quebec, Montreal, and Trois-Rivières. Supplementing and building on the elementary schools were a college run by the Jesuits at Quebec, several vocational schools, and two seminaries. The Seminary of Quebec trained local boys for the priesthood; the smaller Sulpician seminary in Montreal was less a true seminary than a residence for members. While the colony did not have a university in name, the Jesuit college performed some of the functions of a higher-education facility.

The schools of New France were not evenly distributed across the colony. Continuing a trend that had been at work since the rise of towns in the Middle Ages, educational facilities were centred in the towns and their neighbouring parishes, not only because it was there that literate persons were most in demand, but because it was there that the teaching communities were located. As one left the cultural and geographical orbit of the three towns, educational provision fell off dramatically. Indications are that few rural parishes had schools or teachers.

What did the schools of New France look like? Thanks to sketches and paintings of the day, we have a pictorial idea of some of the colony's better-known institutions. The Jesuit college and the Ursulines' convent school at Quebec were favourite subjects of contemporary artists; they were depicted as large and handsome buildings, which squares with Peter Kalm's description of them in his visit to the town in 1749. Another school frequently captured on canvas was Marguerite Bourgeoys's first school in Montreal, which was an abandoned stable measuring thirty-six feet in length and eighteenth feet in width.[13] While this structure did not compare in size and elegance to the two Quebec institutions, it is worth noting that all three buildings were of stone construction. As for schoolhouses outside the urban centres, we know little of their physical features. The few that existed were converted buildings or spare rooms. They were likely wood structures, since wood was abundant in the countryside and the danger of fires spreading less than in the towns. In the rural parish of Lachine, the rectory served as the boys' school for the lay schoolmaster Jean-Baptiste Pottier in 1686. This rectory was later used by the Congregation of Notre Dame for educational purposes before it acquired its own building in 1705. For a number of lay schoolmasters, the home – theirs or their pupils' – served as a makeshift classroom. For example, the seventeenth-century cartographer Jean-Baptiste Franquelin taught students the navigational arts in his Quebec apartment, though a classroom was put at his disposal at the Jesuit college. Similarly, finding, upon his arrival in Detroit in 1760, that the town was without a school, the lay teacher Jean-Baptiste Roucout converted his home into a classroom. For tutors engaged by families to teach their children, the problem of a classroom did not arise; it came with the job.

The division of schools and classes along sex lines was standard practice in early Canada, for it was believed by religious authorities that the mixing of boys and girls in the classroom was morally risky. Indeed, any mixing of the young was cause for concern to the puritanical Bishop Saint-Vallier, who once urged the governor and his wife to set a good example for the townspeople by not holding dances at which boys and girls were in attendance or allowing the sexes to declaim on the same stage.[14] Part of the educational principle involved a ban on male and female teachers instructing children of the opposite sex. In the earliest years of the colony, the proscription on mixed teaching fell victim to the realities of the day, owing to a shortage of teachers.

To judge by the long list of ecclesiastical directives and parliamentary *arrêts* against it, co-education must have been widespread in seventeenth-century France. In spite of the fulminations of authorities, teachers frequently instructed both sexes, since it was a way of supplementing their paltry income. Apparently, the practice of co-education and mixed teaching was fairly widespread in New France as well, for Bishop Saint-Vallier issued two pronouncements against it around 1700, and in 1729 Intendant Dupuy reinforced the clerical position by decreeing that schoolmasters and schoolmistresses not instruct children of the opposite sex except by written permission of the bishop.[15] Two years earlier, in authorizing the lay schoolmaster Raymond Bertrand Junceria to keep a school in Charlesbourg, Dupuy had reminded him that he was only to teach boys.[16]

Other pieces of evidence lend support to the suspicion that the ban on co-education and mixed instruction was not always respected. This is the impression given by a clerical letter of 1735, in which Bishop Dosquet authorized the sending of additional Notre Dame Sisters to Louisbourg. In the letter, the bishop directs the sisters to teach only "those of their sex," as if to imply that the schoolmistresses had been guilty of teaching boys.[17] An examination of notarial contracts reveals that male tutors taught girls as well as boys. For example, in a contract of 1681 the lay tutor Pierre Bertrand promises to take up duties with the Hertel family of Trois-Rivières as soon as he completes his instruction of the daughter of M. Trottier Des Ruisseaux.[18]

Schools in New France were divided into *externat* (day) and *pensionnat* (boarding) institutions. In number and quality, the latter were surprisingly well represented in the colony. The Jesuit college at Quebec had boarding facilities, as did the Ursulines' schools at Quebec and Trois-Rivières. Young men studying for the priesthood at the Seminary of Quebec were lodged at the Petit Séminaire. In addition, most of the schools run by the Congregation of Notre Dame provided living accommodations for girls. The boarding school had many defenders, who considered it superior to the day school on the grounds that the youngster who "lived in" was more receptive to learning. But perhaps the real reason for the spread of boarding schools in New France was less educational sentiment than geographic and demographic realities. It is no exaggeration to say that the boarding school was an absolute necessity in a land whose population was at once small and scattered, whose climate was harsh during a good part of the year, and where distance and slow transportation precluded travel to and from school. The boarding school solved some of the problems connected with education in a frontier society.

Although the schools of New France were in private hands, they showed a public and egalitarian character by providing free tuition and opening their doors to children of all social-class backgrounds. Still, education was not entirely free. Schoolchildren were normally assessed a fee for textbooks and other instructional materials, and boarders were expected to pay for their keep unless they were charity cases. But money was scarce in the colony, and even middle-class families were hard pressed to meet their educational expenses. Only a quarter of the girls enrolled as boarders at the Ursuline school at Quebec in the early years of the institution were capable of paying their *pension* costs in full.[19] Two-thirds of the boarders at the Petit Séminaire in 1700 paid only a part of their maintenance, and the remaining third paid nothing at all.[20]

When families contributed something toward the payment of their children's education, more often than not it was in kind rather than in money. The records of the period are replete with examples of parents paying their educational bills with the likes of cords of firewood, barrels of marinated eels, and pots of butter. Boys boarding at a school in Saint-Joachim in 1690 were charged three *livres* and a bushel of salt per month for their keep.[21]

A curious footnote to the composition of the educational clientele of New France is that, in addition to French and Indian children, it included a handful of English-speaking girls. In their military strikes on New England settlements, France's Indian allies took prisoners, either as hostages or to help replenish their own tribal losses. The captives sometimes included young girls; some of them were brought to Canada and placed in the care of the religious orders, who welcomed the opportunity to tutor these young Protestants in catechism and rebaptizing them in the Catholic faith. Some of the converts opted for the religious life. Mary Sayward, aged eleven when delivered to the sisters of the Congregation of Notre Dame in 1692, later became a nun in the order. Perhaps the most celebrated convert was Esther Wheelwright, who was aged seven when she was carried off by the Abenakis on a raid of her Massachusetts town in 1703. While a captive of the Indians, she was instructed in the Catholic religion by a Jesuit missionary. Later, she was brought to Quebec and placed in the Ursuline convent, where she took the habit in 1713. In 1760, she was elected superior of the Quebec Ursulines, apparently as a gesture to foster good relations with the British military authorities.

The educational aims, curricula, pedagogy, and instructional materials of the schools of New France were largely those of the mother country. The *petites écoles* of early Canada did what elementary schools of Europe had been doing for centuries: teaching children to read, write, count, and know God. On the scale of priorities, the last was the highest, for the cultivation of piety took precedence over the learning of letters. When religious authorities lamented the ignorance of the people, they were referring less to their illiterate condition than to their lack of spiritual enlightenment. Put another way, the school of New France was less a place of mental learning than a centre of moral and religious formation.

Judging from the documentary records of the period, catechism, or religious instruction, was not always a curricular subject in the manner of reading and writing. For example, a contract signed in 1699 by Bishop Saint-Vallier and the authorities of the Seminary of Quebec to authorize the establishment of a boys' school in the town makes no mention of the teaching of religion, only to that of reading, writing, and counting.[22] Yet it would be wrong to conclude from this document that since religion was not listed it would not be taught. On the contrary, such was the overriding importance of religion in education that its place was assumed or left unsaid. Thus, not only were the tenets of religion taught in a more or less systematic fashion, they were reinforced by such subsidiary activities as prayers and hymn singing. Moreover, the secular subjects were enlisted in the cause of Christian learning, as evidenced by the heavy spiritual content of school readers: to learn to read in the schools of early Canada was to be exposed to morally uplifting stories of saints and other biblical figures. The instilling of religious truths in children was ensured by the teacher, who, whether lay or religious, was committed to the primacy of Christian learning. In their act of foundation, in 1686, the Rouillé Brothers, a lay teaching order, promised to instruct Montreal boys in reading, writing, and piety.[23]

The schools of New France were entrusted with moral and social, as well as spiritual and academic, responsibilities. Religious authorities held up the school as the moral antidote to the vice rampant in society. Thus, the central motive for the establishment of the Petit Séminaire in 1668 was, according to its own records, "to remove the children from the corruption of the century, from dissolute ways."[24] In applauding the opening of a girls' school in Quebec in 1691 by the Congregation of Notre Dame, the local *curé* declared that the institution would counter "the immoral ways and other failings" that he said afflicted so many of the young girls.[25] In the opinion of the Ursuline superior, Marie de l'Incarnation, schooling released children from the grip of barbarism. On one occasion, she offered that "without the education that we give our French girls ... they would be worse brutes than the savages."[26]

The educational content of the schools run by the religious orders was steeped in moral and social injunctions. The Congregation of Notre Dame and the Charon Brothers pronounced idleness the colony's most serious social ill and exhorted their teachers to instill good work habits in their pupils. Those teaching under the banner of the Charon Brothers also strove to impress upon their boys the importance of proper moral behaviour, of obeying one's parents, of not lying or showing anger or stealing from others.[27] Students at the Seminary of Quebec were reminded of the moral dangers of frivolous activities such as games of chance, cards, dice, and billiards, and were advised to avoid comedies, farces, operas, and other dubious amusements.[28] Religious leaders alerted schoolmistresses to be on the lookout for signs of affectedness, vanity, immodesty, and other personality faults in their girls. The rules of modesty extended to dress, as well. After a visit to the Montreal school of the Congregation of Notre Dame, during which he spotted examples of pretentious dress among some of the girls, Bishop Saint-Vallier issued a directive condemning "headwear with several lace folds and coiffures supported by more than a single ribbon."[29]

In their reports to Paris, governors and intendants stressed the social benefits to be derived from educational provision, particularly in combatting laziness and anti-social behaviour in the young, as well as their tendency to take on Indian ways. In calling for the opening of boys' schools in the countryside, the eighteenth-century

intendant Jacques Raudot said that their establishment would counteract the influence of rural parents, whom he accused of failing to
demand respect and discipline from their children.

The inhabitants of this land have never had an education. Because of the
weakness that comes from an insane love that their fathers and mothers
have for them in their infancy, in the manner of the savages, they are not
corrected and their character is not formed. As there are also no schoolmasters, they have developed a hard and ferocious character, which falls
often even upon their fathers and mothers, for whom they lack respect, and
upon their superiors and parish priests ... It seems to me ... that it would
be necessary ... to establish schoolmasters in all regions, who, besides the
instruction they would give, would teach them early to be obedient.[30]

Although the sexes studied much the same subject matter in their
respective schools – reading, writing, counting, and religion – girls'
learning was less academic, more practical, and more religious in
emphasis. The distinction lay in the differentiation of sex roles in
early Canada. In general, the province of the male was the world
outside the home, and that of the female was inside the home. Hence,
the rearing and education of girls was geared toward preparing them
for the duties of motherhood and household management, an idea
that lost none of its validity on Canadian soil. Moreover, a girl, even
one from a distinguished family, rarely continued her education
beyond early adolescence; neither law nor tradition required it. She
was judged to have acquired sufficient knowledge to receive first
communion and to assume some adult responsibilities.

In some boys' schools, Latin was taught to those aspiring to continue their education at the Jesuit college. Latin was not offered in
the girls' schools; it was dismissed as intellectually presumptuous
and unnecessary, since there was no secondary school to which they
could go. Girls were destined to become wives and mothers, so basic
subject matter was supplemented by practical instruction in the
household arts, usually sewing, spinning, knitting, and other types
of needlework. Sometimes drawing and painting were taught to girls
from better families. Music instruction probably found its way into
some schools, since religious teachers were frequently trained musi-
cians and instruments such as the violin, the double bass, the flute,
the lute, and the organ were present in the colony. The eighteenth-
century Sulpician schoolmaster Jean Girard, who taught in Montreal

for forty years, was an accomplished organist; it seems likely that he shared his love of music with his pupils.

As the colony lacked a printing press, schools were dependent on France for their texts. While a comprehensive list of school manuals cannot be known, some of the titles were *Le Petit Alphabet*, *Le Grand Alphabet*, and *Les Pensées chrétiennes*. Among the imported pedagogical guides for teachers were the popular *École paroissiale ou la manière d'instruire les enfants des petites écoles*, by Abbé Jacques de Batencour, and Abbé Charles Démia's *La Méthode pour faire les Écoles*. The teacher guides were not, however, slavishly followed. The schools of New France appeared to have ignored the outdated recommendation laid down in *École paroissiale* that Latin instruction precede French instruction in the order of things. Rather, they followed the current practice in France of beginning instruction in the vernacular and taking up the study of Latin later or ignoring it altogether.

Since many of the colony's teachers, like its school-books, were of the imported variety, it follows that classroom methods resembled those of France. As in the mother country, New France's teachers resorted to the orthodox methods of drill and memorization. It is doubtful whether many schools were moved by Montaigne's comment that "a mere book learning is a paltry learning." The point was made earlier that notions of child psychology and soft pedagogy were centuries away from being an accepted part of classroom method. Teachers saw children as society saw them, dependent beings whose duty it was to respond to adult commands and values. Children who failed to manifest the proper interest in their studies or who misbehaved were routinely punished, often physically and sometimes severely. Schools and teachers took their lead from society, which frequently used corporal punishment on wrongdoers.

Yet there is reason to suspect that schoolchildren in New France were treated less harshly than those on the other side of the Atlantic, thanks to a revised notion of childhood. To judge by the reports of colonial officials, children in Canada, and particularly boys, were well-nigh incorrigible – rebellious in behaviour and disrespectful toward their parents, who could hardly control them. Governor Denonville informed France in 1685 that "the great liberty which the light control of fathers and mothers and Governors has exercised over youth ... has reached the extremity that as soon as the children can shoulder a gun the fathers can no longer restrain them and do not dare to make them angry."[31]

On the other hand, a quite different portrait of youth emerges when measured against the laws and traditions of society, which subordinated children to the authority of their parents and especially of their fathers, who, in the fashion of an absolute ruler, were free to govern, reward, and punish their offspring as they saw fit. Those who support this interpretation of childhood in early Canada like to point out that by law children could not marry before the age of majority without parental consent. Perhaps this was the case in better families, but there is evidence to the effect that among the common people young adults married when and whom they pleased.[32]

The true status of children in New France probably lies somewhere between the two extremes, neither the unruly types portrayed in official accounts nor the docile, submissive beings implied by a patriarchal social structure. On balance, it would appear that the children of early Canadian society enjoyed a greater degree of freedom and individual recognition than did their counterparts in France. Their elevated status may be attributed in the first instance to the conditions of a frontier society, which militated against rigid patterns of upbringing. Large families (an average of six children per unit), a small and dispersed population, and certain economic realities had the effect of weakening parental authority. Because parents, especially in rural areas, required the co-operation of their children as contributors to the economic well-being of the family, they were less inclined to rear their children in an overly strict fashion. Another significant variable was the influence of an alternative mode of upbringing. The point was made earlier that Indian child-rearing practices, marked by parental indulgence, much affection, and little punishment, stood in sharp contrast to the traditional French conception of childhood. The notion of permissive child-rearing did not go unnoticed in colonial circles. The Jesuits, according to one writer, gradually recognized "the virtues of an education based on gentleness."[33] Though it cannot be proved, it is possible that the Indian model induced schools and teachers in the colony to exhibit a more enlightened view of children – more inclined to treat them as individuals in their own right, less inclined to anchor instruction in chastisement. By the same token, the more liberal treatment of children may have been a factor in their ability to resist the educational wishes of family and society. Colonial authorities reported to France that children did not take naturally to learning. Pierre Boucher, governor of Trois-Rivières, said, "It is difficult to captivate them with studies."[34]


New France was not a hotbed of pedagogical reform, since it took its lead from France, which itself was slow to adopt new instructional methods. Nevertheless, some new educational techniques managed to make the long voyage across the Atlantic, to become fixtures in the schools of the colony. Part of Marguerite Bourgeoys's educational baggage from abroad was the liberal pedagogy of Abbé Pierre Fourier, who had had a hand in founding the Congregation of Notre Dame in France in 1598. Besides promoting the cause of female learning, Fourier advocated the class system of teaching, which in many parts of Europe took a back seat to tutorial or individualized methods of instruction. He was also in advance of his time in recommending that pupils be divided in the classroom according to their age and ability. And like his contemporary, Comenius, he stood in firm opposition to the use of arbitrary and harsh punishment in schools.

Antoine Forget, a schoolmaster dispatched to Montreal in 1701 by the Sulpician seminary in Paris, is credited with introducing Lasallian pedagogy into the town's schools. Forget had been trained in the classroom techniques of the Christian Brothers' Jean-Baptiste de La Salle and probably had a copy of the founder's *La Conduite des Écoles*, a sort of elementary-school equivalent of the Jesuits' *Ratio Studiorum*.

Before we yield to the temptation of passing sentence on the classrooms of early Canada, it is well to remember that the conditions of learning were far from ideal during the period. If classrooms were dreary places and children often unresponsive or hostile to learning, one reason was the absence of trained teachers. Before the rise of normal schools, in nineteenth-century Europe and America, most teachers came to the job with little theoretical and practical knowledge of how to teach. One of the first to declare war on the dilettante teacher was La Salle, who preached the notion that teachers are made and not born, and that some insight into the child's nature and a grounding in the principles of pedagogy would translate into better schools. To that end, he is credited with establishing some of the world's first normal schools for the training of elementary-school teachers.

Although New France did not have a teacher-training facility, it did not miss the mark by much. The Charon Brothers, a Montreal-based religious order active in boys' education and social welfare, repeatedly attempted to attract La Salle's Brothers of the Christian Schools to Canada, which almost certainly would have led to the establishment of a normal school. On the other hand, the absence in the colony of a teacher-training institution does not mean that teachers embarked on their duties wholly unprepared. Prospective teachers sometimes received informal instruction in classroom management from their religious community before being sent out to teach.

If facilities for teacher training were undeveloped in the colony, one can at least detect the outline of a certification scheme by which those intending to teach were regulated. In theory, anyone wishing to keep school in New France could not do so except by clerical authorization. In a *circulaire* of 1691, Bishop Saint-Vallier commanded his parish priests to satisfy themselves that teachers in their districts were persons of good morals who had made a declaration of faith.[35] Later, the bishop granted parish priests inspection rights over teachers.[36] The certifying role of the bishop was reaffirmed by the civil authority, for in 1727 Intendant Dupuy issued an ordinance prohibiting anyone from teaching who did not have written permission from the bishop.[37] The records of the day do not reveal whether the instructions of the bishop and the intendant were fully respected, but common sense suggests that they were not; given the fact that schoolmasters and schoolmistresses were in short supply in the colony, it is unlikely that rigid barriers were placed before those who wished to teach. It is more likely that any lettered individual desirous of instructing the young was free to do so as long as his or her services were in demand.

Most teachers in seventeenth- and eighteenth-century Canada were born and educated in France and were attached to a religious community. The Sulpicians, who maintained a boys' school in Montreal from the second half of the seventeenth century, relied exclusively on teachers sent to them by the Sulpician seminary in Paris. The Jesuits manifested a preference for European-born teachers, as did the Charon Brothers, whose superiors periodically travelled to France in search of recruits. The Ursulines and the Congregation of

Notre Dame, who together monopolized girls' education, also looked to France for most of their schoolmistresses, though this tradition weakened in the eighteenth century with the Canadianization of their ranks. Marguerite Bourgeoys made several voyages to France in the second half of the seventeenth century, each time returning with schoolmistresses.

Gabriel Souart and Philippe Boucher were a rare breed: they were parish priests who for a time doubled as schoolmasters. Montreal's first *curé*, Souart served concurrently as spiritual leader and boys' teacher in the seventeenth century. Boucher, parish priest of Pointe-de-Lévis in the 1690s and son of the governor of Trois-Rivières, taught local boys their French and Latin letters. Some of his products went on to the Seminary of Quebec.

The truth is that most parish clergy had neither the time nor the inclination to perform as schoolmasters. Their other duties left them with little time for secondary activities such as teaching. In addition to ministering to the spiritual needs of their flocks, *curés* were responsible for keeping parish records, which included the registration of births, marriages, and deaths. Because of a chronic shortage of their number in the colony, some parish priests were charged with the responsibility of overseeing more than one parish, which kept them on the move. Rather, the parish priest's real educational role was that of leader, of making sure that his parish had educational facilities and teachers. To judge by recurring complaints from some bishops, the parish clergy were negligent in exercising their educational responsibilities.

Although few *curés* were schoolmasters as such, they were not free of all pedagogical functions: they organized classes for children in preparation for their first communion. Usually such classes were scheduled during the several weeks preceding communion and were devoted to basic instruction in Christian doctrine and ritual. In the country parishes, what with a scattered population and the lack of resident priests, such instruction was not always possible.

A point of some importance is that the teacher corps of New France included a surprisingly large number of laymen, which demonstrates that education was not entirely a church monopoly. A search of parish registers, notarial acts, and other documentary sources of the period has unearthed the names of fifty-seven lay schoolmasters.[38] Most fit the description of freelancers: like artisans or craftsmen, they were unattached individuals who negotiated their own arrangements. The only example of lay schoolmasters coming together as a group was the short-lived community known as the Rouillé Brothers. Founded in 1686 by six unmarried Montrealers and headed by Mathurin Rouillé, the teaching order folded in 1693 owing to mounting debts and the loss of some of its members.

Some lay schoolmasters taught in a specific location; others, in the manner of the peripatetic Greeks of antiquity, travelled from place to place, peddling their pedagogical wares for a fee. François Labernade was probably the itinerant teacher par excellence. Between 1673 and 1688 he made pedagogical stops in, among other places, Île d'Orléans, Champlain, Pointe-aux-Trembles, and Montreal.

Other lay schoolmasters were in fact private tutors, engaged by families to instruct their children in reading and writing, usually for a fixed period of time. It is worth recalling that tutorial instruction had been for centuries the preferred mode of learning among the better classes of Europe, though it began to lose ground to the institutional school from the seventeenth century – though Rousseau's *Émile*, written as late as 1762, was sketched around the principle of tutorial instruction. Thanks to notarial and other records, we know the names of several tutors and something of their working conditions. In a contract of 1674, Nicolas Métru agrees to "teach reading and writing to the best of his ability" to the children of the Jacques Charrier family of Île d'Orléans. For its part, the family promises to provide Métru with room, board, and heat, to treat him in a humane fashion, and to pay him the sum of eighty *livres* for a year's engagement.[39] In 1681, Pierre Bertrand, who reportedly had attended the University of Paris, promised to serve as tutor to the family of the military figure Joseph-François Hertel of Trois-Rivières, but not until Bertrand completed his teaching engagement with the family of Antoine Trottier Des Ruisseaux of the same town.[40] In a baptismal act of 11 February 1703 at which he was a witness, François Pessureau is listed as tutor to the children of Governor Vaudreuil of Montreal.[41] Lay schoolmasters were also in the employ of religious authorities. Raymond Bertrand Junceria, who received authorization from Intendant Dupuy to teach school in Charlesbourg, near Quebec, was reminded that he was answerable to the parish priest.[42] A number of laymen taught the navigational arts at the Jesuit college at Quebec in the second half of the seventeenth century. Martin Boutet, a married man with a family, was a long-time teacher of mathematics and navigation at the school until his death in 1683. He was succeeded, in order, by lay teachers Jean-Baptiste Franquelin, Louis Jolliet, and Jean Deshayes.

The average lay schoolmaster in New France was in his twenties, a native of France, and a married man. Save for a handful of individuals, rare was the person who held the title of *maître d'école* for any length of time. Lay teaching was marked by instability and impermanence, as individuals slipped in and out of teaching and held other positions before, during, and after their pedagogical stints. Not a few schoolmasters had second jobs. Nicolas Rousselot was at once teacher and precentor in Pointe-aux-Trembles in 1684, as was Pierre-Georges Guelte in Repentigny in 1767. Étienne Marandeau was teacher and bailiff in Quebec in 1688, and Jean Guillon was teacher and merchant in Montreal in 1731. Apparently, teaching and soldiering could be simultaneously managed, for in the death act of his son, dated 23 June 1748, Charles Valins of Quebec is listed as "soldat et maître d'école."[43]

In general, lay schoolmasters entered teaching earlier rather than later in life, only to move on to other pursuits, giving the impression that instructing youngsters was neither socially nor economically rewarding. In other words, for many schoolmasters teaching was a stepping-stone to more lucrative employment. Given their knowledge of letters, it is not surprising to find lay teachers becoming notaries, bailiffs, and clerks of court. Jean-Baptiste Pottier's meagre salary of fifty *livres* from the parish of Lachine – and that was for fulfilling the three jobs of schoolmaster, parish secretary, and precentor – pushed him to search for more remunerative employment during his first year of teaching. He gravitated to the notaryship, preparing his first contract on December 20, 1686. It appears that he never returned to teaching.

Including Pottier, no fewer than eight notaries in New France were former schoolmasters.[44] The transition from teacher to notary presented few obstacles. Like lay schoolmasters, notaries were amateurs in the sense that they did not come to the position with specialized knowledge. In fact, notaries were appointed by the intendant from among candidates who were literate and of good morals.

Not all learning in New France occurred in schools and classrooms. Inasmuch as educational facilities were lacking in many areas of the colony, particularly outside the urban centres, children sometimes learned their letters through casual or informal instruction.

Since such instruction touched individuals more than groups, its impact is difficult to measure. The times dictated all sorts of informal and makeshift arrangements. Soldiers stationed in seventeenth-century Montreal broke the monotony of the long winters by teaching children their letters.[45] A reading of parish histories reveals that lay women sometimes came to the educational rescue in regions where no school or teacher was present. In a seventeenth-century seigneury near Trois-Rivières, the wife of the local notary and another woman taught children to form their letters, invoking the image of the "dame school" of England, where housewives and widows instructed neighbourhood youngsters in their kitchens for a nominal fee.[46] Before the Congregation of Notre Dame opened a school in lower-town Quebec in the 1690s, a married woman used to make her rounds, going from house to house, teaching reading and writing to the young girls of the area.

The family circle was perhaps the centre of casual instruction. In the absence of schools in the far reaches of New France and because of the expense of sending their children to Montreal or Quebec for schooling, some frontier families employed tutors. In 1791, the Pierre Grignon family of Green Bay in northeastern Wisconsin engaged Jacques Porlier, a twenty-six-year-old Montrealer, as clerk for the family business and tutor for its youngest children. After a year with the Grignon family, Porlier left to become a fur trader.[47]

The transmission of literacy skills occurred more often in better families, those convinced of the social and economic benefits which a knowledge of letters could bring. Females more than males took initiatives in this direction, since they were homebodies by tradition. The widow Marguerite Denys, whose husband had been seigneur in Ste-Anne-de-la-Pérade, taught her children reading and writing at the manor.[48] Madame Marie Bégon, whose correspondence constitutes a lively record of polite society in mid-eighteenth-century Quebec, taught her daughter geography, history, and Latin. In a letter to her son in France, she describes her educational day: "I spend the morning ... curling the little one's hair and making her read, write and do all the exercises (she dances also) ... In the afternoon I resume the school and about four o'clock there is sometimes company ... or I write you."[49]

Nor should it be forgotten that the learning of a trade in early Canada also took place in the home, boys being taught a skill by their fathers or acquiring the knowledge via apprenticeship, an arrangement imported from France which flourished in the colony from the late seventeenth century. Apprenticeship training was organized around a personal, tutorial relationship between an apprentice of adolescent age and a master craftsman, the latter providing room and board at his home and promising to pass on his knowledge and skill in exchange for the labour and loyalty of the former.

Whatever one may say about the reach and efficacy of education in New France, it was not without vitality and diversity. While religious authorities were in the forefront of founding, maintaining, and staffing schools, they were not the only participants. Civil officials, lay schoolmasters, artisans, soldiers, and housewives contributed to bringing learning to the youth of early Canada.

### CHAPTER FIVE

# Literacy and Learning

How widespread was education in seventeenth- and eighteenth-century Canada? Most historians are in agreement that education was an exceptional activity in New France – that it did not reach out to the majority of the population. The real challenge thus comes in providing more detailed answers to the question. In other words, did a tenth, a fifth, or half of all youngsters in early Canada attend school? Did more boys than girls attend school? Why were educational facilities greater in the towns than in the country? It must be admitted that because of insufficient data these and other questions do not lend themselves to precise and conclusive answers. We must be content with more general replies, as provided by the fragmentary and largely circumstantial evidence.

Some idea of the spread of learning in early Canada can be ascertained by a tally of the schools that existed. The visiting Swedish naturalist Peter Kalm said in 1749 that every parish in the colony had a school.[1] Like other visitors to the colony, he was either badly informed or given to exaggeration, since other investigations have shown the number of schools to have been far fewer. A more sober estimate is that forty-seven *petites écoles* existed during the life of the colony.[2] The figure is an aggregate one and does not refer to the number of schools in existence at any particular time, which was far fewer, since most schools did not enjoy a long and uninterrupted life. Even so, the figure may be on the high side inasmuch as it mistakes schoolmasters for schools. At any rate, at the end of the French regime in Canada the colony numbered some 123 parishes and districts, of which fewer than twenty had a school or teacher. About half of the known schools or teachers were in the towns of

Quebec, Montreal, and Trois-Rivières. Thus, some good-sized parishes were without educational facilities at the time of the conquest in 1760, including Charlesbourg and St-Thomas near Quebec and St-Charles, Varennes, and St-Vincent-de-Paul near Montreal, each of which had a population in excess of a thousand inhabitants.

On the other hand, the absence of schools and teachers in many areas of the colony does not automatically translate into an educational wasteland. While their impact on learning is difficult to assess, persons other than schoolmasters and schoolmistresses participated in the diffusion of knowledge, Friends and family members lent a hand in instructing the young, which suggests that the situation was not as depressing as it first appears.

SIGNATURE LITERACY

One of the most frequently used methods of determing the extent of education in pre-industrial societies is to inquire into the literacy of the people, the assumption being that a person's ability to read and write is evidence of instruction. However, a drawback of this approach has been the lack of direct and reliable data pertaining to literacy. Although censuses and other forms of mass information have been with us since Roman times, they have not yielded much in the way of pertinent data until recently. Indeed, it was not until the nineteenth century that the modern national census was born, which provided, among other social data, statistical information on the lettered condition of the citizenry. The censuses of New France, though advanced for their day, offered a demographic portrait of people, livestock, grain, and buildings, but were silent as to the learning achievements of the population.

In the absence of direct data on literacy in earlier societies, social historians have tackled the problem from another angle, resorting to indirect sources of information, such as petitions, wills, deeds, and marriage acts. The utility of these sources is that each calls for a signature, which some researchers regard as the key to unlocking the mystery of literacy in pre-industrial societies. The significance of the written signature rests on the belief that a connection exists between the ability to write one's name and basic literacy. The presumption is that a person who can write his or her name is almost certain to be able to write other things; and a person who can write obviously can read.

Those sceptical of this reasoning argue that the significance of the written signature has been overstated, that it represents a specific skill and little more – that even the illiterate person can master it. Some support for this view arises from the fact that master craftsmen in New France sometimes taught their apprentices to sign their own names.[3] A companion argument is that while the ability to sign one's name may be evidence of the ability to write, the making of a mark in lieu of a written signature does not necessarily signify the inability to write. Some persons in early Canada, for whatever reason, declared that they could not write their names when the evidence proved otherwise. There are recorded cases of individuals writing their name on one document, only to make their mark on a later document.[4] On balance, however, such cases have the ring of exceptionality about them and thus do not invalidate the tacit, if not absolute, connection between the written signature and literacy.

In recent years, attempts have been made to validate signature literacy in earlier times. Some of the best work has been done in France, particularly by Furet and Ozouf. Their objective has been to determine whether the written signature correlates positively with more direct sources of information. Using the second half of the nineteenth century as a frame of reference, they compared signature rates on marriage registers with literacy data yielded by the national census and by educational tests given to military recruits. They found a high correlation between the ability to sign one's name and actual literacy, permitting them to conclude, "The signature is therefore a good barometer of literacy."[5]

Of those instances demanding a written signature or a mark in pre-industrial societies, the marriage register is generally acknowledged to be the most reliable source. It enjoys several advantages over other official acts calling for a signature, such as wills, petitions, and notarial acts. First, the marriage register was in place in Canada and France as early as the seventeenth century. In New France, the Ordinance of 1678 decreed that the bride and groom sign the register, and that the presiding priest indicate whether the couple was able to sign. Second, signature data taken from wills and petitions are of limited validity since they are drawn from a select and unrepresentative population and thus their results cannot be generalized. The marriage register, on the other hand, suffers from no such drawback. The clear advantage of the marriage register is that it meets the test of universality – that it embraces a large and representative population, excluding only those adults who do not marry. This has particular relevance to the situation under review, since the adult population of New France was especially attracted to the marriage state, at a rate of almost 95 per cent of that group, say historians. Indeed, even among widows and widowers there was a pronounced tendency to remarry.[6]

Yet there are problems. The parish records of New France are incomplete, and in some cases lost or destroyed. About one-quarter of the parish acts (comprising baptismal, marriage, and death acts) of seventeenth-century Canada are missing. In addition, there is evidence of widespread neglect of the Ordinance of 1678: in almost 40 per cent of the marriages between 1680 and 1699, the priest failed to indicate whether the couples had signed the register.[7] Laxity in record keeping is also evident in the marriage acts of the eighteenth century. In more than half of New France's parishes at midcentury, signature information is incomplete or missing outright, the curé having failed to declare whether the couples had signed the register. On a happier note, marriage-signature data for the colony's three towns and a representative number of rural parishes are virtually intact, providing a solid data base from which literacy estimates can be made.

We begin our examination of signature counts by reviewing marriage acts in the towns of Quebec, Montreal, and Trois-Rivières, and in selected rural parishes, for the periods 1680–99 and 1750–65. The use of two sets of data a century apart serves two purposes. First, it reduces the chance of error or distortion arising from recourse to a single set of figures. Second, it provides a comparative view of literacy estimates in the colony during its infant years and during the final years of the French regime in Canada, when the population was at its height. The collected data, drawn from parish registers, appear in tables 1, 2, and 3.[8]

## URBAN AND RURAL LITERACY

What may be said of adult literacy levels in seventeenth- and eighteenth-century Canada as measured by marriage-signature data? While the incomplete evidence does not permit a precise figure, the least that can be said is that most adults were strangers to literacy and that illiteracy was significantly more widespread in the rural than the urban centres. The rates for urban and rural couples in

Table 1
Brides and Grooms Who Signed the Marriage Registers in Quebec, Montreal, and
Five Rural Parishes, 1680–99

|  | Grooms who signed | | Brides who signed | |
|---|---|---|---|---|
|  | n | % | n | % |
| Quebec and Montreal | 435 | 56.0 | 336 | 43.8 |
| Rural parishes: | 85 | 34.4 | 57 | 22.9 |
| Rivières-des-Prairies |  |  |  |  |
| Varennes |  |  |  |  |
| Ste-Famille (Île d'Orléans) |  |  |  |  |
| Pointe-aux-Trembles |  |  |  |  |
| Beauport |  |  |  |  |

Table 2
Brides and Grooms Who Signed the Marriage Registers in Montreal and Quebec,
1750–65, and in Trois-Rivières, 1750–59

|  | Grooms who signed | | Brides who signed | |
|---|---|---|---|---|
|  | n | % | n | % |
| Montreal | 452 | 44.5 | 396 | 39.0 |
| Quebec | 436 | 46.2 | 328 | 34.7 |
| Trois-Rivières | 34 | 50.0 | 32 | 47.0 |
| Total number and mean % | 922 | 45.5 | 756 | 37.3 |

1680–99 are roughly 50 and 29 per cent, respectively; in 1750–65, they are 41 and 10 per cent.

What must be kept in mind in attempting to arrive at an overall estimate of adult literacy in early Canada is that the French colony was predominantly a rural society. The census of 1754 put the population of Canada at fifty-five thousand souls. Quebec and Montreal were modest towns, with a combined population of twelve thousand inhabitants. Trois-Rivières, with eight hundred inhabitants, had the administrative structure of a town but the population of a village. A simple calculation shows that three-quarters of the colonial population were residing in the countryside, which has the effect of depressing the overall literacy rate. Urban marriage data for 1750–65 show an estimated 41 per-cent signature rate for couples. For the same period, rural couples show a 10 per-cent rate. Although the

Table 3
Brides and Grooms Who Signed the Marriage Registers in Twenty-two Rural Parishes in the Government Districts of Quebec, Montreal, and Trois-Rivières, 1750–65

| District and parish | Grooms who signed | | Brides who signed | |
|---|---|---|---|---|
| | n | % | n | % |
| District of Quebec: | | | | |
| Charlesbourg | 16 | 6.0 | 5 | 1.9 |
| Deschambault | 11 | 13.5 | 9 | 11.1 |
| Île-aux-Coudres | 0 | 0.0 | 0 | 0.0 |
| Neuville | 20 | 21.6 | 27 | 27.8 |
| Ste-Anne-de-Beaupré | 4 | 6.7 | 2 | 3.3 |
| St-Augustine | 2 | 2.5 | 0 | 0.0 |
| St-Ch-de-Bellechasse | 6 | 7.4 | 3 | 3.4 |
| St-François | 9 | 7.6 | 11 | 9.4 |
| Ste-Famille | 5 | 6.6 | 9 | 12.0 |
| St-Joachim | 8 | 11.2 | 4 | 5.6 |
| St-M-de-la-Durantaye | 9 | 6.1 | 9 | 6.1 |
| St-Pierre | 9 | 7.7 | 2 | 1.7 |
| St-Thomas | 26 | 15.0 | 13 | 7.5 |
| District of Montreal: | | | | |
| Lavaltrie | 8 | 6.6 | 7 | 5.8 |
| Longueuil | 14 | 10.5 | 17 | 12.7 |
| Pointe-aux-Trembles | 23 | 16.1 | 24 | 16.9 |
| Ste-Geneviève | 3 | 2.4 | 2 | 1.5 |
| St-Philippe | 12 | 20.6 | 2 | 3.4 |
| District of Trois-Rivières: | | | | |
| Batiscan | 22 | 37.9 | 20 | 34.4 |
| Champlain | 11 | 14.8 | 18 | 24.3 |
| St-François-du-Lac | 22 | 27.8 | 19 | 24.0 |
| Louiseville (1745–54) | 3 | 8.1 | 4 | 10.8 |
| Total number and mean % | 243 | 11.6 | 207 | 10.1 |

data are not complete, they suggest an overall literacy rate of around 25 per cent for the adult population.

The literacy gap between the town and the country was not unique to early Canada. A similar development had been at work in Europe for centuries. Ever since the rise of towns in the Middle Ages, the urban centre had enjoyed a clear superiority over the country in the proportion of its population knowing how to read and write.[9] In eighteenth-century Canada, as elsewhere, the town was the seat of political, commercial, and social life. Those who lived and worked there – political and administrative types, religious personnel, military officers, merchants, and others – were ruled by the written word. As one left Montreal and Quebec, a different way of life asserted itself: a land-based economy that favoured strong bodies over fine minds, where the written word deferred to the spoken word. At the centre of rural life in Canada was the *habitant*, or farmer, for whom pen, paper, and ink were not tools of the trade. Consistent with its need for literate types, the town greatly surpassed the country in educational provision. From the earliest days of the colony, the towns maintained boys' and girls' schools that were well attended. On the other hand, few rural parishes had a school or a teacher.

The tendency of lettered persons to shun the countryside of early Canada is confirmed by other documentary evidence. A reading of parish histories leaves the impression that aside from the seigneur, the parish priest, the militia captain, and the notary, few rural inhabitants knew how to read and write. That each rural parish had its army of illiterates also comes through Attorney General Collet's parish inquiry of 1721. When the inhabitants of each district were offered the opportunity to sign the official report prepared by Collet, few stepped forward, prompting the law officer to insert the phrase "ne savoire escrire ny signer."[10] In the rural parish of Chambly, across the river from Montreal, not a single inhabitant signed the attorney general's report.

Just as there is a significant gap between urban and rural signature rates, so are there striking variations among the various rural parishes for 1750–65. At the low end of the scale is Île-aux-Coudres, where none of the thirty couples signed the register; at the other end is Batiscan, where more than a third of the participants were able to sign. The zero signature rate in Île-aux-Coudres, however depressing, is easily explained. The parish population was small and isolated, living on an island in the St Lawrence River, a good distance from Quebec and other settlements. Another poor performer, Charlesbourg, with a combined signature rate of less than 5 per cent, is harder to figure out. By all measures, it should show a more respectable signature rate. First of all, there was a lay schoolmaster in the area from 1727.[11] The parish also boasted a large population which was organized along the lines of a village – one of the few rural parishes in the French colony to be so structured – the inhabitants were concentrated rather than scattered, a condition that favoured the organization of learning. Finally, Charlesbourg was geographically well situated, only a stone's throw from Quebec, which was rich in educational facilities.

Table 3 shows that the rural parishes in the region of Trois-Rivières were in a class by themselves, with above-average signature rates in three of the four parishes listed. The presence of educational facilities in the area probably accounts for the higher rates. A girls' school under the direction of the Congregation of Notre Dame had been operating in Champlain since 1702. Since the school was equipped to receive both day and boarding students, it seems likely that girls from the neighbouring parish of Batiscan were attracted to the institution. Area families probably also took advantage of the schools in nearby Trois-Rivières. An Ursuline school had been in the town since 1697. It also had had a boys' school between 1720 and 1739, staffed by a Charon Brothers schoolmaster until 1736 and by a lay teacher after that. Notarial records indicate that other lay schoolmasters were active in the region from 1730.[12]

One does not have to look far to find reasons for the widespread ignorance in the countryside of New France. The knowledge of letters had little utility in an environment that favoured land clearers, farmers, fishermen, and hunters. The *habitants* had more pressing concerns than learning to read and write, chief of which was wresting a living from a rough and hostile land. The time and place demanded strong bodies and stout hearts, and the acquisition of letters offered little protection against a bad harvest. On the other hand, the children of rural folk received an education of sorts, but it was informal rather than formal, practical rather than literary, and general rather than specialized. Children were put to work at an early age, boys with fathers and girls with mothers, to help with the demanding tasks of everyday life. Boys learned the arts of farming, fishing, furniture making, carpentry, and animal husbandry; girls were instructed in the arts of cooking, sewing, and weaving. Other conditions that militated against the development of organized learning in the rural districts were a dispersed population, an absence of villages and village life, and a chronic shortage of resident clergy.

Instead of settling in villages, as was the custom in France, the rural population of early Canada opted for a radically different land arrangement which both antagonized government authorities and hampered social and cultural development. The rural colonists elected to settle on *rangs*, or narrow strips of land, that began at the edge of the St Lawrence River and penetrated deep inland. The attractive aspect of these ribbon-like plots was that they accorded the settlers access to the river, which was the colony's principal transportation route and a valuable source of food. By the close of the French period in Canada a row of farmhouses stretched in unbroken fashion along both banks of the St Lawrence between Montreal and Quebec.

While the *rang* land pattern proved popular among the independent-minded colonists, it elicited a different response in official circles. No sooner had Canada become a royal province, in 1663, than Louis XIV ordered colonial authorities to discourage the inhabitants from settling on isolated plots along the St Lawrence, directing that houses be grouped in clusters so as to promote the development of villages like those in rural France. The king's order was not simply another example of royal heavy-handedness in colonial affairs. The Crown was on solid ground in pointing out that the establishment of rural villages would protect the settlers against the assaults of the Iroquois, stimulate agriculture, and lay the foundation for a semblance of community life. Without the rise of villages, declared the monarch, the rural population could not be effectively served by priests, judges, surgeons, and other notables. Intendant Talon tried to give impetus to the royal policy by erecting a village near Quebec, but the experiment was not adopted in the rest of the colony. According to one historical geographer, only six rural villages were born during the life of the colony: Charlesbourg, near Quebec, and La Prairie, Boucherville, Terrebonne, Pointe-aux-Trembles, and Verchères, near Montreal.[13]

The rural colonists' resistance to village life was motivated by political as well as economic concerns – an unwillingness to be ruled from above, whether from Quebec or Paris. Living on their isolated *rangs*, away from the prying glances of civil authorities, the *habitants* were largely free to organize their own lives and to shape their own destinies.[14] The independent life style of rural Canadians was frequently the target of official disapproval and a source of comment from others. The Jesuit historian Charlevoix observed that the *habitant* "breathed from his birth the air of liberty," which prevented him from subjugating himself to others.

Imbued with a spirit of freedom and wanderlust, the Canadian *habitant* had little in common with his rural counterpart in France, who was tied to the land and who answered to the name of *paysan*, or peasant. Like the Indian, whom he frequently resembled in dress and behaviour, the rural colonist was easily distracted, his roving instincts and the lure of quick profits from the fur trade often taking him far afield despite official attempts to limit his movements. A man of many roles and interests, he was at once farmer, woodcutter, fisherman, hunter, trader, and militiaman. One day he would be tilling the soil or netting eels in the productive waters of the St Lawrence; the next day he would be off to distant parts of the upper country in search of furs and adventure, sometimes not to return to domestic living until months later. Such a life style was not conducive to community living and the development of social institutions, one of which is schools. The historian Francis Parkman put it well: "As for the *habitant* the forest, lake and river were his true school; and here, at least, he was an apt scholar."[15]

According to colonial authorities, the combination of a scattered population and the absence of villages constituted the greatest obstacle to the development of learning in the rural parishes. This was summed up in an official report to France in 1718: "The inhabitants not being gathered together in villages and being far from one another ... schoolmasters are not in a position to instruct the young boys, who can come only to the Catechisms that the *curés* hold on feast days and Sundays."[16]

Colonial officials could have added that without villages and village life, opportunities for community action were limited and local government difficult to organize. As we saw earlier, the only semblance of rural government was the *fabrique*, or church council, which occasionally involved itself in educational matters. On balance, however, the concept of the village school initiated and maintained by the rural collectivity is a description of life in eighteenth-century New England, not in that of New France.

The responsibility for organizing learning in the rural areas of the colony rested with the clergy. The point that parish priests had little time or energy to spend on education was driven home in a colonial report of 1685, in which France was alerted to the lack of priests in rural Canada and the harmful effect it was having on organized learning and child rearing. Governor Denonville described as a "pity" the impact that widespread ignorance was having in the countryside, where, in the absence of spiritual leadership, children were being reared in complete freedom and idleness by their parents. He appealed to the minister to provide additional funds so that the number of priests might be increased and the population more adequately served.[17] But a half-century later the scarcity of rural priests was still plaguing the colony. Of the eighty or so parishes in Canada in 1730, only about a quarter had a resident *curé*, the remaining parishes being serviced by itinerant priests and missionaries. The shortage of priests and a dispersed population tended to minimize clerical influence in the rural districts, leaving educational needs unattended.

To judge by Bishop Dosquet's pastoral letter of 1735, the shortage of parish priests in the colony had, if anything, worsened in recent years. The churchman noted that the Séminaire des Missions Étrangères in Paris, which over the years had supplied religious workers for Canada, was no longer providing personnel. (He could have mentioned that the spiritual attractions of New France had diminished in the eyes of the metropolitain church, for there were more exciting spiritual challenges to be found in other lands.) The bishop concluded that the only permament solution to the paucity of rural priests was to train more native sons at the Seminary of Quebec. To that end, he instructed his priests to be on the lookout for boys proficient in Latin and showing an inclination for the religious life.[18]

A related problem was that the rural economy could ill support a full complement of parish priests. The *curé*'s income was normally derived from the *dîme*, or tithe, which by law was one twenty-sixth of the farmer's harvest. While the rate was relatively modest in comparison to European assessments, it constituted a burden on poor farmers – and on all farmers during bad harvests. During such times, the local population contributed little or nothing to the *curé*. In some parishes, the population flatly refused to pay the tithe under any conditions, and official threats from Quebec proved powerless in bringing them into line. Bishop Dosquet told the minister in 1736 that unless the inhabitants paid their tithes in more regular fashion, an exodus of priests from the colony would surely result.[19] While the Crown had subsidized the parish clergy since the earliest years of the colony, the funds allocated had failed to keep pace with expanding needs.

Complicating the problem was the fact that civil and religious leaders were at loggerheads over the stationing of priests in the rural parishes. Crown officials pushed for the establishment of resident priests, as was the case in France. But the bishops, ever since Laval's reign, had regarded the arrangement as a threat to their authority. Determined to make the Seminary of Quebec the focal point of spiritual power in the colony, Laval had worked out a plan whereby the parish clergy would be itinerant in the fashion of circuit preachers, travelling about the countryside to dispense the sacraments and minister to the needs of the people. At the end of the year, the wandering priests would return to the seminary for prayers and spiritual renewal before resuming their travels.

The shortage of rural clergy may also be traced to the urban bias of the Canadian church. In short, where the people were, the clergy were not. For example, in the first decade of the eighteenth century, about four-fifths of the clergy were stationed in the towns, where about one-quarter of the colonial population was living. Put another way, the country parishes, with three-fourths of the population, were served by one-fifth of the secular clergy.[20] To make matters worse, there was no one in the colony to deal effectively with bringing clerical numbers up to strength in the rural districts. Bishop Saint-Vallier was in no position to remedy the situation; he was interned in an English jail outside London, and was not to return to Canada until 1713 – an absence of thirteen years from his diocese.

The spiritual and educational shortcomings of the rural parishes were confirmed in an official inquiry in 1721.[21] On the orders of the king, Attorney General Collet, accompanied by the *greffier*, or clerk, Boucault, was charged with the responsibility of visiting the colony's eighty or so parishes and reporting on their social conditions. As he met with the notables and inhabitants of each parish, Collet was struck by the litany of recurring problems and grievances. Disaffection was greatest in those parishes that did not have a resident *curé*, for the local population was deprived of spiritual care for extended periods during the year, until a roving priest called on the area. As a result, some parishioners heard mass only several times a year, and the sick died without the benefit of last rites. When a roving priest arrived at a settlement little time was wasted, for children had to be baptized, confessions heard, marriages performed, and the catechism taught. The situation in the parish of Chambly, south of

Montreal, was probably typical of many rural districts. The local inhabitants complained to the attorney general that the Recollet priest who was supposed to attend to their spiritual and social needs was rarely around, with the result that few masses were said and children did not receive religious instruction. Moreover, there were also complaints in many parishes that churches were too far removed from the population, requiring parishioners to travel great distances, which was not always possible during the harsh winter months.

It would be reassuring to report that educational facilities existed in those rural parishes that had their own resident priest. However, such was not the case. A reading of parish histories reveals that schools rarely figured in the institutional development of parishes in seventeenth- and eighteenth-century Canada. Rural *curés* channelled their spiritual and physical energies into the building of churches and rectories, preferably of stone construction. The early history of the rural parish of Longueuil, across the river from Montreal, was probably representative of many country districts. On the eve of the British invasion of Montreal, in 1760, the parish, with a population of seven hundred, had a church, a windmill, a watermill, and a cemetery, but no school.[22]

## MALE AND FEMALE LITERACY

Literacy studies on pre-industrial societies have consistently shown not only that men were more literate than women, but that the gap between them was substantial. In a work on literacy in Tudor and Stuart England, it was found that female literacy lagged significantly behind male literacy.[23] In colonial New England, arguably the world's most literate society for its day, a similar pattern was evident. Literacy estimates for men and women in New England in the mid-seventeenth century are 60 and 30 per cent, respectively; in the eighteenth century, 90 and 60 per cent.[24]

Since New France was a political and cultural appendage of France, it behooves us to review the situation in the mother country. Louis Maggiolo's famous inquiry of the last century demonstrated the all-too-familiar disparity in the literacy levels of the sexes in pre-revolutionary France. He determined that for the 1686–90 period, 29 per cent of grooms and 14 per cent of brides across the land signed the marriage register. The figures for 1786–90 were 48 and 27 per cent, respectively.[25] Relying more heavily on urban marriage data, Furet and Ozouf both confirmed and refined Maggiolo's data, adding that the gap between male and female literacy in pre-industrial France reached its widest point on the eve of the French Revolution.[26]

A review of marriage data for eighteenth-century Canada (tables 2 and 3) confirms its status as a traditional society to the extent that males signed more frequently than females. On the other hand, the signature gap between the sexes, characteristic of France and other pre-industrial societies, is seen to be much less pronounced in Canada. The phenomenon finds its explanation in the rural parishes. The urban data reveal a traditional pattern, since 46 per cent of grooms and 37 per cent of brides signed the register. But a different picture emerges in the rural parishes, with signature disparity almost disappearing between the sexes. Brides and grooms in the rural parishes show, respectively, rates of 10 and 11 per cent.

The absence in eighteenth-century Canada of a significant gender gap in the signature rates of rural couples is what differentiates the colony from the mother country. Furet and Ozouf found that the literacy lead of men over women in pre-revolutionary France was greater in the rural than in the urban centres, allowing them to conclude, "The more rural the region the greater are the differences that separate the men from the women."[27] The reason for the difference between the two societies has already been hinted at: the fact that the colony did not resemble France in its rural development. Instead of being concentrated in compact villages, as was the settlement pattern in France, the rural population of Canada was dispersed. Without village life and its accompanying structures, the rural parishes of early Canada neither attracted nor produced male literates, with the result that the traditional literacy lead enjoyed by men disappeared. Put less kindly, male literacy sank to the level of female literacy in eighteenth-century rural Canada.

An underlying assumption of this discussion is that a connection exists between literacy and learning – that the lettered condition of a people reflects, in a general way, educational provision. Although this assumption is probably valid in a stable and traditional culture, it breaks down in the case of an immigrant society, as was New France. In short, many of those who married in Canada between 1750 and 1765 were neither born nor reared in the New World. Thus, their ability or inability to sign the marriage registers says more about educational conditions in France than about those in

Canada. Specifically, the overwhelming majority of these immigrants were urban males. Of the 888 grooms who signed the registers in Quebec and Montreal (table 2), 469, or more than half, were not native to Canada. In sharp contrast, only three of the 724 brides who signed in the two towns were listed as having been born outside of Canada.[28] Put in other terms, it was a case of French males, many of them soldiers, marrying Canadian females. Assuming that the information is correct, it would appear that marriage-signature data for 1750–65 are a truer index of the state of girls' than of boys' education in eighteenth-century Canada.

A continuing debate among historians is whether boys or girls were better educated in Canada during the French period. For the most part, nineteenth-century writers gave the nod to females, citing their greater educational facilities.[29] Most twentieth-century writers, on the other hand, have thrown their support to boys' education, basing their arguments on the higher signature rates of grooms in the marriage registers.

It is suggested that nineteenth-century historians were closer to the truth in affirming the supremacy of female learning. Support for the thesis that educational facilities were greater for girls than for boys draws on three pieces of evidence or proofs: the numerical superiority of female teachers; the higher enrolments in girls' schools; and the longer life of girls' schools.

The attempt to establish the numerical superiority of female teachers must begin with a general discussion of the religious communities, which supplied the colony with the bulk of its schoolmasters and schoolmistresses. In 1759, on the eve of the fall of New France, the colony counted 204 female religious, including seventy Notre Dame Sisters, forty-five Ursulines, and eighty-nine Hospital Nuns. For their part, the male communities totalled eighty-four male religious, including thirty Sulpicians, twenty-five Jesuits, twenty-four Recollets, and five persons attached to the seminary of Quebec.[30] The figures, admittedly, do not do full justice to the male orders, as they fail to mention the Charon Brothers, who had been educationally active in Montreal and in several rural parishes in the 1720s and 1730s before their disappearance, in 1747. In spite of this qualification, there is no denying the numerical superiority of the female communities, which is explained in part by their willingness to recruit Canadian members. In contrast, the Jesuits and Sulpicians, who provided much of the leadership in boys' education, always remained modest in membership by dint of their preference for European members. The Recollets were an exception to the rule, for in 1759 no fewer than seventeen of their twenty-four members were Canadian. The catch in the statistic is that the Recollets were educationally inactive, rarely serving as schoolmasters or taking educational initiatives. The point to be drawn from these data is that the female communities were numerically better situated to provide educational workers. Of the seventy sisters of the Congregation of Notre Dame in 1759, an estimated fifty were probably involved in instruction, representing more than the total number of teachers generated by the male communities.

The numerical distinction between male and female teachers becomes even larger when note is taken of the contrasting occupational roles of the two groups. Female religious were more likely to specialize in teaching, since they were limited in their career choices. For the nun in New France, the choice was between the hospital and the classroom. On the whole, the Ursulines and the Congregation of Notre Dame concentrated on instruction, while the Hospital Nuns devoted their energies to nursing and social welfare. Male religious, on the other hand, were less likely to gravitate to teaching because of competing demands on their services. From the limited pool of male clergy were drawn missionaries, parish priests, military chaplains, explorers, and schoolmasters.

In the countryside, where the bulk of the population lived, educational provision for girls surpassed that for boys. It is a well-established fact that of the religious orders the Congregation of Notre Dame was alone in maintaining permanent schools outside the towns. The sisters' principal competition came from the short-lived schools of the Charon Brothers. To be sure, lay schoolmasters were also active in the rural parishes, but their impact on learning appears to have been marginal. For one thing, few lay teachers remained in teaching for any length of time; for another, their clientele was small in size and was drawn from families and individuals, since few lay schoolmasters kept schools as such. Even more important, lay teachers cannot be an argument for boys' learning, since they taught girls as well.

Schools in early Canada varied in size and enrolment. In the middle of the eighteenth century not only were there more girls' than boys' schools in the colony, but the female institutions appeared to have more pupils. The largest boys' school in Canada was the Jesuit college in Quebec, which was in fact an elementary and secondary school. Although enrolments at the school are difficult to know for any particular year, they probably numbered around one hundred in 1756, since in that year the institution was staffed with five professors and one instructor, the latter serving as teacher in the elementary-school section.[31] Whether the Jesuits still had an elementary school in Montreal at this time cannot be determined, but the Sulpician school in Montreal was still operating and was staffed by two teachers, which suggests that its enrolment was smaller than that of the Jesuit college in Quebec. There is no evidence of a boys' school in Trois-Rivières at this time, or for that matter in the rural parishes, though a handful of lay schoolmasters were active outside the towns.

As for the female communities, the Ursulines had a flourishing school in Quebec and a second one in Trois-Rivières, and the Congregation of Notre Dame had schools in Montreal and Quebec. Furthermore, the Notre Dame Sisters had six country schools from Château-Richer, in the east, to Lachine, in the west. The town schools of the two female orders supported healthy enrolments, probably in excess of one hundred girls, in their Montreal and Quebec establishments. The Congregation of Notre Dame also had a large school in distant Louisbourg, on Île Royale, between 1727 and 1758, and had not the Seven Years' War broken out it is likely that the sisters would have established a school in Detroit.

Girls' schools also showed greater stability and durability than did boys' schools. The Ursulines' two schools and most of those founded by the Notre Dame Sisters were still in operation on the eve of the British invasion of Canada, in 1759. Indeed, in some cases it literally took British shells to knock them out of commission, while others, including that of the Ursulines in Trois-Rivières, operated in uninterrupted fashion throughout the war. With the exception of the Jesuit school in Quebec and the Sulpician one in Montreal, few boys' institutions had a long and unbroken existence. The instability of boys' schools in the colony may be traced ultimately to those in charge of male instruction, who themselves were less than permanent. The Charon Brothers did not succeed in establishing rural schools until the 1720s, and were unable to sustain them much beyond the decade. The Rouillé Brothers opened a school in Montreal in 1686, but it folded seven years later due to financial and personnel problems.

Impermanence also dogged the pedagogical efforts of lay school-masters, few of whom taught for more than a few years.

Just as literacy in early Canada varied according to gender and place of residence, so too did it vary according to socio-economic status. It is indisputable that literacy was universal among the colony's administrative and professional classes, many of whose members had been born and educated in France and were stationed in the towns. I am referring here in the first instance to the ruling élite, including the governor, the intendant, the bishop, the attorney general, and the councillors. Below this group are the lower clergy, judges, military officers, seigneurs, and a host of lesser law and administrative officers such as notaries, clerks of the court, inspectors, and bailiffs. In the town of Quebec in 1750, full literacy was recorded for professionals, army officers, and civil servants.[32] Still, one comes across the occasional law officer, such as the seventeenth-century Montreal magistrate Migeon de Bansaal, who was illiterate.[33]

Less precise is the lettered condition of merchants and craftsmen in early Canada. One historian estimates that two-thirds of the merchants in seventeenth-century Montreal could not or did not read, since books were not part of their possessions as determined by inventories.[34] Common sense suggests, however, that most commercial types were literate inasmuch as accounts, bills of sale, and other written papers were endemic to the business way of life. Louise de Ramezay, the unmarried daughter of the governor of Montreal and a successful merchant in flour and lumber, ordered one of her foremen to set aside an hour each day for writing instruction so that he could manage the books. More significantly, marriage-signature data for Montreal and Quebec for the period 1750–65 show that of thirty-eight grooms listed as merchants, only one could not sign the register.[35] Other research shows a similar pattern. In Quebec in 1750, all six *commerçants* in the town were literate; in 1760, eight of ten were.[36]

As for artisans or craftsmen, a fair percentage of them must have been literate since some of their number gravitated to lettered occupations, becoming notaries, clerks of the court, and magistrates. One estimate is that almost three-fourths of Quebec master craftsmen during the life of the colony could sign their names.[37] In a related study, it was found that between a quarter and a third of apprentices in New France signed their contract of indenture.[38] On the other hand, one does not have to look far to find artisans who were unlettered. Pierre Ménage, a master carpenter and prominent builder in Quebec in the late seventeenth century, was, according to his biographer, illiterate.[39] Similarly, Jean-Baptiste Villain, a seventeenth-century goldsmith, declared at two marriages to which he was a witness that he could not write his name.[40] An overall estimate, based on marriage-signature data, is that roughly half of the colony's artisan labour was literate.[41] Literacy was more prevalent among surgeons, architects, and tanners; less so among carpenters, masons, and bakers.

At the lower end of the socio-economic scale were the common people, who according to most reports were wallowing in ignorance. Describing the situation in Canada after the conquest, General Murray wrote that the *habitants* "are in general extremely ignorant ... few can read or write."[42] Similarly, a French soldier who kept a diary of his experiences during the Seven Years' War portrayed the Canadians as "sincere, kind-hearted, and hospitable ... but the majority are uneducated."[43] There is no reason to doubt the accuracy of these impressions; they square with marriage-signature data, which show low signature counts in the rural parishes, where the bulk of the common people lived.

If literacy, and by implication education, did not reach out to the majority of the population of seventeenth- and eighteenth-century Canada, it behooves us to inquire into the reasons for this. A short answer is that few functions in colonial life demanded a knowledge of letters. Illiteracy was neither a social nor an occupational handicap for most people. Save for those in "clerical" positions in society, which embraced administrative and professional offices, most colonists could earn a living without the benefit of letters. Even some of the skilled trades could be practised in blissful ignorance. The apprenticeship system, which was the standard method of training craftsmen in the colony, set no educational qualifications for boys entering training, and provided no reading and writing instruction during its course. If bakers and shoemakers sometimes knew their letters, it was probably for other than job-related reasons. The point is that most Canadians experienced little inconvenience or shame in their illiterate state. After all, the colonist could work his land, ply a trade, sell his goods, do battle with the Iroquois and English, and win the promise of salvation, all without reference to literacy. Canadians were felled by pestilence, fire, famine, tomahawks, and muskets, but as far as can be determined no one died of illiteracy.

It is sometimes said that literacy can go no further than the written culture takes it. This is to acknowledge the intimate connection between letters and learning – that since antiquity schools have centred their attention on transmission of the written word. As a rule, where the written word flourishes so do literacy and learning. Thus, it is no accident that England and New England were among the West's most literate societies in the seventeenth century. Both supported thriving book cultures, with publishing houses, printing presses, booksellers, and lending libraries – all designed to satisfy the appetite of a sizeable reading class, itself a product of widely available schools.

What was the state of the written culture in New France? All indications point to an abundance of reading matter in the colony. Notarial records, inventories, and wills reveal that persons of standing had reading materials in their possession. One researcher boldly concludes that Quebec surpassed Paris in terms of the percentage of its residents having books, which he attributes to the absence of other cultural outlets in the town, such as theatres and literary clubs. Of 962 inventories left by deceased residents of Quebec between 1690 and 1760, 297, or 32 per cent, listed one or more books among their possessions. In Paris between 1750 and 1759, books were present in 22 per cent of the inventories.[44] In the Quebec sample, there was a strong correlation between social class and the number and types of books held. Not only did members of the ruling and professional classes have more books in their possession, but the holdings tended to reflect a broad range of interests, from religion, law, and history to the arts and sciences. The lower classes not only had far fewer books in their possession, but those they did have were invariably of a religious nature, which suggests that reading was an affair of the élite.

Persons of rank had collections that would be impressive by today's standards. François-Joseph Cugnet, eighteenth-century attorney general, possessed a library of some three thousand volumes, the bulk of which he inherited from his father. The eighteenth-century intendant Dupuy, who was a better scientist than administrator, had a library of more than a thousand books which he had brought from France and which included works from all branches of knowledge. The clergy, both high and low, had books, mostly of a religious nature to be sure, but also a sprinkling of classical texts and occasionally a work by a French modernist. Philippe Boucher, *curé* of Pointe-de-Lévis, had a collection of five hundred volumes; his brother Nicolas, also a parish priest, had more than one hundred works. Military officers were devoted readers and carried books with them wherever they went. Baron Lahontan, who served in Canada during the late seventeenth century, tells of embarking on a military campaign accompanied by such "honest men of past centuries" as Homer and Anacreon. The works of Aristotle, he quipped, were left behind because the boat was not large enough to hold the Greek's syllogisms.[45]

Sometimes the size of personal libraries was dictated more by professional than by literary considerations. If law officers possessed the largest book collections in the colony, it reflected less a cultivated literary taste than a response to an occupational imperative. The law, like religion, was book-based, and its practitioners were required to surround themselves with the written texts to do their job. On the other side of the coin, if merchants rarely had libraries of any size, it was probably due to the nature of business, which was rooted in practice and experience, not in books and heavy tomes.

Like personal libraries, institutional ones were very much in evidence in the colony. Every religious community, house, and hospital maintained a library of some dimension. The Seminary of Quebec, with holdings approaching five thousand volumes by the late eighteenth century, was probably the colony's largest library. While the exact size of the Jesuit college library is unknown, it is believed to have been a well-stocked one. The library of the Charon Brothers in Montreal numbered around 350 volumes, as revealed by a detailed inventory of the community's possessions. Among the female orders, the Quebec Ursulines had a library with more than five hundred volumes.

Turning to the written arts, no small amount of writing was done on Canadian soil, though much of it was of an official character. In the fashion of Gallic societies before and after, New France had a penchant for writing things down, of recording in writing relations between persons, institutions, and property. Civil and religious authorities were indefatigable in churning out decrees, ordinances, notarial acts, judicial rulings, and pastoral letters. A dutiful clergy maintained parish registers, among the most complete of any pre-industrial society, in which are recorded baptisms, marriages, deaths, and censuses. At the same time, whether it was a Jesuit missionary contributing a chapter to his order's *Relations* or Marie de l'Incarnation composing one of her letters or an intendant penning a report to the minister, many wrote not for the population of New France but for that of the mother country. And while no small amount of correspondence passed between Canada and France, most of it was of a governmental and commercial character, including official dispatches, business letters, and trade orders. The evidence suggests that few common people sent or received personal letters.

While the existence of books and other reading materials in the colony cannot for a moment be doubted, it is quite another matter to say that they were in wide circulation. There is evidence to the effect that the exchange of books was common practice among the higher classes.[46] A different picture, however, emerges for the lower classes. Since wills and inventories of the period show that ordinary folk were rarely possessors of books, save for the odd devotional work, they had little to exchange.[47] Peter Kalm, who was sometimes guilty of exaggeration, declared that he never saw a Bible or New Testament in the homes of the common people, which he attributed to the fact that the clergy alone believed themselves qualified to interpret the Scriptures.[48]

On balance, it appears that the class of readers in New France was a limited one, comprising the ruling and professional classes but not extending to the bulk of the population. This is not a rash assertion when taken in conjunction with the fact that the colony lacked the very cultural institutions that support and nourish a sizeable reading class. The lack of printing presses, publishing houses, booksellers, and lending libraries in New France was particularly damaging to the cause of popular culture, since without a press there can be no newspapers or other forms of mass information which serve as outlets for readers. And without a popular written culture, there is little incentive among the common people to acquire a margin of literacy, for which the school is the principal vehicle.

Several unsuccessful attempts were made to introduce printing into the colony. The *Relation* of 1665 tells us that the Jesuits intended to "write and ask for a printing-press and types" in order to help in the learning of the Indian languages.[49] Several decades later, the Montreal Sulpicians petitioned their home seminary in Paris for a press, but were turned down by the superior, Louis Tronson.[50] In 1749, Governor La Galissonière asked France for a printing press to facilitate dissemination of ordinances and other official notices in the colony. Once again, the request fell on deaf ears on the other side of the Atlantic. Some historians have speculated that the refusal of the governor's request was politically inspired – that the Crown feared that the introduction of printing into the colony would result in the appearance of works offensive to the state and the church. A more convincing explanation was offered by Peter Kalm, who was in a position to know, having struck up a friendship with La Galissonière during his visit to Canada in 1749. The Swedish naturalist asserted that the Crown's refusal was economically rather than politically motivated – that France was not prepared to relinquish its monopoly on its profitable book trade.[51]

In the absence of a printing press in the colony, books and other written materials had to be imported, a practice that was both time-consuming and costly. To order a book from abroad meant waiting months, and sometimes years, for delivery, given the distance, slowness of transportation, and lack of an established postal system. The situation was particularly harmful to learning, since educational authorities in the colony were dependent on France for their school manuals and pedagogical guides. They were also at the mercy of the hazards of transatlantic shipping. In 1703, the Sulpician superior in Paris informed the Montreal schoolmaster Antoine Forget that the educational materials he had ordered would not be sent that year because French ship captains were reluctant to leave port for fear of being attacked by the English and the Corsicans.[52]

Books and other reading materials, if not rare in the colony, were not articles of public commerce. They were an affair of a select class of persons who alone participated in their acquisition and exchange. Governors, intendants, and other civil leaders donated books not to ordinary citizens, but to religious representatives. For their part, the Jesuits were in the habit of distributing books as prizes to students who excelled in their studies. From all appearances, the common people were not a party to trafficking in the written word. Being little educated as a class, they were not disposed to seeking out reading matter. Any literary inclinations that they might have had were discouraged by the difficulty of acquiring books. Even had booksellers been in existence, it may be wondered whether the ordinary folk could have afforded to purchase reading materials, what with money being scarce in the colony. The simple act of borrowing a book posed problems unfamiliar to modern society, not the least of which was the absence of libraries as we know them. The religious libraries, however well stocked, were neither public nor lending institutions, and were not inclined to share their intellectual wares with others. Another obstacle facing the potential reader was the location of the libraries. They were in Quebec and Montreal, and were thus destined to serve an urban élite.

In the final analysis, the oral tradition held sway over the written one in early Canada. People spoke and listened more than they wrote and read. Conversation, story-telling, and songs were the "books" of the common people, doubling as a form of amusement and of information. According to numerous witnesses, Canadians were *grands parleurs*, able to relate in lively fashion their experiences and exploits. When officialdom communicated with the people, it resorted to both the written and the spoken word.[53] Although edicts, ordinances, and other official announcements were written down, they were also read aloud to the parishioners from church pulpits and before church doors. In 1728, Intendant Dupuy instructed militia officers, bailiffs, sergeants, and schoolmasters to read the orders of king and intendant before the doors of parish churches.[54]

As it had done for centuries, Christianity relied on the spoken word to communicate with the faithful, as reflected in the orally based sacramental system, though it appears that few worshippers understood the Latin of the service. Peter Kalm said that "it was both strange and amusing to see and hear how eagerly the women and soldiers said their prayers in Latin and did not themselves understand a word of what they said."[55] He went further, offering that Latin was an elusive tongue to many of the clergy as well, as few men of the cloth were able to read and converse in the language of the church with any degree of fluency. He said that the bishop's spoken Latin was so feeble that the churchman avoided his company out of sheer embarrassment.[56]

Befitting an oral culture, the spoken word came in for more praise than the written word in early Canada. Visitors to the colony often commented favourably on the speech of Canadians. Montcalm's aide Bougainville noted that despite their lack of education and their inability to write, "Canadians have natural intelligence, they speak with ease ... their accent is as good as that in Paris."[57] The Jesuit historian Charlevoix expressed a similar view, and the military engineer Louis Franquet, in describing the women of Canada, said that they spoke a pure French without the least trace of an accent.[58]

If colonists could survive in this life without the benefit of literacy, so too could they survive in the hereafter, since the Church of Rome drew no firm connection between learning and salvation. In theory, the high churchman and the lowly peasant had an equal chance to enter the gates of heaven. While religious authorities in New France emphasized the importance of learning, they stopped short of maintaining that the unlettered were doomed to suffer the fires of hell, which may be one reason that the push for learning was not pursued with the same intensity in Catholic Canada as in Protestant New England.

The explanation for this difference lies in conflicting systems of theology. While the two churches both strove to lead man toward salvation, they differed sharply as to how it could be achieved. Roman Catholicism insisted that man could not be saved except through the church, the priesthood, and the sacramental system. In contrast, Protestantism, holding to a more pristine theology, downgraded the role of the institutional church, holding that no church, rite, or formal theology should intervene between man and God. In keeping with this theology, the Protestants scrapped the priesthood of Catholicism and substituted in its place the Scriptures as the emissary between the faithful and the Creator. The elevation of the Scriptures to the priesthood of Protestantism imposed on each believer the duty of acquiring a measure of literacy, for without a knowledge of letters there could be no Bible reading, and without scriptural communication there could be no salvation.

The link between learning and salvation was less firmly entrenched in Catholic theology. Catholicism preached what might be called a "broker theory of education." As the priesthood was the vehicle through which the faithful communicated with God, so it followed that the clergy were first in line for educational attention. In New France, as in other pre-industrial Catholic societies, an educational problem was perceived in the first instance as a clerical one. In the realization that educational facilities in eighteenth-century Canada were not keeping pace with an expanding population, Bishop Dosquet reacted in predictable fashion. In 1735, he ordered his clergy to promote the teaching of Latin in their parishes and to be on the lookout for boys showing an aptitude for the academic and spiritual life, so that they might be recruited for the priesthood.[59] Thus, the educational frenzy that gripped colonial New England was not duplicated in New France. One searches in vain for a Gallic parallel to the Massachusetts Old Deluder Satan Act of 1647, which commanded town children to attend school, "it being one chief project of the old deluder Satan to keep men from the knowledge of the Scriptures."

### CHAPTER SIX

# Boys' Elementary Education

The responsibility for founding, staffing, and operating boys' schools in New France rested with the religious communities, principally the Jesuits, the Sulpicians, and the Charon Brothers. The Recollets, as will be explained later, were not part of this tradition. The male communities were assisted in their educational work by civil and spiritual leaders, lay schoolmasters, and parish clergy. Most boys' schools offered a simple diet of reading, writing, calculation, and religion.

## JESUITS AND OTHERS

In 1616, the Recollet brother Pacifique Duplessis established a school in the area that later became the town of Trois-Rivières. His colleague, Father Le Caron, while on missionary duty among the Montagnais at Tadoussac in 1618, reported that he was kept "busy running a free school, [teaching] the alphabet to some who are beginning to read and write fairly well."[1] Despite these developments, the Jesuits, rather than the Recollets, are traditionally credited with having the first school in Canada, in 1635. The Recollet establishments fail to qualify as legitimate schools in two respects: they had a brief life span, lasting only a matter of months; and they were mission rather than colonial schools. The Jesuit school was a permanent institution, having an unbroken existence through to the end of the French regime in Canada. In addition, though it numbered Indian boys among its early pupils, it catered principally to French boys.

The fact that the Jesuits opened the first authentic school in Canada is not in itself remarkable, since they were the only religious order in New France at the time. The Recollets, it will be recalled, had been replaced by the Society of Jesus in 1632, and other religious communities had yet to set foot in the New World. What is somewhat surprising is that the school established by the Jesuits in 1635 was a *petite école*. Elementary education was foreign territory to the followers of Loyola; their academic training and intellectual bearing better suited them for secondary and higher education. To set the record straight, the founding of an elementary school at Quebec was simply an expediency and not a true commitment to lower education. The Jesuits intended to establish a college in the town, but, realizing that secondary education rests on a foundation of basic learning, they were forced by circumstances to open first an elementary school. With few boys in attendance during its early years, the Jesuit *petite école* rarely required the services of more than a single master. When a residential facility was completed, in 1651, enrolments picked up, and by the end of the century close to a hundred boys were in attendance.[2] The school served the colony well, remaining operational up to and beyond the British conquest of the town, in 1759.

It is possible that the Jesuit school was not the only boys' elementary school at Quebec in the seventeenth century. Around 1685, there were complaints from the local citizenry that the Jesuit institution was not serving the entire population. The problem was that the school was located in upper town, while the bulk of the townspeople were living in the *basse-ville*, or lower town. The residents below the cliff demanded their own school, complaining that their children had trouble walking up the hill to the school, particularly in winter, with the bad weather and poor footing. Whether public pressure translated into a boys' school being established in lower-town Quebec is a moot point. If such a school were opened, and there is no hard evidence that it was, it could have been in 1688, when the parish church in the lower town was rebuilt.[3]

Around the turn of the century, the energetic Bishop Saint-Vallier reasoned that a sufficiently large population existed in the town to justify a second boys' school (which implies that there was no school in the lower town). He approached the authorities at the Seminary of Quebec, asking them to assume responsibility for organizing such a school, to which they agreed. For his part, Saint-Vallier promised a grant of four hundred *livres* a year for operating expenses. In 1699, the two parties entered into an agreement which committed them to supporting a schoolmaster capable of teaching "to read, to write, count, and calculate and other things ... the children of this town of Quebec and areas."[4] However, the projected school did not sit well with the Jesuits, who voiced fears that another school in the immediate vicinity would jeopardize their own enrolments. The bishop dismissed the Jesuits' concerns as unwarranted, and in 1700 the new school opened its doors in a small building, probably a rectory, adjacent to a church. It appears that the school was well attended from the start, since in the second year of operation another schoolmaster was engaged. How long the school functioned, who its teachers were, and the number of boys in attendance remain a mystery.

In the second half of the seventeenth century, several schools can be identified in the neighbouring parishes of Quebec, Saint-Joachim, Château-Richer, and Pointe-de-Lévy. Without the funding and population base of the town schools, these rural establishments disappeared from the educational map in the eighteenth century. Around 1668, Bishop Laval opened a boys' school in Saint-Joachim, some ten leagues downriver from the capital, which offered instruction in the trades as well as in French and Latin letters. Boarding facilities were also available, since parents were assessed "three *livres* and a peck of salt per month" to lodge their sons there.[5]

A boys' school opened in Château-Richer in 1674 also owed its birth and development to Bishop Laval, who donated land and money while the local inhabitants contributed funds for its upkeep. The bishop was seigneur and thus a landowner in the parish, and for a time his manor house served as a schoolhouse. A parish record shows that in 1689 the school was located in the rectory.[6] It is possible that the school was serviced by the lay schoolmasters Charles Roger and Jacques Rondeau, since they are identified as *maîtres d'école* in several parish acts of Château-Richer between 1686 and 1691.[7] As the school was officially known as Petit Séminaire du Château-Richer, it apparently had boarding facilities, though details are sketchy. What is known is that it inherited a larger clientele in 1700, with the arrival from Saint-Joachim of boys who were studying Latin in the hope of attending the Quebec college later. The new students, only a handful, were lodged in the manor. Despite this development, the school was threatened by declining enrolments and rising expenditures in succeeding years. It had only five pupils in 1703, and authorities at the Seminary of Quebec were advised by their superior in Paris to close it as a cost-cutting measure. Not wishing to offend Laval, who was living in retirement in Quebec, seminary authorities decided not to act. The decision to close the school came in 1710, two years after Laval's death.

*Curé* Philippe Boucher kept a school in his parish of Pointe-de-Lévis from the 1690s to the early part of the next century. During his tenure as part-time schoolmaster, he taught his boys the fundamentals of French and Latin, so that they might attend the Jesuit college or Seminary of Quebec. It is not known whether this learned priest taught school until his death in 1721, but it is clear that the parish never boasted a school after this date.

Parish and notarial records show that several lay schoolmasters were active in the Quebec area in the seventeenth century. Pierre Canus was teaching in L'Ange Gardien in 1671, Claude Maugue in Beauport in 1671, and François Labernade and Nicolas Métru in Île d'Orléans in 1673 and 1674, respectively. As was mentioned earlier, it does not necessarily follow that where a schoolmaster was so was a school. It is likely that the above schoolmasters were itinerant teachers or family tutors more than teachers in charge of a school. Certainly this was the case for Labernade and Métru.[8]

## THE SULPICIANS

Montreal kept pace with Quebec in establishing an elementary school for boys at an early date. The Sulpicians arrived in the town in 1657, and within a few years opened a school. Like other schools in New France, that of the Gentlemen of St Sulpice provided free instruction, though the public was asked for contributions to help meet expenses. To their credit, the Sulpicians did not carve out an educational monopoly for themselves, though as seigneurs of Montreal they were in a position to do so. Indeed, the Jesuits opened an elementary school in the town in 1694 with the intention of expanding it into a college, but a lack of funds undermined the project. Besides supporting their own school, the Sulpicians offered moral and financial support to others interested in learning; they provided assistance to the Congregation of Notre Dame and the Rouillé Brothers.

The Sulpicians' first schoolmaster was the priest Gabriel Souart, who along with three others had been sent to Montreal from Paris in 1657 to establish a seminary. Souart's involvement in education testifies to the fact that teaching was not yet a full-time occupation and that it required versatility of its practitioners. Teaching was for Souart, as it was for others in New France, an outgrowth of the religious function, and thus was performed in conjunction with other duties. He was fully occupied, if nothing else: besides instructing boys in basic knowledge, he was superior of the seminary and parish priest to boot.

As the town population grew, Souart looked for educational help. He found it in 1669 in the person of Mathieu Ranuyer, a tonsured cleric, who, in addition to his teaching functions, was treasurer of the seminary. Ranuyer was the first in a long line of schoolmasters dispatched to Montreal by the Seminary of Saint-Sulpice in Paris. In 1672, his position as assistant to Souart was assumed by the sub-deacon Pierre Rémy, recently arrived from Paris. Rémy must have made a favourable impression, since in the same year Souart relinquished his educational responsibilities to him. After performing as schoolmaster for four years, Rémy was ordained a priest and assigned new duties. In 1680, he became *curé* of the parish of Lachine, a post which he held for the next twenty-five years. Rémy never lost his taste for education, as evidenced by his efforts to establish schools in his parish. For a short time during the 1680s, Lachine had both a boys' and a girls' school, a remarkable achievement for a rural parish in early Canada.

With Rémy gone, Souart sent out a call to Paris for an educational replacement. In 1684, Louis-François de La Faye arrived in Montreal, preceded by a less than sparkling recommendation: the Sulpician superior in Paris, Louis Tronson, informed Souart that while La Faye "did not possess great talent, he was obedient and could become a schoolmaster in Montreal."9 La Faye's teaching career lasted several years and did not end, as might be supposed, due to a lack of talent. Rather, the explanation lies in a change of rank, for in 1688 La Faye achieved priesthood. The case of Souart aside, the Sulpicians were not in the habit of employing priests as schoolmasters. Priests, of whom there was always a shortage in New France, were judged too valuable to be "wasted" on teaching boys their letters. They were needed to fill vacancies, especially in the rural parishes, or to serve as missionaires. In the eyes of the Sulpicians, teaching was best left to those in minor orders or to laymen.

Desirous of expanding educational facilities in Montreal and inspired by the example of La Salle's Institute of the Brothers of the Christian Schools in France, Souart and La Faye lent moral and material support to a lay teaching community. In 1686, they donated one thousand *livres* and a two-room building across from the seminar on Notre Dame Street to a group of six unmarried laymen, headed by Mathurin Rouillé.[10] In their act of foundation, on 15 September 1686, the Rouillé Brothers promised to devote themselves exclusively to the education of Montreal boys and to "instruct the children, to show them how to read and write and to rear them in piety, and in other good principles."[11] To help subsidize their teaching activities, the brothers purchased a working farm bordering on the St Lawrence, but the enterprise proved to be a poor investment.

Unfortunately, we know little of the educational work of this teaching community. In any case, owing to financial and personnel problems, the Rouillé Brothers folded in 1693. In the fall of that year, Rouillé himself took legal steps to have the community dissolved, citing mounting debts and the recent loss of two of his teachers – Nicolas Barbier had been killed in battle against the English at La Prairie, and Jacob Thoumelet had taken a wife. Pierre Gaulin had died earlier. Thus, in a contract of 17 September 1693 the community was dissolved, ceding all educational rights and possessions to the local parish and the Sulpicians.[12] Rouillé became an associate of the Charon Brothers' hospital in Montreal and Philibert Boy returned to France, where he trained for the priesthood, only to come back to Canada in 1701. Although the Rouillé Brothers had operated for less than a decade, the existence of this lay teaching community demonstrates that learning in New France was not the exclusive preserve of the clergy – that religious representatives both welcomed and depended on lay participation.

The disappearance of the Rouillé Brothers dealt a blow to the cause of education in Montreal. The town had lost one of its two boys' schools. There remained only the Sulpician school, now headed by Léonard Chaigneau. He lamented the fact that the *fabrique* was incapable of filling the educational void left by the Rouillé Brothers, noting, "The parish council is poor and cannot support the said schools ... because the revenues ... are not sufficient for the maintenance of schoolmasters, for repairs that must be done on their buildings."[13]

Like his predecessors, Chaigneau had been sent to Montreal by the Sulpician seminary in Paris and was not a priest. Upon assuming his duties as Montreal schoolmaster he took steps to expand the school's curriculum, adding the teaching of Latin grammar and the study of classical authors. The gesture did not sit well with Louis Tronson in Paris; he refused to send Chaigneau the requested Latin texts, saying that the change would provoke tensions with the Jesuits, who had a monopoly on the teaching of Latin at their schools in Quebec and Montreal.[14] But Tronson's successor, Leschassier, felt differently, expressing no opposition to the teaching of Latin in the Sulpician school in Montreal. As a result, from the early years of the eighteenth century the school maintained Latin classes, designed to serve the sons of gentlemen who looked to acquire a sufficient knowledge of the ancient language to enable them to enrol in the Jesuit college at Quebec. Because the regular schoolmasters were a bit shaky in the language, priests had to be employed on a part-time basis. The Sulpician directory lists five *maîtres de latin* in the eighteenth century: Guillaume Chambon, Mathieu Guillon, Jean-Claude Mathevet, Claude de Metry, and Jean-Baptiste Curratteau.[15]

The arrival in Montreal from France in 1701 of one new schoolmaster, Antoine Forget, and two returning ones, Armand Donay and Jacques-Anne Boësson, augured well for the town's educational future.[16] Forget was the key figure. Here was the type of teacher that the local Sulpicians had been hoping for. Like others who had preceded him, Forget had been sent to Montreal by the Sulpician seminary in Paris; unlike his predecessors, he came highly recommended and well qualified. Prior to coming to Canada he had completed a six-month training course at the Christian Brothers' teacher seminary near Paris, where he had studied the pedagogical theories and methods of La Salle. At a time when elementary-school teachers were rank amateurs – when few of them came to the classroom with any knowledge of pedagogy – Forget was the happy exception. He possessed other virtues, including a strong devotion to duty, for he realized that the position of Montreal schoolmaster carried no salary – only living expenses would be provided. He also came to Montreal with the warning that the post could not be looked upon as a stepping-stone to the priesthood.

Forget is credited with introducing Lasallian pedagogy into Montreal classrooms and possibly into other schools in the colony. If Forget was true to Lasallian principles, he probably ran a quiet, well-ordered school in which children were grouped according to grades or classes, anticipating the elementary-school organization of today. And while it is unlikely that Forget dispensed with corporal punishment entirely, as a disciple of Lasallian methods he probably deplored its use and resorted to milder forms of correction. Forget brought with him to Canada a number of pedagogical and religious texts produced by the Christian Brothers; later he ordered others from Paris.

Forget served as Montreal schoolmaster until 1715, when he fell ill and returned to France to recover his strength. The following year, feeling well again, he asked to be allowed to return to Canada to resume his teaching duties. The Sulpician authorities in Paris refused his request, believing that his health was not good enough. Forget's replacement in Montreal was the minor cleric Jacques Talbot, who arrived from Paris in 1716. In 1724, he was joined by Jean Girard in response to a growing school-age population in the town. Talbot and Girard had remarkable and remarkably similar careers: both taught school in Montreal for almost forty years. Talbot died in 1756, at the age of seventy-seven, and was succeeded by Jean-Baptiste Curratteau, who had arrived from Paris two years earlier.

From the middle of the seventeenth century to the end of the French period in Canada, the Gentlemen of Saint-Sulpice maintained an educational presence in Montreal, principally through their support of an elementary school for boys. In providing free tuition to the school, the Sulpicians practised a form of educational democracy by opening their classrooms to boys from all social backgrounds. As we have also seen, they were not hesitant about extending assistance to lay schoolmasters, being the benefactors of the Rouillé Brothers. Moreover, the Sulpician *curé* of Lachine, Pierre Rémy, himself a former schoolmaster, engaged as parish teacher the layman Jean-Baptiste Pottier in 1686.

## THE CHARON BROTHERS

The point has already been made that the great majority of New France's educators were born, reared, and educated in the mother

country. One who was not was François Charon. Born in Quebec
in 1654, he received part of his schooling in France. Had Charon
followed the script, he would have come to education through the
church. Instead, he started out in the unlikely role of businessman,
rising in the second half of the century to become one of Montreal's
most prominent fur merchants. In 1687, however, a serious illness
turned his life around. So thankful was he at having regained his
health that he vowed to devote his life and wealth to good works.
To that end, he founded a community of brothers, officially known
as the Brothers Hospitallers of the Cross and of St Joseph, but more
popularly known as the Charon Brothers.

Thanks to land grants from the Sulpician superior, Dollier de Casson, and from Mathurin Rouillé, and to money gifts from other
Montrealers, Charon set about founding a *maison de charité*, which
became Hôpital Général. The general hospital was so named because
it operated as a social-welfare institution for males, caring for the
elderly, the destitute, the handicapped, and orphan boys. The last
signalled an educational obligation, spelled out in the king's letters
patent of 1694 authorizing the Charon Brothers "to teach trades to
the said children, to give them the best education they are able, all
for the greater glory of God and for the well-being and utility of the
colony."[17]

Although Charon was committed to the care and instruction of
orphan boys at the hospital, he had more ambitious projects in mind.
At first, he aspired to gaining control of all boys' education in Montreal and concentrating it in Hôpital Général. For this to happen,
the Sulpicians would have to be persuaded to relinquish their rights
to boys' education, which they were not prepared to do. On the
advice of their superior in Paris, the Montreal Sulpicians resisted the
educational encroachments of Charon.

Charon also had his eye on the rural parishes, where ignorance
was widespread owing to a lack of educational facilities. Charon's
attempts to remedy the situation by bringing a measure of organized
learning to the countryside through the placement of teachers was
a long, drawn-out affair. Almost two decades were to pass before a
number of schools were established. The long delay in bringing educational relief to the rural parishes may be traced to several factors.
First, since teachers were not available in Canada, they had to be
recruited in France, which necessitated time-consuming voyages to
the mother country by Charon and his successors. Second, funds

were lacking for the maintenance of schoolmasters in the rural parishes. Although the king had awarded the Charon Brothers an annual subsidy of one thousand *livres* in 1700, the monies were earmarked for welfare, not education. Moreover, the establishment by the brothers of the brewery, a flour mill, and other small industries in later years failed to produce much in the way of supplementary income. Third, as much as Charon was keen in promoting rural education, his priority at the turn of the century was spiritual – to establish the Charon Brothers as an authentic religious community. With the blessings of Bishop Saint-Vallier in 1701, the male community adopted a modest but distinctive uniform. The following year, the six-member community pronounced its religious vows. But when the king learned of this action on the part of the Charon Brothers, he slapped an interdict on the community. In the hope of getting the Crown to revise its position, Charon spent five years, from 1707 to 1712, in France vainly arguing his case. During his long absence from Montreal, the work of the Charon Brothers came to a standstill and membership declined. In 1716, the community numbered only four members, including the founder.

The long struggle to establish boys' schools in the rural districts of New France began, paradoxically, in France. While on a teacher-recruitment mission in France in 1700, Charon tried to interest La Salle's Christian Brothers in coming to Canada. Charon felt that the French teaching order was an ideal choice, since it was experienced in the training of teachers and in elementary-school teaching. However, the Christian Brothers showed little interest in the Montrealer's invitation, possibly scared away by his community's involvement in social welfare, with which they had little experience. The tenacious Charon was not discouraged, and persisted in his attempts to get France's largest teaching order to change its mind. In 1718, his efforts seemed to have paid off, for Brother Barthélemy, La Salle's successor as director of the institute, announced, "By all appearances we shall soon have an establishment in Canada."[18] Indeed, four brothers with tickets in hand were prepared to board ship for Canada. But two days before their scheduled departure, La Salle personally intervened to abort the voyage, though his reasons for doing so are unclear. One interpretation is that the founder feared for the spiritual discipline of his brothers in Canada, believing that as rural schoolmasters they would come under the authority of the parish *curés*.[19]

The enterprising Charon was not without schemes. At one point he lobbied the government in Paris to give approval to a plan linking the Charon Brothers, the Christians Brothers, and the Sulpicians, in effect creating a triple association. According to Charon's thinking, the Sulpicians would give his community spiritual legitimacy, while the Christian Brothers would give it pedagogical expertise. Although there was early support in government circles for the projected merger, it was ultimately rejected in 1718. The Sulpicians in Paris, for their part, greeted the decision with much relief. In a letter to the Sulpician superior in Montreal, François Magnien, procurator of the Sulpician seminary in Paris, wrote that while he could not say why the Council ruled against Charon, he regarded the decision as "the divine Providence."[20]

Since the turn of the century, Charon had sought funding for his plan of posting teachers in the country parishes of Canada. He found a valuable ally in Intendant Jacques Raudot, who told the government in Paris in 1707 that the absence of schoolmasters in the rural parts of the colony was having a corrupting influence on youth. Because of the lack of teachers, wrote the administrator, children in the countryside were growing up entirely in the presence of their parents, who reared them in the Indian manner – namely, with much indulgence and little discipline. Raudot added that this mode of upbringing was producing boys of "hard and ferocious" character, which translated into violent behaviour. The intendant argued that the presence of schoolmasters in the educationally starved rural parishes would serve to counteract the ill effects of a defective upbringing and thus appealed to the king to increase his annual subsidy to the Charon Brothers from one to three thousand *livres*.[21] When the Crown failed to act on his recommendation, Raudot pressed his case the following year by writing to the minister Pontchartrain, emphasizing that nothing would be more beneficial to the welfare of the colony than if the Charon Brothers could accomplish for rural boys what the Congregation of Notre Dame was achieving for rural girls.[22] Governor Ramezay of Montreal added his voice to the appeal, arguing that increased financial support from the king would greatly contribute to the welfare of Canada.[23]

More than a decade would pass before the Crown decided to increase its subsidy to the Charon Brothers. In 1718, Louis XV authorized an annual payment of three thousand *livres* to the Montreal community for the support and maintenance of six rural schoolmasters. This time colonial officials protested, the governor and intendant claiming that the funds should have been used to finance the dowries of sixty girls chosen from among the colony's poorest families.[24] The king said that the grant was awarded because "young boys lacked learning" in the countryside, while young girls received schooling at the hands of the Congregation of Notre Dame.[25] Here again was official confirmation of the fact that outside the towns educational provision was greater for girls than for boys. The king was later to rule that the three thousand *livres* was intended to support eight rather than six schoolmasters (six in the rural parishes and two at the Montreal hospital) and that the schoolmasters were forbidden to charge for their instruction.[26] That an eighteenth-century monarch would tie a subsidy to free education should serve as a reminder that pre-revolutionary France was not always unenlightened in matters of learning.

Having received funding for the maintenance of rural schoolmasters in 1718, Charon promptly sailed for France in search of teachers, returning to Montreal within the year with six recruits in hand. However, the recruitment campaign turned sour; the new arrivals lost their interest in educational matters upon setting foot in Canada, forcing the tireless Charon to sail again for France. His shopping tour was successful, as he recruited eight candidates and a like number of artisans. All left for Canada aboard the king's vessel *Chameau* in June of 1719. But a few weeks into the voyage to Canada Charon died, and was succeeded as superior later in the year by Louis Turc, one of the eight recruits on board.

Since the new arrivals did not take up teaching duties until a year or two later, it may be wondered whether in the interim they did not undergo a period of teacher training at the hospital. In other words, did the Charon Brothers maintain a normal school of sorts at their facility? Some support for this thesis is found in the king's letters of confirmation for Hôpital Général, dated February 1718, which speak of "preparing in this hospital schoolmasters" for the country parishes.[27] On the other hand, it is doubtful whether his document can be interpreted as signifying the existence of a teacher-training facility; the time and place argue against such a possibility. A more logical explanation is that the king's letters merely recognized the right of the Charon Brothers to recruit and place teachers. This is not to preclude the possibility that teachers destined to be posted to the rural parishes received some informal instruction in teaching methods and classroom management.

Governor Ramezay of Montreal, who earlier had rallied to the side of the Charon Brothers, attacked the community in 1721, saying that it was failing in its social and educational responsibilities. In a letter to the colonial office, he accused the Charon Brothers of having opened only one rural school: "I feel obliged to inform the Council that they [the Charon Brothers] are not fulfilling any of their duties, neither for the instruction of children nor for the care of the eleven elderly who are in the hospital ... There are seven brothers in the community, of whom only two are experienced, one of whom is stationed in Pointe-aux-Trembles, the others not doing anything but using up the goods of the poor."[28]

Ramezay's allegations, contained in a letter of 4 October, are contradicted by other documentation, including the Charon Brothers' own records[29] and parish registers,[30] which show that five rural schoolmasters were in place in 1721. The schoolmaster in Pointe-aux-Trembles to whom the governor alluded was Jean Jeantot, who had been teaching there since 1706. Nor was Jeantot the only schoolmaster before 1720. Until his death, in 1714, the Charon Brothers' Mathurin Durand had kept school in Boucherville. At any rate, parish records confirm that in 1720 Louis Pillard was teaching in Boucherville and Antoine de la Girardière in Trois-Rivières, and that by the summer of 1721 François Simmonet was teaching in Longueuil, and Nicolas Datte in Batiscan.

The Charon Brothers were not the first schoolmasters in these rural parishes, though they were probably the first full-time ones. Parish records indicate that they were preceded, albeit at some time previous, by lay schoolmasters who may or may not have kept schools as such. For example, in 1666 René Remy was a tutor in Trois-Rivières, as was Pierre Bertrand in 1681. The long-time notary of the town, Séverin Ameau, whose career spanned the second half of the seventeenth century, did some part-time teaching there.[31] The parish records of Boucherville show that the area had had three schoolmasters before the arrival of the Charon Brothers. Julien Beaussault was there in 1689, J.B. Bau dit Lalouette in 1695–96, and Jean-Baptiste Tétro from 1703 to 1711; the latter, like others, quit teaching to be come a notary. Pointe-aux-Trembles had two known teachers in earlier years: Nicolas Rousselot was schoolmaster and precentor in the parish in 1684, and the well-travelled François Labernade taught there between 1684 and 1688.

By perusing the parish acts of the 1720s, in which the names of the Charon Brothers frequently appear as witnesses in baptisms, marriages, and deaths, we are able to trace the comings and goings of rural schoolmasters during the decade. In 1723, Jeantot was recalled to Montreal to serve as counsellor at Hôpital Général, though he returned to teaching around 1727, this time in Champlain, near Trois-Rivières. His replacement in Pointe-aux-Trembles was Laurent Bruno, whose name surfaces in numerous parish acts between 1723 and 1726. René-Guy Gournay was a teacher in Longueuil for the years 1722 and 1723, which means that for a time the parish had two schoolmasters, since Simmonet was not transferred to Trois-Rivières until 1724. A similar situation prevailed in Boucherville. In addition to Louis Pillard, who taught there throughout the 1720s, Jacques Viel was also schoolmaster in the parish in 1723, to judge by the parish register.

Gervais Hodiesne, Joseph Delorme, and Frère André, all Charon Brothers, are listed as witnesses in several marriage acts in the St-Jean parish of Île d'Orléans for 1723 and 1725.[32] The question arises as to what they were doing there. Since none of them is identified as *maître d'école* in the parish acts, it cannot be stated conclusively that they were schoolmasters in the area. On the other hand, there seems to be no other explanation for their presence in the region – certainly not as witnesses in a number of marriages – for the Charon Brothers' sole activity in the countryside was an educational one. In addition, this was precisely the period during which the male community was establishing schools in the rural parts of the colony.

It will be recalled that Louis Turc succeeded Charon as superior of the Montreal community following the founder's death at sea in 1719. Like his predecessor, the new superior was deeply interested in education (he was also a teacher at the hospital), but unfortunately he lacked Charon's administrative *savoir-faire*, as future events would testify. Like Charon, Turc discovered that recruiting teachers was one thing, but that keeping them was quite another. In the years 1722–24 he recruited a total of fifteen teachers in France, only to find that upon reaching Canada their pedagogical interests waned, some returning to France and others turning to other lines of work in their adopted land.

To overcome the chronic problem of teacher defections, Turc reopened negotiations with the Christian Brothers, hoping to effect a union between the two communities. When nothing came of the talks he looked elsewhere for a solution, hatching a scheme which, though not lacking in boldness and promise, sowed the seeds of his downfall and seriously compromised the reputation and work of the Montreal male order. While in France in 1723, he proposed that the Charon Brothers establish a normal school on that side of the Atlantic, which would select and train teachers before shipping them off to Canada. The site envisaged was the seaport town of La Rochelle, which was an embarkation point for ships bound for the New World. Bishop Champflour of the town promised funding for the proposed institution if boys from his diocese could be trained there as well. When the members of the Charon Brothers gave approval to their superior's plan in 1724, the way seemed clear for its realization.[33] But it was not to be. The project collapsed when evidence came to light of financial irregularities on Turc's part; he had borrowed heavily against funds for the proposed normal school. Unable to satisfy his creditors, he made things worse by dipping into the regular funds of the community which were earmarked for ongoing educational activities. In 1725, Turc fled to a Caribbean island, leaving the Charon Brothers leaderless and in a state of financial confusion. Though a new superior was appointed in 1727, the damage had been done; the Charon Brothers never quite recovered.

Not a great deal is known about the schools run by the Charon Brothers, save for their location and the names of their schoolmasters. The best source of information is the community's constitution of 1723, approved by Bishop Saint-Vallier, which contains regulations pertaining to the boarding school at the hospital, the organization of the school day, and the administration of rural schools. The document leaves no doubt as to the spiritual purpose of the Charon Brothers' schools: "The children who want to be received in order to be instructed in the schools of the Frères Hospitaliers ought to know that the principal end for which one receives them is to teach them to know God, to love Him, and to serve Him so they can be truly happy."[34]

The school at the hospital in Montreal received both day and boarding pupils. Although the number of boys in attendance is unknown, enrolments must have been fairly large, to judge by the size of the facility. A hospital inventory taken in 1719, after the death of Charon, refers to a "large room to hold the classes."[35]

The regulations contained in the constitution offer some insights into boarding-school life at the hospital.[36] No boy below the age of eight was to be admitted as a boarder; nor were any allowed to remain beyond the age of eighteen. The rooms of the boarders were to be kept separate from those of the brothers. Each boarder was to have his own bed and living space, which was enclosed by a curtain in order to discourage boys from sleeping together. Parents could visit their sons at the hospital, but were prohibited from seeing them in their quarters. In addition to the regular school subjects, boarders were taught good work habits, which included making their beds, sweeping the floors, and doing other chores demanded of them. Like other religious communities in New France, the Charon Brothers were bent on stamping out idleness in the young.

The school day at the hospital was, by today's standards, a short one. Classes were held in the morning from eight to ten o'clock and in the afternoon from two to four o'clock. Mornings were taken up with instruction in reading, writing, and spelling, and afternoons with Latin and arithmetic. The spiritual side of education was not neglected. The day began and ended with prayers, and on Wednesdays and Fridays regular instruction gave way to one-and-a-half hours of catechism. In addition, boys were encouraged to practise their devotions outside school; to say their prayers upon waking each morning and upon retiring each night; to attend church regularly; and, in the case of older boys, to attend confession once every two weeks. At the same time, the Charon Brothers lectured their charges on the importance of proper moral conduct, of obeying their parents, of not lying to or mocking others, of not showing anger or impatience, and of not stealing from others. In the eyes of the Charon Brothers, education was an intellectual, spiritual, and moral undertaking.

Like the Jesuit college in Quebec, the school at Hôpital Général provided instruction in hydrography. Apparently it was of good quality, since Governor Ramezay enrolled his two sons at the hospital in 1707 to study navigation and fortifications. Moreover, the fact that one of the original aims of the Charon Brothers was to teach orphan boys the methods of farming and other manual skills suggests that the hospital also functioned as a trade school.[37] As a matter of fact, the community favoured the recruitment of brothers who possessed a manual skill and who in turn were capable of passing on this knowledge to young boys. The stress on manual training was designed, according to the community's constitution, to overcome idleness in the young, which is described as the source of all sins in the colony.[38]

The constitution also includes regulations governing the organization and administration of rural schools. Before opening a "mission" school, the superior was advised to seek the advice of his fellow brothers as well as to secure authorization from the bishop or his delegate. The superior was also responsible for organizing living arrangements for the schoolmasters posted in the rural parishes, as well as for appealing for charity from the local population. In contrast to the hospital school in Montreal, those in the country districts were exclusively day schools, for, unlike the Congregation of Notre Dame, the Charon Brothers lacked the financial resources to support boarding facilities. A three-year posting was standard for a country teacher, though the regulations allowed for an extension of the contract were the superior and the teacher to agree. The regulations also commanded rural teachers to keep the superior informed of spiritual and educational problems in their parishes.[39]

By 1730, half of the rural schools maintained by the Charon Brothers had closed. The precise reason for this is unclear, though the community's mounting debts and ineffective leadership were probably contributing factors. Louis Pillard, François Simmonet, and Antoine de la Girardière were alone in continuing their pedagogical duties into the next decade. Pillard taught in Boucherville until 1733, following which he returned to Montreal as bursar at the hospital. Later he quit religious life, accepting in 1735 an appointment as royal notary in the Quebec area. In 1737, he married. After teaching in Boucherville until 1730, Simmonet moved to Trois-Rivières, where he kept school for at least five years. In a parish act dated 12 May 1735, he is listed as "frère, maître d'école," proving that he was still schoolmaster in the town.[40] Girardière, who had taught in Trois-Rivières in the early 1720s before leaving, returned to the town at about the same time as Simmonet. Parish records confirm his presence there until 1736, during which time he was also employed as church chorister and sacristan. He was succeeded as schoolmaster by the layman Pierre-François Rigault, who had originally come to Canada as a soldier.

The decline in the Charon Brothers' educational activities in the country parishes brought a reproach from Louis xv in 1730, who accused the Montreal community of neglecting its responsibilities.[41] A year later the king took punitive action by withdrawing his educational subsidy of three thousand *livres* for the maintenance of schoolmasters.[42] The bishop of New France added insult to injury by imposing a recruitment ban on the Charon Brothers. Stripped of their government subsidy and reeling from accumulating debts, the order once again appealed to France's Christian Brothers to come and establish themselves in Canada. The overture bore fruit, for in 1737 the French teaching order dispatched two brothers to Montreal for exploratory talks. The discussions proved successful, as the two sides signed an *acte d'association* which proposed no less than a merger of the two communities. According to the terms of the protocol, the Christian Brothers would take control of educational matters and assume the debts of the hospital. For their part, the Charon Brothers agreed to adopt the regulations and dress of the Lasallian order, though they would be allowed to continue their social-welfare activities.[43] Ratification of the agreement seemed but a formality, as one of the Christian Brothers remained in Montreal to be with his "new brothers," while his colleague returned to France to conclude the accord.

The protocol, however, remained a dead letter. One problem was that others in the colony had designs on Hôpital Général. Louis Normant, vicar general and superior of the Sulpician seminary of Montreal, who had a hand in establishing the Sisters of Charity under Marguerite d'Youville, wanted to see the female order installed in the hospital. Normant's intentions so concerned Governor Beauharnois and Intendant Hocquart that in 1738 they wrote to Count Maurepas, urging the secretary of state to facilitate the proposed merger between the Charon Brothers and Christian Brothers, and to restore the king's subsidy of three thousand *livres* to the Montreal community.[44] Complicating matters was the shifting attitude of the Christian Brothers, who seemed to have second thoughts about the merger. If one is to believe a report of the Ministry of Marine in 1739, the French teaching order was frightened off by the enormous debts of the hospital.[45] When Bishop Pontbriand pronounced in favour of Normant's scheme in 1741, all hopes for the Christian Brothers coming to New France were effectively dashed. The high churchman's victory was the colony's loss, for had the

Lasallian order come to Canada around 1740 instead of a century later, boys' education might have taken a more prosperous turn.

As things turned out, the fate of the Charon Brothers was officially sealed in 1747, at which time the male community folded, ceding the hospital and its possessions to the Sisters of Charity, or the Grey Nuns, as they were popularly known. At the time of their demise, the Charon Brothers numbered two aging brothers, were in deep debt, and their hospital was in a state of disrepair. In hindsight, it may be wondered whether the founder did not overextend himself in setting the dual course for his community of maintaining a social-welfare facility and promoting education in Montreal and in the rural parishes. At any rate, the disappearance of the Charon Brothers at mid-century is a harsh reminder of the fragility of organized learning in early Canada, however well intentioned its supporters.

## THE RECOLLETS

The educational contributions of the Recollets appear to have slight. It will be recalled that the Franciscan order returned to Canada in 1670, after an absence of forty years, ostensibly to assist in the missionary campaign. It is well known that their reappearance on Canadian soil was also generated by political motives, the king seeing them as a counterbalance to the influence of the powerful Jesuits. Shortly after their return to the New World, the Recollets found themselves locked in religious combat with Bishop Laval, who accused them of abandoning the spiritual life and aligning themselves too closely with the civil authority. The bishop's charge was not without foundation, as the Recollets had joined with the governor and the intendant in ridiculing the Jesuits, accusing them of inflating their missionary achievements and meddling in commerce and other secular affairs.[46]

The Recollets were nothing if not active. The retiring life of the monastery did not suit their adventurous, temporal nature, which saw them play many roles in New France, from Newfoundland to Detroit. Unlike the Jesuits and the Sulpicians, they were not above recruiting Canadians, which had the effect of increasing their ranks. While initially committed to evangelization of the Indians, they also took on other tasks, becoming parish priests, confessors to civil and religious leaders, explorers, and military chaplains. During its existence, Lake Champlain's Fort Frédéric counted a total of eleven chaplains, all of them Recollets. Whether the Recollets opened schools or served as schoolmasters is highly doubtful, though it is possible that they did some casual teaching in the forts of the upper country. But the evidence fails to sustain the assertion of several historians that the Recollets, in the fashion of the Jesuits and Sulpicians, were active in colonial education.[47]

If it is true that the Franciscans were schoolmasters, why are such persons so difficult to identify? As far as can be determined, no historian has succeeded in naming a single Recollet teacher in seventeenth- and eighteenth-century Canada. Of forty-three Recollets listed in the *Dictionary of Canadian Biography* between 1670 and 1760, only two are described as having pedagogical connections. Prior to being admitted to the Recollets in 1756, Leger-Noël Veyssière taught school for the Sulpicians in Montreal.[48] Patrice René's biographer credits him with opening a boys' school in Acadia around 1708.[49]

What may be said of the assertion that the Recollets maintained schools in Quebec, Montreal, and Trois-Rivières? No one doubts that the male community had churches and religious houses in the three towns, but such establishments must not be confused with schools. Indeed, there is not a shred of evidence to indicate that the Recollets ran schools in Quebec and Montreal. Architectural plans of the order's buildings in Montreal give no hint of the existence of a school or of educational activities.[50] At Trois-Rivières, the evidence of a Franciscan presence in education is at best circumstantial, though as parish clergy of the town from 1671 to 1683 and from 1693 to 1777 the Recollets were well placed to furnish teachers and to exercise a margin of leadership.[51] As was indicated above, Trois-Rivières was not without schoolmasters during the French regime in Canada. Their names are known by dint of parish and notarial records, and not a one is a Recollet. They include the laymen Séverin Ameau, Pierre Bertrand, Jean-François Janelle, René Remy, and Pierre-François Rigault, and two Charon Brothers, Antoine de la Girardière and François Simmonet. The declaration by a Franciscan historian that Recollet teachers succeeded the lay schoolmaster Rigault after he quit teaching around 1739 is not backed by hard evidence.[52]

Leaving aside the question of schoolmasters, did the Recollets of Trois-Rivières take educational initiatives? In other words, did they take responsibility for establishing a school and engaging the lay schoolmasters who operated in the town? The case for a Recollet school appears to rest on a single piece of documentary evidence, an 1821 petition addressed to Lord Dalhousie by the citizens of the town in which the petitioners declare that the Recollets "have constantly maintained a free school for the small boys in this town."[53] At the very least the statement is ambiguous, for it is unclear whether the petitioners were referring to Recollet involvement since the conquest of 1760 or since 1671, when the male community first arrived in the town. At any rate, the statement is difficult to reconcile with the fact that the Recollets died out in Canada before 1800. Until more reliable evidence is forthcoming, the traditional belief that the Recollets participated in education in Trois-Rivières during the time of New France cannot be embraced with conviction.

Curiously, the key to unlocking the mystery of Recollet participation may lie in Louisbourg, an eastern-seaboard port town on Île Royale. Perhaps the most significant aspect of this eighteenth-century town is that it had a girls' but not a boys' school: from 1727, the Congregation of Notre Dame operated a well-attended school there. As a thriving seaport and garrison town bursting with administrators, clerks, merchants, military officers, and other lettered types, and boasting a population of three thousand inhabitants by 1740 and perhaps triple that number on the eve of the Seven Years' War, Louisbourg was fertile ground for a boys' school. To be sure, the town had several teachers, possibly clerks, who tutored the children of better families. Boys were sent to Quebec or France for their formal schooling.

The glaring absence of a boys' school in Louisbourg may be ultimately traced to the clerical situation. The parish clergy and military chaplains of the town and of Île Royale were Recollets, who, in keeping with their humble origins and scanty education, did not attach much importance to the diffusion of learning. Their detractors, who included the civil leaders of the town and the bishop of New France, accused them of ignorance and spiritual indiscretions, and tried unsuccessfully to have them removed in favour of more learned clergy. One of the Recollets' severest critics was Bishop Saint-Vallier, who charged them with fraternizing too closely with ordinary folk. In 1727, the bishop wrote to the Recollet provincial in Brittany, requesting priests for Louisbourg who were "more learned and more reserved in their conduct, eating among themselves and not looking to dine and sup with ship captains and fishermen who think only of drinking."[54] But thanks to the support of the common people, who liked and respected the Recollets for their simple piety and unpretentious ways, they survived the attacks of civil and religious leaders.

Thus, if the Recollets of New France were involved in education, it is a well-kept secret. The documentary evidence does not support such a role. Perhaps Peter Kalm was not far off the mark when he portrayed the Recollets in Canada as intellectually second rate, saying, "They do not torment their brains with much learning."[55]

### CHAPTER SEVEN

# Girls' Elementary Education

## THE CONGREGATION OF NOTRE DAME

Of the female communities participating in New France education, none was as active and as greatly admired as the Congregation of Notre Dame. Civil and religious leaders were united in praising the work of the Notre Dame Sisters. Intendant Jacques Raudot told France in 1707 that because of the sisters, a good proportion of the youth of the colony had been rescued from a state of ignorance.[1] The bad-tempered governor of Montreal, Claude de Ramezay, who quarreled with just about everybody and who in 1721 accused the Charon Brothers of not doing their job, had only kind words for the female community, describing it as indispensable to the life of the colony.[2] Similar acclaim came from bishops Laval and Saint-Vallier and from the Sulpician superior, Dollier de Casson. The praise, if sometimes exaggerated, was not misplaced, for the congregation chalked up solid achievements in the domains of education and welfare. No religious community in Canada founded and operated more schools; until the Charon Brothers came on the scene, it was virtually alone in maintaining schools in the educationally impoverished rural parishes.

The reputation of the congregation was enhanced by the fact that it was not perceived as posing a spiritual or political threat to others. Moreover, the Notre Dame Sisters practised what they preached, sometimes sharing in the poverty of those to whom they lent assistance. And if the sisters demonstrated a soft spot for the lower classes, they faithfully strove to meet the learning needs of all girls, irrespective of their social origins. Marguerite Bourgeoys reminded her companions that their duties must be "performed with purity of intention, without distinction of poor or rich, relatives or friends, pretty or deformed."[3] For this reason, it may be suggested that the notion of popular education in Canada found its first true expression in the work of the Congregation of Notre Dame.

The point was made above that a lack of funds rather than a want of zeal was frequently the determining factor in whether a school would stand or fall in the colony. For the congregation, which was dedicated to the simple life and did not have an independent source of income, the financial question was a real and perennial one. In the pursuit of social and educational work, the female community was heavily dependent on the generosity of others in the form of money gifts, buildings, and properties. Fortunately, the sisters did not lack friends on either side of the Atlantic. The bishops of New France and the Sulpicians were regular donors to the community. In the late seventeenth century, Laval financed the construction of a school for the Notre Dame Sisters in Château-Richer, including an annual maintenance grant of three hundred *livres* for the support of two schoolmistresses. Laval's successor, Bishop Saint-Vallier, financed many of the congregation's educational ventures. In addition, he called on the population in the rural parishes to build schoolhouses for the sisters, promising that once they were erected he would pay for their upkeep.

But it was not only the great and powerful who sustained the Congregation of Notre Dame in its work. In 1685, the parish priest of Sainte-Famille on Île d'Orléans, François Lamy, donated "three acres" upon which he said the sisters could build a school.[4] Louis Geoffroy, parish priest of Champlain in 1700, sold most of his personal belongings, including his "books, his furniture, and his pendule," so that the sisters might run a school in his district.[5] The longtime *curé* of Lachine and friend to learning, Pierre Rémy, willed all his income plus one-half of his grain, fowl, pigs, butter, oil, and other provisions to the Notre Dame Sisters. He hoped that the inheritance would help the sisters to erect a stone house near the church so that they could continue in the care and instruction of orphan girls in the parish.[6]

Despite the generous help of others, the congregation could never distance itself from financial problems, forcing it to suspend some activities and put aside others. The sisters' financial difficulties were not made any easier by their commitment to free instruction. The congregation's *Reglemens* of 1698 expressly prohibited the assessment of tuition fees, though the regulations allowed for the billing of pupils for books, pens, ink, and firewood.[7] Sometimes Marguerite Bourgeoys put her pupils to work after class and into the evening to compensate for free tuition. On the other hand, girls enrolled as boarders were expected to pay for their keep. Those attending the *pensionnat* at Château-Richer in the late seventeenth century were assessed thirty-six *livres* and twelve bushels of wheat.

In addition to the ever-present financial woes, both the Notre Dame Sisters and the Ursulines were harassed by the twin scourges of the era – fire and pestilence. In 1683, the mother house of the Congregation of Notre Dame in Montreal was destroyed by fire, resulting in the death of two novices. In 1650 and again in 1686, the Ursulines in Quebec saw their convent ravaged by fire, which required a new building in each case. The house and school of the Ursulines of Trois-Rivières was levelled by a terrible fire which swept through the town in 1752. Infectious diseases also intervened to disrupt learning: in 1703 an epidemic struck the Quebec Ursulines and led to the suspension of classes.

As was noted earlier, the educational work of the Congregation of Notre Dame in Canada dates from 1658. In April of that year, Marguerite Bourgeoys opened a *petite école* in Montreal in an abandoned stable, receiving a handful of local children, some of whom were of pre-school age. The modest school was a bit daring for its time, since it included boys as well as girls. This breach in educational protocol was repaired later, when the Sulpician Gabriel Souart opened a boys' school near the seminary. Realizing that her school would need more hands if it were to grow and prosper, Sister Marguerite sailed to France in the autumn of that year in search of schoolmistresses. During her absence, she entrusted her school to two Hospital Nuns from Quebec. She returned to Canada the following year with four recruits, three of whom were promptly put to work as teachers.

In 1673, Marguerite Bourgeoys had reason to be pleased. Her community legally existed in the eyes of church and state; the rundown stable had been replaced by a larger and more suitable building; and school enrolments were on the rise. Four years earlier, Bishop Laval had granted spiritual recognition to the Congregation of Notre Dame, and the female order had received its letters patent from the king after Marguerite Bourgeoys's two-year lobbying effort in France. Furthermore, on the superior's return from France in 1672 she was accompanied by nine females, ranging in age from sixteen to thirty, who had been recruited as schoolmistresses. The increase in the number of educational workers allowed the congregation to receive more pupils. Soon an estimated one hundred girls were learning their letters and catechism at the *petite école* in Montreal.

Since the 1660s, pressure had been building for the establishment of a second girls' school in the town, in particular a boarding facility. The influx of new settlers included families of higher social standing who wanted a type of school befitting their station. They were seconded in their demands by parents who complained of the inconvenience, danger, and expense of sending their daughters to Quebec for a convent-school education. Initially, there was talk of inviting the Ursulines to come and set up a boarding institution in Montreal, the likes of their *pensionnat* in the capital. But Marie de l'Incarnation said it could not be done in the absence of financial assistance from the government. Into the gap stepped the resourceful Marguerite Bourgeoys, who around 1676 opened a boarding school in the town. The census of 1681 shows that seven girls between the ages of six and thirteen were in attendance.

Sister Marguerite's concern for the spiritual and social condition of poor girls translated into yet another educational facility in the second half of the century. The superior's concern was at first met by allowing girls to remain in the *pensionnat* beyond the normal leaving age, until the age of eighteen in some cases, as well as bringing together adolescent girls on Sundays to hear lectures on piety. Ever fearful that adolescent girls, if left to their own devices, would lapse into impious behaviour, she then founded the House of Providence, a sort of vocational school for poor girls between the ages of twelve and eighteen. The aim of the facility was to teach needy girls domestic skills so that they could fend for themselves after marriage.

The House of Providence, which moved to Point St-Charles in 1668, combined practical training, religious instruction, and work experience. Though the institution catered to adolescent girls, the temptation to label it Canada's first secondary school for girls must be resisted. In the first place, Providence was more workhouse and welfare centre than school, though the institution may have been an early forerunner of French Canada's family institutes of the first half of the twentieth century. Second, the documents of the day do not use the term "college" – the standard designation for a French secondary school – in referring to the institution. Nor could Providence answer the description of a normal school, in spite of the fact that some of its girls went on to become teachers: Bishop Saint-Vallier reported that from "Providence have come several schoolmistresses who went to different parts of the colony, where they taught catechism to children and gave useful courses to older girls."[8]

Whatever the precise character of the House of Providence, it drew raves from the right quarters. So taken was Bishop Saint-Vallier with the institution in his visit to it in 1685, during which he counted twenty "grandes filles" in attendance, that in the following year he purchased a house with a court and garden in upper-town Quebec and asked the Notre Dame Sisters to convert it into a second workhouse.[9] The Quebec House of Providence opened in 1686.[10] Direction of the new facility was entrusted to two sisters, one of whom was Marie Barbier, the community's first Canadian-born member, who had been teaching school on Île d'Orléans. Not much is known about the activities of the Quebec workhouse, save that its mandate, like that of the Montreal institution, was to receive poor girls and "to teach them to work and earn their living honestly in the fear of God."[11] Bishop Saint-Vallier laid down three regulations for the Quebec institution, which were designed to promote a turnover in enrolments and to ensure that the facility paid its own way. First, it was decreed that only girls having reached the age of eleven or twelve would be admitted, since such girls were of communion age and would thus see fit to leave after a reasonable time. Second, girls who failed to pay their *pension*, or boarding costs, would not be allowed to stay more than a year. Third, girls whose parents did not do their laundry would be assessed a fee of thirty *livres*.[12] The curious feature of these regulations is that they seem to be directed at girls who presumably could pay, which suggests that the Quebec House of Providence received not only poor or needy girls.

The Quebec workhouse had a short life; in 1689 it became Hôpital Général, which was less an institution for the sick than a shelter for the homeless, the helpless, and the aged. Five years later, the House of Providence in Montreal closed its doors, a casualty of insufficient funds; when the Sulpicians cancelled their annual subsidy that year, the Congregation of Notre Dame was unable to come up with replacement funds.

In 1691, the Notre Dame Sisters opened a girls' school in lower-town Quebec, using revenues from the sale of their workhouse to finance the institution. The decision of the female community to establish itself educationally in the capital was in response to appeals from several quarters. The steep trail to be climbed to reach the Ursuline school in the upper town was so treacherous that some inhabitants used *grappins*, or grapnels, to pull themselves up. Before the school of the Notre Dame Sisters was established, lower-town families had engaged the services of a married woman, who went from house to house giving lessons for a small fee. When this proved unsatisfactory, a male teacher was engaged, but he fell afoul of the clerical ban on mixed teaching. The town *curé*, François Dupré, welcomed the new girls' school in the belief that the presence of the sisters would raise the moral level of the young girls in the area. By accompanying them to church and by instructing them in piety and modesty, said the parish priest, the sisters would combat the "licentiousness and other improprieties" that afflicted so many of them.[13]

Not everyone welcomed the congregation's appearance in the capital. Quebec had been the educational fief of the Ursulines for more than a half-century, and protocol dictated that the Montreal community respect this tradition. The Ursulines were critical of the new school, claiming that it would undermine their own institution by robbing it of girls. Dupré came to the defence of the Congregation of Notre Dame, saying that Quebec could easily support two girls' schools, especially in view of the town's substantial school-age population. He added that since the school in the lower town had opened (four months earlier), only three girls had "defected" from the Ursuline institution.[14]

Indications are that the school run by the congregation in lower-town Quebec was a popular success. In appealing for public funds for the school in 1714, Bishop Saint-Vallier reminded parents that they were fortunate to be able to send their daughters "daily to a school which the sisters acquit with so much care" and where they were "well brought up, instructed, and formed in piety by the sisters."[15] According to the 1716 census of the parish of Notre-Dame-de-Québec, six schoolmistresses were teaching at the school, which translates roughly into an enrolment figure of around one hundred girls.[16] The school was a going concern until 1759, when British bombardment of the town forced it to close.

The Congregation of Notre Dame probably made its most notable contribution to education in New France outside of the urban centres. It was alone among the male and female communities in maintaining schools in the countryside from the last quarter of the seventeenth century to the end of the French regime in Canada; the Jesuits, the Sulpicians, the Rouillé Brothers, and the Ursulines confined their educational efforts to the towns. Bishop Laval's recognition of the Congregation of Notre Dame as a religious community, in 1669, included the mandate to diffuse learning throughout the colony. As a non-cloistered community, itself an innovation for its time, the congregation was supremely fitted for the task, its members possessing the qualities of mobility and adaptability needed to carry the banner of learning to every corner of the colony. By 1700, the Notre Dame Sisters had schools in Château-Richer near Quebec, in Sainte-Famille on Île d'Orléans, in Champlain near Trois-Rivières, and in Lachine and Pointe-aux-Trembles on the island of Montreal. In the eighteenth century, rural schools were also established in the parishes of Boucherville, La Prairie, and Saint-Laurent.

Maintaining schools in the rural parts of New France was no easy accomplishment, as there were many challenges. An indifferent public, a dispersed population, poverty, and inadequate facilities all worked to undermine the stability of organized learning in the country parishes. In the second half of the seventeenth century, learning was sometimes disrupted by Indian raids. An educational victim of the Indian incursions was the congregation's school in Champlain, which remained closed between 1683 and 1702. Another school, that kept by the sisters in Lachine, though not directly affected by the Iroquois massacre of 1689, lay moribund until 1692. Further threats of Indian attacks on the area forced the school to close again in 1701. However, the congregation was coaxed back the following year by the promise of better facilities. Using much of his own money, the curé Pierre Rémy had constructed for the sisters a handsome two-storey stone building, which served as residence, orphanage, and school.

Despite the problems indigenous to rural education, the schools of the Congregation of Notre Dame did more than survive; most of them enjoyed a long life. The schools established in the parish of Sainte-Famille in 1685 and in Château-Richer in 1689 had an unbroken existence until 1759, when the threat of advancing British troops forced them to close. Similarly, three rural schools in the

Montreal region, at Lachine, La Prairie, and Pointe-aux-Trembles, were still in operation in the eve of the British conquest of the town in 1760.

The existence of girls' schools in the countryside seems to have paid educational dividends, as evidenced by the incidence of higher signature rates for females. In parishes for which information is available, more brides than grooms signed the marriage register, suggesting a higher literacy rate. Lachine did not have a boys' school in the eighteenth century, but it had a girls' school, and the impact is reflected in signature data for 1730–49, which show a 36 per-cent rate for brides and a 21 per-cent rate for grooms. Similarly, the marriage-signature rate in Sainte-Famille in 1750–65 was 12 per cent for brides and 7 per cent for grooms; for the same period in Champlain the figures are 24 per cent and 15 per cent, respectively; in Pointe-aux-Trembles, 17 per cent and 16 per cent.[17]

In spite of the demonstrated success of the Congregation of Notre Dame in bringing a margin of learning to the rural parishes of the colony, an occasional dissenting voice could be heard. Louis Franquet, a military engineer stationed in Canada in 1752, condemned rural education as a "slow poison" that turned the heads of country girls. He charged that as soon as a rural girl educated by the sisters reached the age of a young lady, she disowned her agrarian roots and fled to the town. He called on colonial authorities to reform rural education so that girls' learning would be limited to religious instruction given by the local *curé*. In this way, suggested Franquet, young ladies would not entertain ideas contrary to their class and would thus remain on the farm, helping to populate rather than to depopulate the countryside of Canada.[18]

Clerical approval was required before the Notre Dame Sisters could open a rural school. The request for a girls' school was first placed with the parish *curé*, following which the bishop or his delegate ruled on it. In keeping with the regulations of the congregation, two sisters were initially posted to a country district. There were social as well as logistical reasons for this arrangement. In addition to the importance of companionship, each sister performed a different task: one taught school and the other occupied herself with housekeeping and administrative chores. Since some of the rural schools were equipped to receive both day and boarding pupils, the sisters needed to provide care as well as instruction. The congregation's *Reglemens* enjoined rural schoolmistresses from charging fees for their instruction but allowed them to impose an annual charge of "vingt sols" to cover the cost of school books.[19]

Until a rural parish could furnish the schoolmistresses with their own residence, they were forced to live among the people, which sometimes proved socially awkward. The sisters were also pained to discover that in matters of learning the rural folk were far less enthusiastic than town dwellers. As can be appreciated, the lot of the rural schoolmistress in early Canada was not an easy one – even for the Notre Dame Sisters, who were trained to have little regard for their own personal comfort. A rural posting meant hardship, sacrifice, loneliness, and sometimes danger, conditions of which the superior was very aware. From time to time, Marguerite Bourgeoys visited her companions in the country districts, checking on their progress and encouraging them in their duties.

For Marie Barbier, one of two sisters posted to Sainte-Famille on Île d'Orléans in 1685, the experience of being a country schoolmistress almost proved her undoing. She wrote, "We arrived at Île d'Orléans almost dead from the cold, and we suffered much during the first winter."[20] Since the building intended to serve as their residence and school was not yet ready, Barbier and her companion, Anne Mayrand, had to move in with a local widow, who ran a boarding house at which there was a common table. Complicating matters was the fact that the parish church was situated a fair distance from where the sisters were lodged, requiring a long walk each day. One November day, while returning from church, the two sisters were caught in a sudden and violent snowstorm and separated. Unable to see her way, Barbier took refuge in a ditch. Nearly frozen, she was snatched from almost certain death by passing farmers who mistook her black dress for one of their fallen cattle.

It was one of Bishop Saint-Vallier's fondest hopes to see schools established in the farthest reaches of New France. He had intended to open a school in Acadia and put the Congregation of Notre Dame in charge of it, but the ceding of the territory to the English by the Treaty of Utrecht in 1713 compromised the project. Conditions were more favourable in Louisbourg, on Île Royale, where in 1727 he dispatched Sister Marguerite Roy and two lay assistants to open a girls' school. Before the year was out, the school had attracted twenty-two girls. Strangely, the bishop's action had neither the approval of the minister in France nor that of the superior of the Congregation of Notre Dame in Montreal. France had repeatedly turned a deaf ear to appeals from Louisbourg officials for financial support to establish a girls' school, saying that the time was not yet ripe, though by the 1720s more than three hundred children of school age were living in the garrison town. For her part, the Montreal superior had advised against the venture, saying that adequate funding was lacking and that Louisbourg was without secular clergy, to whom the sisters normally reported.

The superior's concerns about funding were borne out by developments. Having received a subsidy of 1,500 *livres* from the Ministry of Marine in 1730, Marguerite Roy squandered the sum on the purchase of land and buildings, which left the Louisbourg enterprise in deep debt. The new bishop of New France, Dosquet, lost confidence in the administrative abilities of Roy, and replaced her with Marguerite Trottier in 1733. No sooner had Trottier arrived in Louisbourg than she asked the bishop for reinforcements, saying that the school was understaffed and the sisters overworked, adding that without the aid of domestics they had to do their own housekeeping and cleaning. Like his predecessor, Saint-Vallier, Bishop Dosquet was a friend of education and responded to the request by sending staff, bringing the total of Notre Dame Sisters to six in 1734. Still, financial problems continued to dog the operation during the 1730s; the sisters constantly flirted with bankruptcy, unable to meet the payments on their properties despite some financial assistance from France. What probably saved the congregation from financial collapse was a windfall inheritance in 1742. The governor of Louisbourg, Isaac-Louis de Forant, had died in 1740 and left the enormous sum of thirty-two thousand *livres* to the sisters, who invested the money in France and used the interest to pay off their debts. The terms of the governor's will also provided for the subsidization of eight places at the boarding school for officers' daughters. Despite recurring financial problems in succeeding years, which necessitated a pared-down operation – in 1752 only three sisters were at the school – the Congregation of Notre Dame maintained an educational presence in Louisbourg until 1758, when the town fell to British arms.

While much is known of the financial struggles of the Notre Dame Sisters in Louisbourg, surprisingly little is known of their pedagogical activities.[21] Tradition and assumption, rather than hard evidence, suggest that the sisters proceeded along well-established lines in their curricular offerings and teaching methods. Nor do we have any firm statistical data on enrolments at the Louisbourg institution. But given the fact that the school employed four or five teachers at its height after 1734 and knowing something of teacher-pupil ratios in other schools run by the female order, it is speculated that enrolments approached one hundred. Like other schools of the congregation in New France, that in Louisbourg accommodated day and boarding pupils, the former surpassing the latter by a good margin. Boarders were assessed a fee, but the sisters were in the habit of reducing the amount for hardship cases, which reportedly earned the female community the esteem of the townspeople.[22]

Consideration was also given to sending Notre Dame schoolmistresses to Detroit, at the other end of New France. Like Louisbourg, Detroit was both garrison town and colonial settlement, the largest in the western country. Established as a military post by Cadillac in 1701, it was slow to attract colonists. In 1749, a growing number of people were attracted to Detroit thanks to a liberal immigration policy launched by Governor Galissonière, by which settlers were promised free land, farm animals, and supplies. The influx of colonists coincided with demands for a school.

At the urging of the inhabitants of Detroit, Bishop Pontbriand wrote the minister in 1746, seeking approval for sending several Notre Dame Sisters to the town to establish a girls' school. This marked the first official attempt in almost a half a century to open a school in the area. In 1703, Cadillac had proposed a school for the joint instruction of French and Indian children, but was rebuffed by the home government.[23] The choice of the Notre Dame Sisters as prospective schoolmistresses for the town was dictated by logic and logistics. Of the teaching communities of New France, the congregation was alone in being educationally active outside the urban centres of Canada. It was also the only community that was sufficiently large to supply educational workers.

In his letter to the minister in 1746, the bishop argued that a school in Detroit "would be useful for the instruction of the young and it might induce the inhabitants to settle down there."[24] Minister Maurepas demonstrated no interest in the project, probably not wishing to commit the government to fresh expenditures. Further letters from the bishop to the minister in 1747 and 1748 went unanswered. Not easily discouraged, Pontbriand took another tack by writing to Maurepas's successor in 1749, promising that the project would be of no expense to his Majesty as the townspeople would bear the costs of maintaining the sisters.[25] The churchman could have added that the number of settlers justified a school: town census of 1750 put the number of girls below the age of fifteen at ninety-five.[26]

The minister procrastinated, saying that the project ought not to be hurried and that, in any case, the governor and the intendant would have to be consulted. Pontbriand's failure to win France's approval for sending schoolmistresses to Detroit had other consequences as well. It meant that the town lost out on the charity of Louis, Duke of Orleans, who had established a fund of one thousand *livres* to be paid annually to the Congregation of Notre Dame in New France, one-tenth of which was earmarked for the Detroit school, should the sisters be installed there.

The military and parish clergy of Detroit, like those of Louisbourg, were Recollets and were inactive in education. A possible exception was Bonaventure Liénard, *curé* of Detroit at mid-century. In 1755, Father Liénard wrote to Governor Duquesne on behalf of the townspeople, once again asking for school teachers. The absence of a girls' school in the area, explained the priest, forced local parents to send their daughters to Quebec, Montreal, or New Orleans, the expenses of which were prohibitive. He added that settlers were reluctant to come to an area in which there was no school. If the teaching sisters were sent, he concluded, the inhabitants of Detroit would build them a residence and furnish them with firewood and other necessities.[27]

No sooner had Duquesne given his approval to Liénard's request than he was succeeded in the governorship by Vaudreuil. The new governor in turn wrote the minister in France, assuring him that not only would Detroit get its teaching sisters, but that they would not cost the king anything: "I will make arrangements to promote the establishment of two Sisters of the Congregation at the post to educate the Children without its costing the King one sol."[28] After Vaudreuil's letter we hear nothing further of the matter. It is certain that no schoolmistresses were dispatched to Detroit, for the official history of the congregation would surely have mentioned it. Education, never a high government priority during the life of New France, was even less so in the final years of the French colony, with the gathering of war clouds.

If Detroit failed to get its teaching sisters, it did get a schoolmaster, if belatedly. Several months before Major Robert Rogers and his

British garrison arrived in Detroit to receive the surrender of the town in 1760, a school was started up by the layman Jean-Baptiste Roucout, about whom little is known except that he was a native of France. Roucout's title was schoolmaster and choirmaster of St Anne's parish, which suggests that he was employed by the church council. For the next thirty years he taught French children in his home, though the records are silent as to the lessons taught, the methods used, and the number of youngsters in attendance. It is unlikely that he had many pupils, since he had no schoolhouse and since most of the French families had moved to outlying rural areas with the arrival of the British. According to a report of 1776, ignorance was widespread among the French in the Detroit area. Lieutenant-Governor Hamilton reported, "The Canadians at Detroit are mostly so illeterate [sic] that few can read, and very few can sign their names."[29]

Thanks to the Congregation of Notre Dame's *Reglemens*, we know something of the educational policies and practices of the female community, whether in Montreal, Château-Richer, or Louisbourg. In their day schools the sisters received girls of different ages, though they were reluctant to accept those below the age of six in the belief that such children were uneducable. They also refused admission to married girls, to those engaged to be married, and to those with communicable diseases. Boarders were admitted from the age of five and could remain until the age of eighteen, or longer, with the permission of the bishop.

According to the *Reglemens*, the schools of the congregation were to teach girls "the fundamental truths of the religion, and at the same time teach them to read, write, count, and to work with prudence and charity, on every occasion, the hate of sin, the fear and love of God."[30] The spiritual aim of their schools was reinforced by the saying of prayers at the beginning and the end of classes each day.

The point was made earlier that girls' schools in pre-industrial societies sometimes ignored or played down the teaching of writing as being unnecessary for females. It is clear that New France's Notre Dame schools were not part of that tradition. Not only was writing instruction a stated aim in the *Reglemens*, but various school inventories contain references to writing desks, ink bottles, feathered pens, and pen holders. For example, an inventory of a 1722 classroom lists "six pinewood tables to make the children write ... fourteen pen holders."[31] A 1757 inventory of a large classroom mentions "12 bottles for ink ... 15 pen holders."[32]

To academic and spiritual learning in the congregation's schools was added practical education. Befitting their future station in life, girls were taught to knit, sew, and spin. The teaching of practical subjects also found its rationale in Marguerite Bourgeoys's defence of the work ethic, suggesting that the Calvinists did not have a monopoly on the principle. The superior lashed out at idleness, which she described as the mother of every vice. Believing that the unattended youngster succumbs to the lazy, unsettled life, she commanded her sisters to form girls in the habits of industry by putting them to work.[33] To that end, pupils were kept busy in all types of useful work, from the making, mending, and washing of clothes to helping in the kitchen. Sister Marguerite's prescriptions were not directed only at young girls. She advised her companions to "shun idleness, above all things ... we should be occupied at something ... and whatever we have to do, let it be done cheerfully. God loves the cheerful giver."[34]

An examination of the rules governing the operation of the *pensionnat* of the Congregation of Notre Dame reveals that the girls in attendance were subjected to the regulated and disciplined life of a Christian boarding school. The *Reglemens* provide that "boarders will have a separate bed, surrounded as much as possible by a curtain, without which they could sleep together ... They will be extremely modest in their habits, and in the manner of being dressed ... They will not have any books or writings without having them shown to their teachers, and will neither write nor receive letters without the same permission. They will not be allowed to eat outside the four meals ... "[35]

Although the schoolmistresses of the congregation did not undertake their teaching duties without some preparation, it would be rash to call it a formal program of teacher training. Still, lectures were given by the superior to the candidates on the topic of instructional methods and the means of promoting virtue in the young. Marguerite Bourgeoys had learned her pedagogy in France, and indications are that she communicated this knowledge to teacher aspirants. Her pedagogy was neither as elaborate nor as sophisticated as that of the Jesuits and the Christian Brothers, for she believed that the attitude and personality of the teacher took precedence over classroom techniques. On the other hand, like the Lasallians she opted for simultaneous instruction, grouping of children along ability lines, and the frequent use of slate and blackboard. While admitting that the teacher must seek out knowledge and the means of transmitting it, Bourgeoys insisted that her sisters bring to the classroom the qualities of goodness, sacrifice, and love for those under their care. This stress on the moral qualities of the teacher is spelled out in the *Reglemens*, which says that the good teacher shows "patience, moderation, and an equal charity toward all children, and a true courage to fight constantly against impatience, boredom, disgust, anger, lukewarmness, and other obstacles that are frequently met on the job."[36]

By injecting a measure of social humanitarianism into teaching, Marguerite Bourgeoys and the Congregation of Notre Dame anticipated the child-centred theories of Rousseau, Froebel, and Pestalozzi. Thanks to the influence and reach of the community's teachers and schools, the classrooms of New France were less a place of threats and beatings. The superior advised her sisters that when the punishment of children was called for, it was to be applied with "prudence, modesty and moderation, through respect for God, at all times, present."[37]

### THE URSULINES

We have already spoken of the educational work of the Ursulines, of how Marie de l'Incarnation and her companions on arriving in Quebec in 1639 promptly set to work instructing French and Indian girls. When the nuns' convent was completed, in 1642, they began to receive boarding pupils. Until girls' schools were established elsewhere in the colony, the Ursuline convent school attracted a cosmopolitan clientele, drawing girls from near and far. In 1668, Sister Marie reported that the "French bring their daughters from more than sixty leagues from here."[38]

In educational terms, the Ursulines and the Notre Dame Sisters had much in common. Both communities shared a deep commitment to the care and instruction of girls; both subscribed to a curriculum grounded in moral and spiritual learning, literacy learning, and training in the household arts; both manifested an egalitarian spirit in providing free tuition and opening their classrooms to girls of all social levels, not to mention Indian children; and both were equipped to receive day and boarding students. On the other hand, there is no disputing the fact that the female orders differed significantly in their educational reach. Whereas the Congregation of Notre Dame established schools far and wide in New France, the Ursulines established but two schools, one in Quebec and the other in Trois-Rivières. The explanation for this difference has already been hinted at. The Ursuline order was traditional and cloistered, and thus its members were physically and educationally tied to the convent. Put another way, the foot-loose Notre Dame Sisters brought learning to the people; the Ursulines brought the people to learning.

Owing to sketchy data, it is impossible to get a fix on annual enrolments at the Ursuline school in Quebec. A further problem is that the data are largely restricted to boarding students. One estimate is that between 1642 and 1739 the institution housed an annual average of twelve boarders.[39] This figure may be on the low side. In 1669, Marie de l'Incarnation wrote of the *pensionnat* normally having between twenty and thirty girls.[40] The annalist of the Ursulines reported that at the beginning of the eighteenth century there were almost sixty *pensionnaires* at the school, adding that enrolments fell to forty in 1703 because of an epidemic.[41] Enrolment figures for day students are harder to come by, though it is certain that day pupils surpassed boarders by a good margin because they could more easily be accommodated. At one point, Sister Marie admitted ignorance of the number of day pupils in attendance, saying that a reliable figure could not be provided since many of the children were absent because of the severe cold and heavy snow.[42] On balance, indications are that enrolments continued to rise over the years, permitting the observation that the Ursuline school at Quebec was a thriving institution during the French regime in Canada.

The clientele of the Ursuline school was split along social-class lines. In general, the day school was the school of the people, attracting local girls of modest means, while the boarding facility tended to draw girls from more affluent families. On the other hand, it would be incorrect to portray the boarding school as a finishing school for upper-class girls, since all classes were represented. Of the eighty-one families who sent their daughters to board with the Ursulines in the two decades following the opening of the *pensionnat* in 1642, nine were identified as nobility, forty-one as bourgeoisie, and the remainder as lower class.[43] For what it is worth, Marie de l'Incarnation spoke badly of the boarders, describing them as undisciplined, flighty, and in need of constant supervision. In a letter to her son in France, she complained, "Thirty girls give us more work in the boarding school than do sixty in France."[44] It is impossible to determine whether the superior's view was a representative one.

The social distinction between day and boarding pupils may be explained in part by economics. Schooling was free for all pupils, but boarders were charged for room and board. In the seventeenth century, the annual boarding fee with the Ursulines was 120 *livres*, roughly the equivalent of the yearly wage of a skilled worker in the colony. The records suggest that few parents paid their educational fees in full.[45] In 1660, Marie de l'Incarnation complained that parents contributed little or nothing toward the education of their daughters, adding that it was more expensive to feed and lodge French than Indian girls.[46] In order to keep the boarding school open to girls from all social backgrounds, the Ursulines applied a sliding scale of fees, providing low-cost or free maintenance to girls whose families were too poor to pay. Student bursaries, known as *fondations*, funded by donations from the lay foundress Madame La Peltrie and the neighbouring Jesuits, were also available. About three-quarters of the boarders in the seventeenth century were recipients of study or maintenance grants, though the evidence also shows that middle- and upper-class girls were given preferential treatment in the distribution of awards.[47]

Notwithstanding the fact that the Ursulines were a cloistered order, there was a worldly quality to their educational program. The nuns never lost sight of the fact that the great majority of their pupils would become wives and mothers, and thus required an education consistent with their secular station in life. As a result, in addition to the staples of reading, writing, arithmetic, and religion, the Ursulines instructed their girls in the arts of embroidery and needlework, for which they were famous. In comparison to day pupils, boarders were exposed to an education that was at once more advanced and more refined, both because they were with the nuns longer and because their number included girls from the colony's social élite. The Ursulines realized that girls of gentle birth sought an education that would initiate them into the ways of polite society. To that end, the nuns instructed them in the arts of letter writing and conversation, and impressed upon them the importance of good manners and etiquette – in other words, those accomplishments proper to a cultivated lady. Nor were the Ursulines contemptuous of the physical and recreational side of learning, as if to belie the sombre reputation of a convent education. The school day was interrupted by periods of play and innocent games in the recreation room or on the playground.

Since schools of that period were not graded or structured according to a fixed number of years, the length of time a girl remained in school varied with the individual and the circumstances. As a rule, boarding students stayed longer than day students. In one of her letters, Marie de l'Incarnation mentioned day pupils attending school for only a year, during which time the schoolmistress had to struggle to teach them "to read, write, count, the prayers, the Christian morals, and all that a girl ought to know."[48] On the other hand, the duration of schooling was not entirely unscheduled, since it aimed at preparing girls for their first communion. During a visit to the Ursuline school in 1749, Peter Kalm was told that girls generally came to the nuns at around the age of ten or eleven and stayed for two, three, or four years, until such time as it was judged they had achieved sufficient maturity and learning to receive communion.[49] Thus, the school-leaving age for such girls coincided with puberty and the first rites of communion, as if to announce the end of childhood and the dawn of adulthood.

In 1697, a second Ursuline establishment was founded in the colony – in Trois-Rivières, at the time a town of several hundred inhabitants. The new facility differed from its Quebec counterpart in containing both a school, for day and boarding pupils, and a hospital. The founding of a dual institution to treat the sick and to instruct girls was enthusiastically welcomed by the townspeople, who for some time had been asking for a girls' school. The town had not seen a schoolmistress for more than thirty years. Marie Raisin, a sister of the Congregation of Notre Dame, had taught in the town in 1666. However, her tenure as schoolmistress had been a brief one, as she resigned her position before the year was out to enter the Ursuline convent in Quebec.[50]

The Ursuline establishment in Trois-Rivières bore the signature of the energetic Bishop Saint-Vallier, whose name is indelibly linked with educational progress in the colony. Having returned to Canada after a three-year absence in Europe, the churchman promised the nuns suitable facilities were they agreeable to operating a school and hospital in the town. He negotiated the purchase of a property bordering on the St Lawrence River, which included a handsome two-storey mansion that had been the residence of the governor. Thus, the Ursulines of Trois-Rivières did not have to start from scratch, as had their counterparts in Quebec. When the enterprise suffered financial difficulties in its third year of operation, the bishop again came to the rescue, injecting his own monies into the faltering facility.

Like the Ursuline school in Quebec, that in Trois-Rivières initially provided instruction for Indian and French girls, though as time passed the former disappeared from the enrolment lists. The Trois-Rivières institution approached the record of the Quebec school by providing almost uninterrupted service to the local population to the end of the French period. Even the terrible fire of 1752, which destroyed the convent as well as most of the town, failed to disrupt the educational work of the nuns. Almost without missing a beat, the Ursulines continued to hold classes following the conflagration, this time in the Recollets' house, which was lent to them until new facilities were constructed. Two years after the fire, the Ursulines moved into their new quarters, which had been subsidized in part by Bishop Pontbriand. And, as Trois-Rivières was little touched by the Seven Years' War, the Ursuline school remained operational during and after the conflict.

The Ursulines were also educationally active in the southernmost region of New France. At the invitation of Governor Bienville of Louisiana, six Ursulines from France arrived in New Orleans in 1727 to open a girls' school and to oversee the hospital. According to one of the nuns, they were given the "finest building in town," a two-storey structure that had once been the residence of the governor. In no time at all, the nuns' convent school was flourishing, receiving colonists' daughters and a sprinkling of Indian and slave girls. In its second year of operation, the New Orleans school counted twenty boarders and a large number of day pupils. In 1734, the Ursulines moved into a new building that had been constructed specifically for them.[51]

As we saw in the case of the Charon Brothers, the hospital in New France sometimes doubled as an educational facility. The Hospital Nuns of Quebec, whom it will be recalled first set foot in Canada in 1639, founded Hôtel-Dieu in the town and later assumed authority over Hôpital Général as well. Apparently, some informal instruction was provided at Hôtel-Dieu from the earliest years of the institution, but it was at Hôpital Général that a more formal educational role was spelled out. In 1725, with the financial backing of Bishop Saint-Vallier, a girls' boarding school was established at the institution. In the absence of hard data, little is known of the *pensionnat*, who its schoolmistresses were, and the number of girls in attendance. While it cannot be substantiated, it is possible that an Ursuline from the Quebec convent was in charge of the boarding school.

Although the number of *pensionnaires* at Hôpital Général averaged fifteen per year between 1725 and 1760, the statistic fails to distinguish between pupils and women living permanently at the hospital.[52] On the other hand, since the latter group rarely exceeded three in any year – to judge by the records before 1725 – it is reasonable to suggest that the boarding school lodged an annual average of between ten and fifteen girls. Some of the subjects taught at the boarding school were reading, writing, religion, violin, and glazing.

The Grey Nuns, who succeeded the Charon Brothers at Hôpital Général in Montreal in 1747, also played an assisting role in education. In 1749, Madame d'Youville promised the Crown that, were her female community to be granted official recognition, it not only would attend to the needs of the poor and the helpless, but would undertake the education of orphan girls.[53] It appears that the Grey Nuns' instructional role did not begin until much later, for the community's own records speak of the sisters "taking charge of education" in 1760.[54] In 1763, d'Youville asked the France-bound Montgolfier, who was the order's confessor, to carry a message to religious authorities there. The gist of the request was that the Montreal hospital required three sisters: one to care for the newly born; another to care for children who could walk; and a third "for those who have to be taught."[55] The request is interesting from another perspective: it demonstrates that religious ties between Canada and France had not been severed by the British conquest of New France.

### CHAPTER EIGHT

# Secondary, Professional, and Vocational Education

## SECONDARY EDUCATION

Institutions, like children, sometimes come into the world before their time. Such appears to have been the case of the Jesuit college in Quebec, which saw the light of day in 1635, when the town was little more than an outpost. Nine years earlier in France, Nicolas Rouault, Marquis de Gamaches, had contracted with the Society of Jesus to leave part of his future inheritance to its Canadian mission. At the time there was no mention of the gift being earmarked for education. But in 1634, when the inheritance was due to be awarded, a dispute arose over the terms of the agreement. In the ensuing negotiations, the marquis proposed that the inheritance be used to found a college in Canada, a gesture which the Jesuits accepted.

While the Quebec superior, Paul Le Jeune, greeted with joy the announcement of an endowment to finance the establishment of a college in the town, he must have wondered whether the time was opportune for such a project. It is clear that Le Jeune and his fellow Jesuits were not psychologically and logistically prepared to pour their energies into establishing a French secondary school. Their interests and priorities lay in other directions. Like the Recollets before them, the Jesuits had come to New France to evangelize the Indians, not to instruct colonial boys. There was also the question of clientele. Could the small settlement at Quebec support a college? After all, Quebec was little more than a village, and villages, at least in seventeenth-century France, were not in the habit of hosting colleges. Moreover, of the several hundred French inhabitants around Quebec, few were children of school age. An estimated ten French boys between the ages of seven and fifteen were living in the region in 1635.[1]

Although the obligation of providing for the educational needs of the colonists did not excite the Jesuits in Canada, they were not inclined to disobey orders from their provincial in France, or to allow an endowment opportunity to go unattended. As a result, they proceeded to act on the terms of the endowment by establishing a school of sorts in 1635. As was pointed out in a previous chapter, the Jesuit college began not as a secondary school but as an elementary one, a characteristic which it never lost; while it was to evolve eventually into a true college, it never shed its elementary-school section, which served as a preparatory school for the college. In any case, in its early years the Jesuit college was something less than its name, being essentially an elementary school with one instructor, a handful of pupils, and a basic curriculum. The Jesuit Charles Lalemant taught a bit of reading, writing, counting, and religion in a small rectory of the local church. It would be some time before the Quebec school could be favourably compared to a college in France.

Over the next several decades, the Jesuit institution struggled to become an authentic college. The process was painfully slow owing to a small colonial population, the lack of suitable facilities, and the Jesuits' consuming interest in Indian souls. The issue of a proper building was resolved in 1650, when the Jesuits saw the completion of their college and adjoining residences for boarding students. By 1664, the college was offering the outline of the standard secondary-school curriculum, allowing Bishop Laval to inform Rome that "the Jesuit fathers have a college where the humanities classes are flourishing and where the children ... are brought up in the same manner as in France."[2]

Notwithstanding Laval's comments, the Jesuit college was still a modest institution three decades after its official founding. In 1665, it was staffed by four teachers, one of whom was responsible for the elementary-school section. Of the others, one taught rhetoric, another grammar, and the third philosophy and theology. While the precise number of students is not known, it was likely around twenty. But the future looked brighter. Two years earlier New France had become a royal province, and with this status came the promise of a more vigorous immigration policy. At the moment, the town of Quebec, from which the college drew most of its students, had a population of five hundred, few of whom were boys of secondary-school age. Bishop Laval's decision to establish the Petit Séminaire in 1668 augured well for the college, since it guaranteed the school a regular supply of students. Because the small seminary was essentially a residence for boys in training for the priesthood and not involved in instruction, the young seminarians were sent to the Jesuit college for their academic learning.

It is impossible to know with precision the number of students in attendance at the Quebec college in any given year; the records of the period, many of which were lost or destroyed, allow no such luxury. Yet the scattered pieces of evidence are such as to permit the building of a general pattern of enrolment over the years. Indications are that enrolments took off in the second half of the seventeenth century, though expansion was greater among day students, since they were easier to absorb. As a rule, the ratio of day to boarding students was two to one. One estimate is that in the late seventeenth century the college had a yearly average of between 130 and 150 students.[3] Enrolments declined in the early years of the next century because of damaging fires at the seminary, which deprived the college of some of its regular clientele. The fortunes and enrolments of the college rebounded around 1742, with the physical expansion of the school and an increase in its teaching staff. The enlarged facility was a source of pride to the Jesuits and, in the words of a prominent visitor to the town, "the finest building in the town."[4] As was pointed out earlier, some Indian boys attended the college, though few remained for any length of time. To all appearances, the Jesuit college did not enrol any Indian students after 1700.

Before the eighteenth century, the Jesuit college drew its students principally from the Quebec area. While the difficulties and hazards of travel and the cost of a boarding-school education worked against boys from other parts of New France, there is also an academic explanation. Entering students were expected to have an elementary grasp of Latin, but until the late seventeenth century the only schools equipped to teach the ancient language were in the Quebec region. One problem was that the teaching of Latin was regarded an exclusive privilege of the Jesuits, which means that elementary schools in Montreal and elsewhere were unable to prepare boys for college entrance. Quebec boys thus enjoyed an educational advantage in the scramble for places at the Jesuit college, at least before the eighteenth century and the rise of Latin schools in other population centres. It will be recalled that the Jesuit college began as an elementary school,

157 Secondary, Professional, and Vocational

one of whose objectives was to give boys a grounding in French and Latin letters. On the whole, the favoured educational situation of Quebec youth remained intact during the life of the French colony, as the Jesuit college was Canada's sole secondary school.

Innovation and originality were not the strong suits of the Jesuit college. The Quebec school did not break new ground, frame a new curriculum, or spawn new teaching methods. To judge by comments of the day, the school's most engaging quality was precisely its faithfulness to tradition – that it did not depart in any fundamental way from the Jesuit colleges in Europe. Joseph Germain, who was teaching philosophy and theology at the school in 1712, informed his provincial in France that "as regards the Quebec College, everything exists or is done there as in our colleges in Europe and perhaps with greater regularity, exactness, and fruit." The Jesuit teacher also spoke favourably of his students, describing them thus: "Very intelligent, have excellent dispositions, and are capable of succeeding well in everything that we can teach them."[5] Thus, in outlook and character the Jesuit college was neither a novel institution nor one native to Canada; it was an institution made in France and exported to the New World.

An ironic twist is that the Jesuit colleges of France, after which the Quebec school modelled itself, were themselves imitative institutions. When they made their appearance on the European scene in the sixteenth century as the Catholic educational response to the spiritual challenges of Protestantism, they adopted the standard curriculum of the day. Catholics and Protestants may have been deeply divided over religious doctrine and the role of the institutional church, but they were in remarkable agreement over the type of learning befitting the educated man. The *collège* in France, the *Gymnasium* in Germany, and the grammar school in England all subscribed to the Renaissance definition of the educated man as a Christian steeped in classical language and literature.

No bold innovators or starry-eyed theorists, the Jesuits left their educational mark on the European scene by packaging a better product than their competitors. As was noted earlier, their European colleges were models of efficiency and thoroughness, combining solid learning, firm but humane discipline, and close supervision of students, the methods and procedures of which were codified in the *Ratio Studiorum*. The Jesuit curriculum, whether in Paris, Madrid, or Rome, consisted of two sections, a lower one covering five years and an upper one of three years. The first three years of the lower section were devoted to the study of Latin and, to a lesser extent, Greek. In the fourth year, the reading of classical authors was begun; in the fifth year, rhetoric. The upper section, called the philosophy course, continued the literary tradition of the lower section while adding instruction in philosophy, science, and mathematics.

If the Quebec college was not an exact replica of its European parent, it was not far off the mark. Structurally, the Canadian institution, when fully developed, offered a program of study that was a year shorter than its counterpart, though the division of the curriculum into a lower and an upper section was maintained. The seven-year curriculum was split into a five-year lower and a two-year upper section. Like the European school, that at Quebec was a school of classical learning in its lower section. Boys entered the school at around the age of ten and were expected to have a reading knowledge of Latin and French. The first three years of the lower section were spent chiefly on Latin grammar, though some Greek and French were apparently taught as well. Interestingly, Greek was taught through the medium of Latin. In the fourth year students were introduced to classical literature – the works of Cicero, Virgil, Ovid, and the like. The fact that the works of Corneille and other French masters were read indicates that vernacular literature was not entirely neglected. In the final year of the lower section, the emphasis switched to rhetoric, which may be defined as the art of speaking well. Students were called upon to recite the speeches of Cicero and other distinguished orators of antiquity, as well as composing their own works in Latin. Prizes were awarded to boys who demonstrated excellence in written and spoken Latin.

It may be helpful to pause and reflect on the reasons for the linguistic bias of the Quebec college. At first glance, the situation seems almost absurd to the modern reader, with students concentrating on a language that was little used in daily commerce, particularly in a frontier society. Rather like the tribal boy of modern Africa, the student of New France experienced the educational sensation of studying a language other than his own, which had the effect of making the school a bilingual institution. As anomalous as the situation may appear to the modern eye, there are solid reasons for the primacy of Latin in secondary education in earlier times. What must be recognized is that the vernaculars – that is, French, German, and English – were relatively new kids on the block, having little tradition as a literary force in Europe before the seventeenth century. While it is true that ever since the epic poems of the Middle Ages a written vernacular literature had been in evolution, it had neither the status nor the output of the classical languages. Indeed, it was not until the Protestant Reformation of the sixteenth century that the Bible was translated into the national languages. As for Latin, it was no upstart; it had been the language of Christianity and scholarship in the West since the fall of Rome and boasted a vast literature, both sacred and profane. Moreover, in clerical circles Latin was judged to be more suitable than the vernaculars for the recording of the written word, with its rich vocabulary, stable grammar, and reliable spelling. In short, the time had not yet arrived in Western life when one could speak confidently of an educated man without reference to classical learning. Even the Protestant leader Martin Luther, who did much to popularize the vernaculars by translating the Latin Bible into German and by laying the foundation of German-language elementary schools, allowed them no place in his secondary-school curriculum.

Historians differ as to the place of Latin and French in the Quebec college. An extreme view is that in the middle of the seventeenth century all instruction in the school was in Latin.[6] This assertion is suspect on practical grounds, since it implies a competence in the language among teachers and students; it also implies that non-literary subjects such as science and mathematics were taught in the ancient language. Another theory is that "from the first days of the college pupils learned to write French in a satisfactory fashion."[7] If this is true, it implies a far greater emphasis on French in the Quebec college than in its European number, in which French was rarely taught before the eighteenth century. Still, the evidence that French was studied at Quebec from the earliest days of the school is circumstantial, based on the existence of French textbooks and the observation that graduates of the college seemed to possess a reasonable ability in the language.

One of the educational strengths of the Jesuits was their ability to fuse profane and sacred learning in such a way as to make their schools attractive to the secular and the religious mind. The upper, or philosophy, section of the Quebec college is a case in point. For seminarians lodged at the Petit Séminaire, the upper level offered an excellent pre-theology preparation, equipping them with the rational tools for engaging problems in religion. For lay boys in search of more practical learning, the upper level provided knowledge in mathematics, navigation, surveying, and physics, useful subjects in a largely uncharted land.

In a sense, the philosophy section of the curriculum may be regarded a form of higher education, since it offered more advanced and specialized learning for those who had a grounding in ancient learning. It should also be noted that the appellation "philosophy" carried a wider construction in those days, embracing not only logic, metaphysics, and ethics, but also mathematics and physics. Appearances aside, the philosophy section did not represent a turning away from classical learning, only a consideration of a different side of it. If Cicero was a central figure in the lower curriculum, Aristotle occupied a similar status in the upper one. In logic Aristotle's *Organon* was read, in ethics his *Nichomachean Ethics*, in philosophy his *Metaphysics*, and in science his *Physics*. However, Aristotle's place in the curriculum went beyond that of the contribution of learned commentaries on every facet of human knowledge. Roman Catholicism was in debt to the versatile Greek for providing the intellectual weaponry in defence of rational Christianity. In the thirteenth century, the theologian Thomas Aquinas, in attempting to reconcile faith and reason, seized on the logic and syllogistic system of Aristotle to make his case. What eventually evolved as Thomistic Christianity was essentially the application of Aristotelian thought to spiritual questions. "Never deviate from Aristotle in matters of importance," runs a line in the *Ratio Studiorum*.

The place of mathematics and hydrography in the Quebec college curriculum deserves elaboration, if only because it represents one of the few instances in which local conditions exercised a direct influence on the program. Mathematics was introduced into the course of study in 1651 and was taught in a commercial fashion, presumably to respond to the needs of an evolving merchant class in the country. Hydrography, which was normally taught in conjunction with mathematics, and frequently by the same teacher, blossomed into a course of some importance. As New France was dotted with waterways, few of which were properly mapped, the course met a need. Hydrography made its curricular début in around 1671, when the layman Martin Boutet, who had been teaching mathematics at the Jesuit school, added navigation to his load at the urging of the intendant Jean Talon. New France's administrator dreamed of founding a marine academy which would train navigators, ship pilots, surveyors, and cartographers. While the academy never went beyond the conceptual stage, the hydrography course at the Jesuit college satisfied some of the same objectives, since it was designed to prepare pilots, surveyors, and map-makers.

The hydrography course was a bit of an anomaly, being a vocational rather than a liberal-arts subject and hence alien to the spirit of disinterested learning. Somewhat similar to a modern-day continuing-education course, its students were drawn from within and without the school, and some of them were fully employed adults who were desirous of upgrading their qualifications. A Jesuit letter of 1676 says that the lay teacher Martin Boutet "has instructed most of the captains who bring vessels to this country."[8] Classroom, or theoretical, instruction, which was usually given in the winter months, began with arithmetic and moved on to geometry, astronomy, geography, and possibly some physics. The summer months were set aside for practical instruction. Students learned the use of navigational and astronomical instruments, particularly the magnetic compass and the sextant; the reading and making of charts and maps; and the recording of sea logs and the calculation of tide tables. Impressed with Boutet's course, the Crown decreed that no surveyor in the colony would be permitted to practise without a certificate from him.

Boutet's death, in 1683, deprived the colony of its only teacher of hydrography. Two years later, Governor Denonville petitioned the minister for a replacement, saying that such a person was much needed. The appointment in 1686 of Jean-Baptiste Franquelin as king's hydrographer at state salary demonstrated that France was aware of the importance of navigational instruction to the well-being of the colony. The tradition of royal hydrographer continued right to the end of the French period in Canada, though from the early eighteenth century the post was held by Jesuits, some of whom had distinguished themselves as map-makers. Antoine Silvy, the first in a long line of Jesuit teachers of hydrography at the college from 1708, had previously been stationed at Hudson Bay, where he taught mathematics aboard ships.

The popularity and practicality of the navigational arts were such that they were taught beyond the walls of the Jesuit college. Franquelin gave lessons in his private quarters near the school, though it is suspected that the arrangement was dictated more by personal preference than by heightened demand. Moreover, he did not take willingly to teaching since it interfered with his first love, map-making. In the 1690s, the teaching of hydrography spread to Montreal under the auspices of the Jesuits. Claude Chauchetière, who had been dispatched to the town by his Quebec superior, reported, "I have pupils who are good fifth-class scholars; but I have others with beards on their chins, to whom I teach navigation, fortification, and other mathematic subjects. One of my pupils is pilot on the ship which sails to the north."[9] And, as we saw in an earlier chapter, the Charon Brothers taught navigation at their hospital.

Île Royale was also a centre of hydrographic instruction. In 1726, Jean-René Cruchon arrived in Louisbourg from France in the hope of being appointed royal hydrographer for the area. The location augured well for the recent graduate of Saint-Malo's school of hydrography – Louisbourg was filled with naval types and young-sters who aspired to maritime careers. But France's Ministry of Marine was not prepared to subsidize a hydrographer in Louisbourg as it had done in Quebec, and therefore Cruchon was left to fend for himself. Drawing on a natural clientele, he taught theoretical and practical navigation to prospective mariners for a fee. Cruchon's course was well regarded and apparently a financial success, since he was able to support a family on the fees collected until his premature death, in 1738.

Despite the fact that physics, astronomy, and navigation were taught at the Jesuit college, in both the philosophy section and the hydrography course, it should not be concluded that science was a mainstay of the curriculum. It is doubtful whether the physics taught in the philosophy section was science in the strict sense at all, for it drew heavily on the syllogistic teachings of Aristotle and eschewed experimentalism. As for the science of the hydrography course, it more properly deserves to be called applied mathematics.

What must be recognized is that science and the scientific method, as we have come to know them, were slow to make an impression on the schools. Science often failed to penetrate the school door in earlier times, not only because it was suspect in some religious circles owing to its materialistic or physical orientation, but, perhaps more importantly, because it was seen as a threat to the supremacy of classical learning.

The absence of experimental science at the Jesuit college was probably due less to outright opposition than to the strength of humanistic learning. In curricular terms, the Jesuits were educational conservatives; their attachment to classical learning was responsible for keeping science and other emerging studies on the sidelines. The little science taught at the Jesuit college was ancient rather than modern, bookish rather than experimental, deductive rather than inductive. One searches in vain in the long history of the school for mention of a laboratory. Had the Oratorians rather than the Jesuits been the college teachers of New France, the cut of the curriculum would surely have been different. (It will be recalled that the Oratorian colleges in seventeenth-century France were renowned for their science teaching and well-equipped laboratories.)

In general, the science pursued in New France was natural rather than physical, and occurred beyond the pale of the school; thus, it did not raise any awkward questions or pose a threat to classical learning. As a largely undiscovered land, New France was a naturalist's paradise, yielding for collectors numerous new and exciting species of plant and animal life. According to the visiting botanist Peter Kalm, the study of natural science was further advanced in eighteenth-century Canada than in the English colonies to the south, where "the sciences were held in universal contempt."[10] Kalm's statement must be put in perspective, since it is believed that he was referring to official government efforts. While the English colonies had their share of prominent naturalists – Kalm had visited Benjamin Franklin, John Bartram, and other active scientists there – they had no one at the high government level the likes of Governor La Galissonière, who used his office to promote the study of the natural sciences.

Those who took an interest in science in early Canada were on the whole neither schoolmen nor professional scientists; nor were they rank amateurs. Rather, they tended to be men of position and cultivation, whose turn of mind and talents led them in scientific directions. If the French colony did not produce a Lennaeus or a Kalm, it did spawn a host of modest naturalists who contributed to the expansion of knowledge. Some of the self-made naturalists were civil leaders whose investigations served to give impetus to the work of others. Pierre Boucher, long-time governor or Trois-Rivières, contributed one of the earliest studies of the natural history of Canada.[11] La Galissonière, a military leader who was governor of New France between 1747 and 1749, put his officers to work collecting data on natural history and astronomical phenomena. Before coming to Canada, he had been in charge of organizing scientific expeditions to foreign lands.

As a group, it was probably the medical fraternity that produced the greatest number of naturalists in New France, thanks in part to the close connection between herbal medicine and plants. Foremost among this breed of part-time scientists was the prominent physician Michel Sarrazin, whose broad range of interests and activities epitomized the cultured man of the period. Despite his demanding medical duties, Sarrazin found time to pursue his interests in botany, zoology, mineralogy, and agriculture. Named correspondent of the Royal Academy of Sciences in Paris, he collected, sorted, and classified plant species, some of which he forwarded to France. His scientific curiosity also led him to a study of Canadian fauna, particularly the ubiquitous beaver and muskrat, which were the staples of the fur trade. To mention Sarrazin is to speak of Jean-François Gaultier in the same breath. Gaultier, like Sarrazin, was a physician by profession who dabbled in botany, zoology, meteorology, and herbal medicine. Hubert-Joseph de La Croix, a surgeon at Hôtel-Dieu in Quebec, also collected plant specimens for botanical authorities in France. The link between medicine and natural science does not stop here. Catherine Jérémie, a midwife by trade, was among the many eighteenth-century amateur botanists who devoted their spare moments to the collection and identification of plants. Like Sarrazin and others, she was particularly interested in discovering the medicinal properties of plants used by the Indians to effect cures. Her brother Nicolas made his mark by contributing a valuable scientific account of the little-known animal life of the Hudson Bay region.

The scientific fraternity of New France also numbered several clerics. The Jesuit missionary and explorer Joseph-François Lafitau, who is best known for his study of eighteenth-century Indian culture, was an inveterate collector of flora, and is credited with having discovered ginseng in North America. Jean-Baptiste Gosselin, an eighteenth-century parish priest, was an active collector of plant specimens. That Joseph-Pierre de Bonnécamps, a Jesuit teacher of hydrography at the Quebec college in the 1740s, dreamed of building an observatory on the school's roof should not surprise us. The Jesuits had long been interested in astronomy and meteorology, and some of their European colleges maintained observatories. Whether

Bonnécamps succeeded in constructing his observatory is a bit of a mystery. The correspondence of intendants Hocquart and Bigot in the 1740s noted that the Jesuit had not received the scientific instruments he ordered from France.[12] In a separate enterprise, Father Bonnécamps, at the request of La Galissonière, accompanied a military contingent to Ohio in 1749; during the voyage he kept scientific notes and mapped the territory.

As in other schools of the period, drill and memorization were pedagogical staples at the Jesuit college. Where Jesuit instruction differed was in its thoroughness; every point was driven home and sustained by constant review and repetition. There was little pretence of disinterested learning, for students were not rewarded for initiative or originality of thought but for their ability to accept and digest a fixed body of knowledge rooted in spiritual and academic orthodoxy. What also set the Jesuit school apart from others was its emphasis on competitive learning; the followers of Loyola were high on the educational value of competition, which they felt brought out the best in learners. Accordingly, Jesuit teachers resorted to prizes, public disputations, and a system of rivalry in which each boy was paired against another. Formal debates pitting student against student were periodically held. The debate, or disputation, was a sort of dialectic joust as participants clashed wits in Latin, armed with the weapons of Aristotelian logic. Two forms of debate can be identified as to time and place. The *sabbatine* was a class disputation held on Saturdays and at the end of the month. The *menstruale*, in spite of its name, was an end-of-the-year public debate, presented against the background of a festive occasion. The first *menstruale* was held on 2 July 1666 and was attended by the leading lights of the colony, some of whom participated. A special feature of the affair was the participation of the intendant Jean Talon, whom it was said argued well in Latin.

If debating proved to be a popular extra-curricular activity at the college which doubled as public entertainment, so too did play acting. The school's first director, Paul Le Jeune, who had acquired an appreciation of the dramatic arts while a student at Collège La Flèche in France, introduced the tradition at the Quebec institution. Students performed plays, some of which were written by their teachers, to celebrate special occasions such as the arrival in the colony of a new governor or intendant. But the thespian tradition sometimes fell prey to church censorship. Seeking a form of distraction for his officers and society in 1694, Governor Frontenac made preparations for the showing of Molière's *Tartuffe*. Bishop Saint-Vallier, whose strait-laced brand of Catholicism allowed for no such amusement, issued a *mandement* prohibiting the local inhabitants from attending the performance.[13] The church, at least in this instance, triumphed over the state, and for a time plays were not presented at the college or in the town.

The teaching staff of the Jesuit college was a mixed bag, composed of priests, brothers, seminarians, and some laymen. One gets the impression that the Jesuits did not assign their best talents to the school, fueling the thesis that education of the colonists played second fiddle to conversion of the Indians. Indeed, the job of teaching seems to have been relegated to clerics just starting out or to those in the twilight of their careers. The latter tended to be older missionaries, some of whom were physically and psychologically spent from working many years in Indian country. In the words of a Jesuit historian, the teachers at the college included old missionaries "broken by the years and the labours."[14] A representative figure is Father Claude Pijart, who after stints among the Nipissings, the Algonkins, and the Hurons, became in 1657, at the age of fifty-seven, a teacher at the school; he taught classes in rhetoric and philosophy there until the age of eighty. For some missionaries, the college represented a form of rest and recuperation before plunging again into the wilderness. After labouring for fourteen years in the upper Great Lakes region, Louis André was recalled to Quebec in 1684, where for the next six years he taught classes in philosophy and Latin. In 1690, at the age of sixty, he was sent to the Saguenay region, one of the most demanding assignments on the missionary circuit.

To novice priests the instruction of French boys was regarded as a stopgap, something to tide them over until they embarked on the real business of saving Indian souls. Such teachers were in effect transients, engaged to teach until they had sufficiently mastered an Indian tongue, which qualified them for a posting in a field mission. The Jesuit Claude Chauchetière, who was sent to Montreal in 1694 to teach letters and navigation, described himself as a bird on a branch ready to take flight, telling a friend in Bordeaux that he was holding himself in readiness to go among the Iroquois.[15]

Was the colony educationally deficient in having only one college? The question touches on demographic, geographic, and cultural factors. It is well to remember that the population of the French colony was always modest. At its demographic height, on the eve of the British invasion, it numbered fewer than sixty thousand persons. In the eighteenth century, it was not unusual for a French provincial town of comparable population to have but one college. The flaw in the comparison is that seventeenth- and eighteenth-century Canada did not resemble a French provincial town. Its predominantly rural population was scattered along the shores of the St Lawrence River from Quebec to Montreal. Less than one-quarter of the population was concentrated in Quebec, Montreal, and Trois-Rivières, and only the first two deserved to be called towns. The point is that with a single college, located in Quebec, the other areas of the colony were educationally disadvantaged, even for a pre-industrial society. Parents in Montreal and elsewhere in the colony were reluctant to send their sons to Quebec for schooling, not only because it meant paying boarding fees but because the journey to the capital was long, costly, and sometimes dangerous. In the seventeenth century, the warring Iroquois made no distinction in their attacks between ordinary folk and aspiring scholars.

It is worth noting that several unsuccessful attempts were made to establish a college in Montreal. Before the end of the seventeenth century, the citizens of Montreal were on record as calling for such a school, complaining that they could not afford to send their youngsters to Quebec. The Jesuits prepared the groundwork by opening an elementary school in the town in the 1690s, intending to expand it into a college when funds were available. That the lack of funds was the stumbling block to realization of the project came out in a petition from the Montreal citizenry to Governor Beauharnois in 1727.[16] The petition emphasized the social advantages to be derived from such a school: that it would cure Montreal youths of their riotous behaviour born of ignorance and idleness, and would make of them obedient servants of church and king. Beauharnois lent his support to the petition, and appealed to the minister to provide financial assistance. But the minister rejected the governor's request, saying that the establishment of a college in Montreal would be financially "too costly" for the king.[17] The Crown's decision may have been influenced by the suspicion that Intendant Dupuy was seen as imprudent in financial matters.

Dupuy having been recalled after only two years as colonial administrator, Beauharnois, in collaboration with the new intendant, Hocquart, again appealed to France for financial aid in support of a college for Montreal. In their letter to the minister, the colonial leaders advanced the Jesuit suggestion that the 1,500 *livres* recently sliced from the annual subsidy of the Charon Brothers be diverted to the proposed college.[18] But the Crown was unmoved by the argument and again turned down the request, leaving Montreal in the cultural shadow of Quebec and demonstrating that the government could be foe as well as friend to education. It was not until the British period in Canada that a college surfaced in Montreal.

### TRAINING OF PRIESTS

Realizing that Canada could not depend entirely on France for clerical workers, Bishop Laval founded the Seminary of Quebec in 1663 to train young men for the priesthood, so that they could serve as *curés* in the colony's parishes. The role of the seminary was, in the words of the founder, "to teach young men all they need to know to make a good cleric."[19] In order that boys from all corners of the colony could attend the seminary, Laval established the Petit Séminaire in 1668 as a residence for seminarians. An important point is that the pre-theology course was the responsibility of the neighbouring Jesuit college. Thus, each day seminarians could be seen leaving the "little seminary" and making the short walk across the town square to study with the Jesuits. The training of the secular clergy was lengthy, even for its day, as evidenced by the fact that theology constituted a two- or three-year programme following the completion of the seven-year course at the Jesuit school. The theology program was centred in scholasticism, the system of philosophical teaching dating from the Middle Ages, based chiefly upon the authority and writings of Thomas Aquinas, and characterized by marked formality in methods and arguments. Until the eighteenth century, at which time the Seminary of Quebec imported teachers, the theology course was taught at the Jesuit college.

When the number and quality of professors at the Jesuit school declined, in the eighteenth century, the authorities at the seminary entertained the idea of instructing their own senior students. Their superiors in Paris approved the scheme in 1726 and dispatched two instructors to Quebec, one to teach philosophy and one to teach theology. In effect, the Jesuit monopoly on higher education in Canada was broken. From that time forward, the Seminary of Quebec more closely resembled a true seminary, both training and educating candidates for the priesthood, though junior seminarians continued to receive their pre-theological instruction from the Jesuits.

At the beginning of the eighteenth century, enrolments at the seminary stood at fifty. On the average, from five to eight new boys were admitted each year, most between the ages of nine and twelve. One of the enduring characteristics of the French-Canadian clergy over the centuries has been its classless nature; talents from all social classes have been represented. This egalitarian tradition may have begun in the French period. The early records of the Seminary of Quebec point to students from all social-class backgrounds and from every region of the colony. Study bursaries and maintenance grants ensured that no boy was denied entrance on financial grounds. On the other hand, an unsettling statistic shows that only a minority of the seminarians completed their studies. Of almost 850 boys who were in residence at the Petit Séminaire between 1668 and 1758, fewer than two hundred stayed the course, and of this number only about half achieved priesthood. The high drop-out rate at the seminary explains in part the colony's chronic shortage of priests.

A perusal of student records of the Petit Séminaire from 1668 offers clues as to why so many seminarians fell by the wayside.[20] Not a few dropped out for academic reasons – they were unable to cope with the course of study, which was both long and intellectually demanding. For example, the entry for François-Borgia Gauvreau shows that he was admitted to the seminary in 1697, at the age of nine, and left in 1705 because he lacked an aptitude for Latin. Others abandoned their studies in the realization that they were not cut out for the religious life. The phrase "Not having an inclination for the ecclesiastic state" appears frequently in the records. Still others were asked to withdraw because they were found morally wanting by seminary authorities. Joseph Amiot, who entered the seminary in 1676, was requested to leave on 23 May 1680 for "licentiousness." Ill health also accounted for a number of dropouts. Beside the names of some departing students are written "bad headaches," which may have been caused by wretched lighting and the resulting eye strain. On the brighter side, if most seminarians did not complete their studies, they did not leave empty-handed. They had acquired a solid, if partial, education along the way that stood them in good stead as future members of the colony's ruling and administrative class. The dropouts from the seminary became civil servants, notaries, magistrates, merchants, and the like. Moreover, some boys came away with a knowledge of a skilled trade. It was the custom at the Seminary of Quebec to provide academically weak students with training in the vocational arts. The entry for Jean Gagnon reads that he was admitted to the seminary in 1672 but, "not being able to succeed, he left having learned the carpentry trade."

One of the rare glimpses into seminary life is provided by *Règlement Particulier*, the collection of rules and regulations of the Seminary of Quebec before 1682.[21] The document offers ample evidence of the regimented way of life of seminarians in seventeenth-century Canada. Nothing is left to chance. Every waking moment of the seminarian's day, from the ringing of the rising bell at five in the morning to retirement at nine in the evening, is accounted for. Every activity, from prayers, devotions, meditation, class, and meals to recreation, is scheduled with clockwork precision. In addition, detailed explanations are spelled out for every activity so that no student is in doubt as to what is expected of him. It is clear that the seminarian had little time for himself. Seminary life was a communal affair; students dined, studied, prayed, and played together.

Viewed from a different perspective, *Règlement Particulier* is a code of conduct, a set of rules defining the proper behaviour of a seminarian. Some regulations have a social as well as a spiritual purpose. In the section on meals, the seminarian is encouraged to come to the table in a spirit of penitence and mortification; he is advised against eating too much meat, complaining about the food, drinking undiluted wine, and speaking badly of others. In the section on recreation, the seminarian is told to avoid games of chance, cards, dice, and billiards, and to stay away from public presentations such as comedies, farces, and operas. He is also warned against frequenting restaurants, cabarets, and other places where liquor is served. Walking seems to have been one of the few forms of recreation and relaxation open to him, provided it was done in groups and that contact with persons of the opposite sex and those of questionable character was avoided.

The section on schooling is primarily a definition of acceptable classroom behaviour, and is presumably aimed at senior students. The time spent in class was surprisingly brief, comprising two short periods during the day. The morning schedule calls for breakfast at 8:15, followed by class until ten o'clock; in the afternoon class runs from 2:30 to four o'clock. Students are urged to arrive early to class, to observe a strict silence, and to show respect toward the teacher, as a representative of the Lord. They are told to write clearly and correctly in their notebooks, to listen attentively, and to apply themselves as best they can. In class discussions they must not show themselves to be opinionated, and they must treat their classmates honestly both in and outside the schoolroom. During the times of day set aside for private study, seminarians are commanded to read *le Traité* and other religious works recommended by the director.

In 1692, Bishop Saint-Vallier wrote to the authorities of the Seminary of Quebec complaining about the hard regimen of seminary life, and about the toll it eventually took on clerical workers.[22] The bishop was troubled by the "burn-out" of priests in the colony; they were physically spent at an early age, which he attributed in part to an overly taxing seminary education. In his letter, he called on the authorities to moderate their regulations so that graduates of the seminary left refreshed rather than exhausted, better able to withstand the physical rigours of religious life. Specifically, he recommended that the seminarians' daily duties and spiritual obligations be relaxed and reduced, that they be allowed more time for recreation and leisure, that their diet be increased during the colder seasons, that the conventional rising hour of four o'clock be changed to 4:30 in the summer and to five o'clock in the winter, and that they be permitted to remain standing during prayers (presumably to save wear and tear on the knees).

In their reply to the bishop, seminary authorities said that some of his suggestions had already been implemented and that others were under consideration. They refused, however, to budge on the question of modifying the seminarians' rising hour, noting that four o'clock had long been the standard in the religious houses of the colony. They added that the present schedule assured the students of eight hours of sleep, saying also that the public was not interested in seeing the hour changed.

## LAW AND MEDICAL TRAINING

Ever since the Middle Ages, universities in Europe had maintained faculties of law, medicine, and theology. Since New France did not have a university and, more significantly, looked to the mother country for most of its professional manpower, the colony was only marginally involved in the training of physicians, law officers, and the like. Of professionals, only clergymen were educationally accounted

for in Canada, being trained, as we have just seen, at the Seminary
of Quebec and the Jesuit college. Less formal patterns of training
were established for those aspiring to careers in law and medicine.

The legal and judicial system of New France was headed by the
intendant and administered by the attorney general, councillors,
judges, justices of the peace, and lesser officers. The highest court
in the colony was the Superior Council (known as the Sovereign
Council before 1703), which heard cases, established legal prece-
dents, and interpreted the Custom of Paris in light of local conditions. In addition, a network of lower courts was scattered around
the colony. A curiosity of the justice system in New France is that
it did not recognize lawyers in legal proceedings, which means that
the people often pleaded their own cases. The first French advocate
to practise law in Canada was Guillaume Guillimin, who was
licensed by Governor Murray in 1765.

On the whole, access to the legal ranks in New France required
neither formal training nor the possession of a credential. Save for
attorneys general, who were graduates of law schools in France, rare
was the judge or magistrate who had been professionally trained.
Some attempts were made to introduce legal training into the colony,
though it is presumptuous to conclude, as some historians have, that
these efforts resulted in the founding of *écoles de droit*, or law
schools.

In 1712, Mathieu-Benoît Collet, who had been a lawyer in the
Parlement of Paris, was appointed attorney general of New France.
He was dismayed to discover that judges and other legal officers in
the colony had little knowledge of the law they were expected to
administer. To that end, Collet undertook to give lessons in French
law and legal procedures to interested persons, and asked France to
supply him with legal texts. In 1717, the minister agreed to subsidize
Collet's course on the condition that he provide instruction free of
charge. Collet received the requested law books from Paris and proceeded with his teaching, though it appears that his course was not
particularly successful.

Collet's successor as the colony's chief law officer, Louis-Guillaume
Verrier, who arrived in Canada in 1728, began where Collet left off.
Starting in 1732 and continuing for the next twenty years or so, the
enterprising attorney general offered weekly lectures on law. Verrier's
course attracted few students in the early years and no financial
backing, for France doubted that he could make a go of it. In 1738,

he had seven regular students, but thanks to rising enrolments two years later he decided to give a second weekly lecture. Surprised and not a little impressed with the growing popularity of Verrier's course, France awarded the attorney general a subsidy of four hundred *livres*, increasing it to six hundred *livres* in 1751.

Verrier founded no law school; his lectures were not intended to prepare legal specialists. In style and purpose they resembled an adult-education course, designed for office holders or for those aspiring to positions in the legal hierarchy for whom a general knowledge of law would be useful. He taught, declared Verrier, those who had "no tincture" of jurisprudence.[23] His students were of all ages and backgrounds. They included young men from good families who saw career advantages in knowing something about the law, and seasoned professionals, the likes of Jean-François Gaultier and Michel Berthier, king's physician and surgeon, respectively.

The Superior Council was presided over by the intendant and composed of sixteen councillors appointed by the king, few of whom had a background in law, inviting the suspicion that patronage rather than legal ability and training was the determining factor in appointments. For example, the king's storekeeper, François Foucault, was appointed to the Superior Council in 1737, though he was without knowledge of the law. An encouraging trend was that those who attended Verrier's lectures were increasingly favoured in appointments to the Superior Council. Jean-François Gaultier proved to be an excellent student, and was subsequently rewarded with an appointment to the Superior Council in 1744.

Few details are known of Verrier's course, save for some of the legal texts used and the attorney general's pedagogical approach. He taught his students as he himself had been taught, relying on a Cartesian instructional mode. He began by reading or introducing a principle of law, following which he explained it. When he was satisfied that the students had grasped the principle, he showed them examples of it in the civil and criminal law. Verrier's students probably received more than a cookbook education. He was a cultivated man and possessed a large library, including works by contemporary as well as classical authors, which he likely shared with his students, some of whom were men of taste and learning themselves.

Since Verrier's lectures never attained the status of compulsory learning, most of the colony's administrative and legal officers came to their positions without training or special knowledge. Certainly this was the case for notaries, who were useful persons because of the strength of the written law and the diminished role of lawyers in a Gallic society. Like the mother country, New France was a contract society and relied heavily on notaries to exercise many of the functions normally reserved to lawyers in Anglo-Saxon cultures, from the drawing up of deeds, wills, and other contracts to the serving of writs, decrees, and ordinances. Considering the specialized nature of their duties, one would have expected notaries to have been trained in the manner of architects and surgeons, via the apprenticeship route, but this was not the case. Notaries were appointed by the intendant (in exceptional cases by seigneurs) from among candidates who were literate and of good moral character. No experience or knowledge of administrative law was required, which perhaps explains why a fair number of notaries were ex-schoolmasters.

One historian paints a dreary portrait of the notary in New France, describing him as poorly paid and placed too low on the administrative hierarchy to reap any honours or prestige.[24] So unappealing was the notaryship, so few its material and social rewards, that intendants were forced to look for candidates from all walks of life, wherever a lettered person could be found. Thus an artisan, a merchant, a soldier, or a teacher turned notary was not a rare occurrence. At the same time, owing to a shortage of clients and paltry salaries, the notaryship was a part-time occupation, and many notaries worked at other jobs. The former schoolmaster Jean-Baptiste Pottier was at once surveyor, court clerk, royal bailiff, and notary. A number of notaries were also surgeons and schoolmasters. Antoine de Adhémar de Saint-Martin must have been the moonlighter par excellence in the colony. Besides being a popular and busy notary, he was a process-server, a prison keeper, a clerk of the court, and a surveyor.

The practice of medicine in early Canada fell chiefly on the shoulders of surgeons and physicians, though a mixed bag of apothecaries, healers, midwives, and charlatans were also involved. On the whole, it was surgeons rather than physicians who provided medical care for the population, for the colony numbered many surgeons but few physicians. The distinctions between the two types of medical practitioner were, however, more than quantitative; the Middle Ages had bequeathed a separation of function and social status. Physicians were by tradition and training cultivated men, products of universities who brought an academic perspective to the healing arts. Over the centuries, the self-respecting physician had shied away from dissections and surgical operations, judging them to be undignified and unworthy of his office. The messy jobs of blood-letting, lancing wounds, and amputation were left to the socially and professionally inferior surgeons, who were not formally educated and who were vocationally linked with barbers, due to the widespread belief in bleeding as a remedy for most ills, coupled with the notion that surgery required mainly a sharp knife and a steady hand. The peppermint pole that stands before the modern barber shop is a grim reminder of the historical barber-surgeon alliance.

Historical differences aside, neither physicians nor surgeons possessed much in the way of sound medical knowledge. In seventeenth- and eighteenth-century Canada medicine was still in its infancy, less a science than an art – and a crude one to boot. In the absence of anaesthetics, surgical operations other than amputations were sparingly performed, and when carried out often ended in disaster, since little was known of the dangers of infection. Medical types were largely ignorant of the origins and causes of diseases, with the result that their remedies were often ineffective, and sometimes lethal. They were particularly helpless against the outbreaks of smallpox, typhus, scarlet fever, and other pestilences that ravaged the French and Indian populations. It is sometimes said that more Hurons and Iroquois were killed off by infectious diseases brought by the white man than by armed conflict. A ship arriving in the colony was a mixed blessing, for while it carried a cargo of people and supplies, it was sometimes the bearer of a dreaded disease. Twelve days after he disembarked at Quebec in 1740, the newly appointed Bishop Laubervière was dead, a victim of a fever which had swept through his ship during the voyage. It is suspected that the physician Gaultier, who died in 1756 at the age of forty-eight, was a victim of typhus brought by the ship *Léonard*.

Smallpox periodically reached epidemic proportions in the colony. The disease was of such virulence in 1732 and 1733 that it carried away almost two thousand lives in Quebec alone, transforming hospitals into mortuaries. What chance did bleedings (the aspirin of its day), herbs, poultices, and prayers have against the unrelenting pestilence? As the records show, children were particularly susceptible to contagious diseases. Rare was the colonial family that did not lose one or more of its offspring to smallpox or other contagions. Nor were medical families spared these afflictions. Michel Sarrazin, New France's most celebrated physician, lost three of his seven children to disease.

By the seventeenth century, the social and professional gap between physicians and surgeons showed signs of narrowing. Though physicians continued to enjoy a higher status, they were no longer averse to performing surgery. Michel Sarrazin began his career as a military surgeon in 1685, only to return to France later to study medicine for three years and earn the title of doctor. As a physician-surgeon, Sarrazin performed autopsies in addition to his regular medical duties. As the same time, surgeons had risen in the medical fraternity. The "sawbones" of an earlier day was becoming more of a general practitioner, also diagnosing and treating illnesses and injuries by non-surgical techniques, though his connection with barbers would remain intact until the middle of the eighteenth century.

Despite the aforementioned changes, time had not radically altered the pattern of training physicians and surgeons. The colony's handful of physicians, headed by Sarrazin and Gaultier, had been formally trained in Europe, but the vast majority of New France's medical practitioners – surgeons, for whom no academic preparation was required – continued to acquire knowledge through experience and apprenticeship. Not a few came to Canada in the capacity of ship's surgeon or military surgeon. Others came to medicine via the apprenticeship route, which was well established in the colony by the late seventeenth century. The apprentice surgeon attached himself to a master surgeon who provided him with bed and board and taught him the skills and techniques of medicine. Simon Soupiran, a barber-surgeon in early-eighteenth-century Quebec, had four apprentices under his care, to whom he entrusted the running of his barbershop and who accompanied him on house calls and visits to Hôtel-Dieu, where he performed operations.

Family tradition played an important role in the forming of surgeons, sons often following in the footsteps of their surgeon fathers. Joseph Mathon and Claude LeProust, both of Neuville, had surgeon fathers.[25] Michel Sarrazin sent his eldest son to Paris to study medicine, but he died of smallpox before completing his education. Sometimes fathers transmitted their medical skills to their sons. Soupiran trained his son to be a surgeon, and he in turn taught the art to his son. A Montreal surgeon, Jean Martinet de Fonblanche, received as apprentice his brother-in-law in 1674.

The year 1685 saw the creation in Canada of the Corporation of Surgeons and Barbers, which was charged with the supervision of its members. Though the corporation's activities remain obscure to this day, surgeons were officially accountable to the king's physician at Quebec. The fact that several generations of Soupirans became surgeons without any knowledge other than that passed down from father to son suggests that there was little supervision of surgeons in the seventeenth century.[26] Government establishment of licensing procedures for surgeons dates from the early eighteenth century. The Superior Council ruled on 3 August 1716 that a certain Pierre du Verger would not be recognized as a surgeon and be allowed to practise medicine until he presented himself for examination before Michel Sarrazin, the king's physician.[27]

Indications are that by the middle of the century, licensing procedures were taking hold, with the result that the outline of a medical fraternity free of amateurs and quacks was taking form; this was reflected in the decision of the surgeons to divest themselves of the companion trades of barbering and wigmaking. In 1750, Intendant Bigot decreed that newcomers to the colony wishing to practise medicine must submit themselves to examination before the king's physician, failing which they could be liable to a fine of two hundred *livres*.

## VOCATIONAL TRAINING

The uniqueness of manual training in New France is that it occurred mainly outside of the regular schools and was little dependent on church or state for its regulation and development. Though the colony had several arts and crafts schools under clerical direction, the fact remains that the great majority of locally trained artisans and craftsmen were products of the apprenticeship system, which prospered in Canada from the late seventeenth century.

From its earliest days, Canada required the services of skilled workers to assist in the building of a new society. Before the eighteenth century, the colony looked to France for most of its tradesmen, as an army of indentured labourers, or *engagés*, crossed the ocean to ply their skills. It is often said that of the ten thousand immigrants to Canada during the French period, almost four thousand were *engagés*. What drew this multitude of workers to a distant land was not patriotic or settlement motives; they were lured by attractive salaries and generous benefits, for colonial officials had to pay dearly to entice reluctant workers to come to Canada, if only for several years. The result was that the recruited worker won a contract whose provisions would be the envy of a modern labour union. The standard contract called for a fixed term of service – three years was normal – and provided the worker with salary, maintenance, transportation to the colony, and sometimes return passage to France. Often the salary took effect from the signing of the contract in Paris, constituting a bonus of sorts, since the *engagé* did not begin his actual duties until months later, the time it took him to travel to the seaport of La Rochelle or other point of embarkation, and then across the ocean to Canada.

As a society that had to be built from scratch, Canada needed workers with various skills. In the early years, physical strength counted for more than fine skills, since the colony had to be literally hacked out of the wilderness. Land clearers and wood-cutters were needed to prepare the land for crops and buildings; carpenters, sawyers, masons, and joiners to erect structures; locksmiths to keep the colonists' weapons in good working order in anticipation of attacks from the Iroquois and the English. Religious authorities were heavily dependent on imported labour, whose high cost put a strain on finances. The Jesuit college, the Seminary of Quebec, and the Ursuline convent were all active employers of *engagés*, from carpenters and sculptors to servants and cooks. Marie de l'Incarnation wrote her son in 1644, "Our workers have arrived from France that we have engaged for three or more years. We have ten of them who work for us."[28] In 1681, the Congregation of Notre Dame in Montreal had thirteen *domestiques* in its employ, some of whom were imported workers. The Jesuits tried to reduce labour costs by activating the medieval *donné* system, whereby lay workers of religious bent attached themselves to a religious community in exchange for maintenance and protection. However, the *donnés*, some of whom served with the Jesuits in their field missions, were never of sufficient number or skill to preclude the engagement of skilled workers.

Owing to the high cost of imported labour, coupled with the reality of an expanding population, the colony began to train its own craftsmen from the late seventeenth century. On an informal level, artisan fathers passed on their skills to their sons; on a formal level, the apprenticeship system, which since the Middle Ages had supplied Europe with skilled workers, gradually became the standard method of preparing skilled workers in the colony. Because of local conditions, apprenticeship in New France evolved as a stripped-down version of its European parent; guilds and other organizational practices associated with the European craft tradition did not take root in Canadian artisan soil. On the whole, the marketplace, rather than craftmen's associations or government regulation, was instrumental in determining standards of practice and quality of work in the skilled trades. In brief, apprenticeship in early Canada was a private training scheme between a master craftsman and an apprentice, the former promising to reveal the secrets of his trade in exchange for the labour and loyalty of the latter.

Apprenticeship was an adolescent phenomenon. Though apprentices ranged in age from ten to twenty-five, most were in the fourteen-to-eighteen age bracket. The period of training was normally three years, but four or five years were not unusual. The apprentice lived in the master's home at the latter's expense, which always included bed and board, and sometimes a clothing allowance as well. As we move into the eighteenth century we find an increasing number of masters paying wages to their apprentices, often in lieu of a clothing allowance. The wages paid were roughly equivalent to those earned by servants and farm labourers. Were the apprentice to run away before the completion of service or fail to show obedience to the master, he was liable for fines, extension of service, and even prison. In 1734, Intendant Hocquart empowered François Gauthier dit Larouche, a master maker of edge tools in Quebec, to arrest his apprentice, Étienne Auger, who had illegally quit his service. The order granted Gauthier the option of conducting his apprentice to the nearest prison.[29] On the whole, however, masters showed considerable leniency in the case of errant apprentices, in whom they had invested both time and money. On the other side of the coin, mistreatment of the apprentice by the master was grounds for voiding the contract.

The relationship between master craftsman and apprentice was normally defined in law, and formalized in a written contract prepared and validated by a notary, which spelled out the length and conditions of service and, occasionally, the penalties for breach of contract. The following contract, in which eighteen-year-old Pierre

Campagnas is apprenticed to Nicolas Doyon, a master gunsmith, in the year 1705, is typical of the period.

Was present Pierre Campagnas son, aged eighteen ... son of Pierre Campagnas, inhabitant of Cap Rouge, and of Anne Martin, his wife ... who voluntarily agree to release him as apprentice for three entire and consecutive years without interruption from this day to Nicolas Doyon, gunsmith, residing in this town at present, and accepting him in the quality of apprentice for the said three years, during which he promises to demonstrate and teach his trade of gunsmith and all that is related to the said Campagnas, who promises to learn it as diligently as he is able and to serve and obey the said Doyon in all that will be honestly and legally ordered him with all the loyalty required; this engagement and apprenticeship transaction to be done on the condition that the said Doyon treats him humanely and to feed, house, to wash, and to maintain coats, underwear, and working clothes and service during the said three years, according to the quality, and at the end of the time to furnish him ... with his old suits, underwear, and clothes, and also ... a clean and honest suit that will serve him only during the last ten months of his apprenticeship for feast days and Sundays ... [30]

The Canadian apprentice enjoyed a financial advantage over his counterpart in France, who was charged fees for the privilege of training. With the exception of several trades, principally those of gunsmithing and clothing, apprenticeship was free in New France.[31] Hence, with free tuition in the regular schools and free instruction in most trades, a measure of educational democracy was present in the colony. Furthermore, apprenticeship in New France was not a dumping ground for orphans and poor children, as was frequently the case in the English colonies to the south. Indeed, Canadian craftsmen balked at accepting them; they were generally hired out as domestic servants until they reached adulthood. In other words, apprenticeship in New France remained a "choice" institution, attracting boys who elected to go in that occupational direction.

It would appear from the preceding discussion that of the two parties, the apprentice came off better, receiving as a rule not only free training but sometimes a modest wage as well.[32] Before we shed a tear for the financially beleaguered master, however, it is well to consider the following fact. Normally the time it took to train an apprentice fell short of the contract period, which means that after a time the master had at his disposal a worker who was both skilled and cheap. The apprentice was thus in the second stage of his contract and was akin to an indentured labourer, filling the role traditionally occupied by journeymen. Canadian journeymen existed, but they were a special breed. Being of independent habit, like so many of their contemporaries, they showed a disinclination to work for other artisans, preferring to be their own bosses by selling their labour to the government or to private merchants, who as a rule paid better wages than master craftsmen. It is also worth mentioning that it was customary for apprentices to offer their labour free of charge to their masters upon completion of the contract.

In spite of the apparent economic benefits enjoyed by the Canadian apprentice, there is no disguising the hard regimen of the boy in training. His day was long, often stretching from five in the morning to eight or nine in the evening. And while apprenticeship was essentially a form of specialized training, not all of the boy's time was spent on relevant or productive activities. Unless specifically prohibited by the contract, apprentices were expected to do what was ordered by the master – that is, to perform tasks not directly related to the skill being acquired. Consequently, they were put to work performing lowly domestic chores such as gathering firewood, making fires, carrying water, and sweeping out the shop. If the apprentice was living in a rural setting (apprenticeship was largely an urban phenomenon), his duties might assume the character of general farm work. Though the apprentice had Sundays off, he was expected to attend church. The abundance of religious holidays, however, offered a welcome break from the routine of work and training.

In pedagogical terms, apprenticeship was a variation on tutorial instruction, the boy learning directly from the hand of the master through on-the-job training. The closeness of the relationship was enhanced by the tendency of many masters to accept only one apprentice at a time. Since many of the skilled trades did not require a knowledge of letters, instruction in reading and writing was rarely a part of the apprenticeship experience, though there are reports that some masters taught their trainees to write their names. Apparently a fair number of boys came to apprenticeship possessing a margin of literacy, as evidenced by signature rates on the contractual agreements.[33] At any rate, it is clear that New France did not duplicate the practice in colonial New York, where apprentices were routinely given leave to attend school. At most, younger apprentices in

Canada were sometimes released by their masters to attend catechism classes offered by the parish priest in preparation for first
communion. Normally, leave was given to apprentices only for personal or family reasons.

Craftsmen in New France eventually represented about a "fifth of
the adult, male population, and they were concentrated in the
towns."[34] The crafts themselves drew candidates from across the
colony, though farmers' sons appeared to have a preference for the
physical and outdoor trades such as carpentry, masonry, and joinery.
Like other occupations, the skilled trades differed as to wage and
prestige levels. At the top of the social scale were apothecaries, surgeons, silversmiths, and wood carvers; at the low end of the scale
were millers, butchers, shoemakers, and stonemasons.

Civil leaders in seventeenth-century Canada expressed interest in
establishing trade schools to supply the colony with skilled labour
and to provide an educational outlet for boys lacking an aptitude
for academic learning. While intendants and governors vacillated,
clerical authorities acted, founding several *écoles des arts et métiers*.
These arts and crafts schools, of which there apparently were three
– one in Quebec, one in Montreal, and one in Cap Tourmente –
aimed at training wood carvers, painters, and silversmiths, for the
clergy required expert hands to decorate and embellish its churches.
Although these trade schools represented an institutional alternative
to the preparation of skilled workers, they never threatened the dominant position of apprenticeship. One estimate is that the arts and
crafts schools turned out about seventy artisans, which is a far cry
from the nine hundred or so notarized apprenticeship contracts.[35]

Bishop Laval is believed to have established an arts and crafts
school around 1668 (though the name as such does not appear in
any document of the period) at Cap Tourmente, in the parish of
Saint-Joachim, about fifty kilometres east of Quebec.[36] The unusual
location of the school is explained by the fact that the churchman
maintained two farms in the region, Grande-Ferme and Petite-
Ferme, where seminarians from the Seminary of Quebec vacationed
in the summer months. Part of the large farm was used to house and
instruct boys learning a trade; part of the small farm served as a
boys' elementary school.

Laval's purpose in teaching the trades at Cap Tourmente was two-
fold: to prepare expert hands to build and decorate churches in what
was still an infant colony, and to provide an educational alternative

for boys who were unsuccessful in their academic and sacerdotal studies, to give them the opportunity to learn a skill so they would not be a burden to themselves or others. An examination of the records of Petit Séminaire in Quebec reveals the names of boys who were sent to Cap Tourmente for manual training. An entry for 1678 reads: "J.B. Lamusette entered 8 July, was sent to Cap Tourmente, from where he left having the trade of mason."[37]

The priest Louis Soumande, who was in charge of the two farms, was also put in charge of the trade school, a position he held during the life of the institution. Soumande's background and personality were right for the appointment. Though he had been educated by the Jesuits, his father had been a master maker of edge tools, and he himself was an architect and builder. He was also a generous man. In 1693 he established a foundation of eight thousand *livres*, the income from which was to pay the boarding costs of three boys studying the trades at Cap Tourmente. In the same year, Laval, then in retirement, established a similar foundation for six boys, declaring, "These children ought to be from the country, of good morals, inclined toward work; they will be chosen by the superiors and the directors in order to be fed, maintained, and instructed in good morals, in piety, to read, to write or be formed to work, or [to be assigned] to someone from the trades who practises them there."[38]

What trades were taught at Cap Tourmente? To judge by the variety of craftsmen engaged, including, among others, tailors, masons, shoemakers, locksmiths, sculptors, and decorators, instruction was available in many skills. Some of the artisan-teachers were from France, including the wood carvers Michel Fauchois and Samuel Genner; Jacques Leblond de Latour came to Canada in 1690, and his name, along with those of his students, is linked to a number of impressive church carvings. Still, the exact character of trade instruction at Cap Tourmente is unclear. Was it given in a regular classroom setting – that is, students learning the trades as they would reading and writing – or did it proceed along apprenticeship lines – boys learning directly at the foot of an artisan? A variation of the latter tradition seems a more plausible explanation in light of the fact that the artisan-teachers were themselves products of the apprenticeship system.

From the sketchy data available, it appears that enrolments at the trade school were modest. In his first visit to the Saint-Joachim region, in 1685, Bishop Saint-Vallier found that thirty-one boys were attending school there, of whom twelve were studying the trades.[39] In 1690, some forty boys were attending school in the parish, but the proportion of those learning a trade cannot be determined by the documentary evidence.[40] In any case, the demise of manual training at Cap Tourmente coincided with the death of Louis Soumande, in 1706.

Instruction in the trades was also given at the Seminary of Quebec. Governor Denonville reported to France in 1685 that the seminary had two houses, one of which included boys who had a taste for letters, the other of which was for those who were learning a trade.[41] The governor's report is corroborated by the records of the Petit Séminaire, which indicate that some boys remained at the seminary for trade instruction instead of going off to the Jesuit college for their academic studies. An entry for 1681 says that Jacques Chevalier of Beauport, who entered Petit Séminaire in May of that year, was taught to be a shoemaker.[42]

In the letters patent of 1694, the Charon Brothers of Montreal's Hôpital Général were authorized by the king "to teach trades" to poor orphan children under their care.[43] Five years later, royal approval was given to the brothers to establish several "manufactures d'écoles et métiers" at the hospital.[44] Whether these authorizations translated into a trade school is a moot point. At the turn of the century, the Charon Brothers attempted, in collaboration with the sculptor Charles Chaboulié and the painter Pierre Le Ber, to found such a school; when Chaboulié lost interest in the project and turned his attention elsewhere, the proposed school seemed to flounder. On the other hand, this did not rule out all vocational instruction at Hôpital Général, as some of the craftsmen employed there took on apprentices. A contract of 1695 shows the Charon Brothers acting as sponsor for Antoine Fortier, aged fifteen, who agrees to be apprenticed to Martin Noblesse, a master craftsman employed at the hospital. The contract adds that Fortier is to receive two years of training, and in return is to offer his labour to Noblesse for the remaining two years.[45] It is also likely that Le Ber, who was a member of the Charon Brothers and who lived at the hospital until his death, in 1717, taught painting to boys under his care.

Hôpital Général was also the site of several manufactures, which may have produced opportunities for boys to learn trades. On his last trip to France, in 1719, Charon persuaded André Souste and François Darles to come to Montreal to establish a factory for the production of silk and woolen stockings. It appears that the enterprise spilled over into craft training, for in the same year the Charon Brothers engaged Pierre Chauvet, aged fifteen, who had recently been expelled from the military because of his young age, as apprentice to learn the stocking trade at the hospital.[46]

On balance, craft training was one of Canada's most successful educational ventures, inviting the comment that the colonists were gifted with their hands. The Jesuit historian Charlevoix declared in a letter to a French duchess that, while he was unable to confirm the widely held belief that the Canadians were unfit for the sciences, "no one can deny their excellent genius for mechanics ... some have succeeded in all trades without ever having served an apprenticeship."[47]

# Conclusion

The seventeenth century witnessed the arrival in New France of missionaries in search of Indian souls. Education was an important tool in the evangelization campaign, for it was believed that religious conversion was best secured when preceded and underscored by instruction in Christian doctrine and ritual. Sometimes learning went beyond catechism to include instruction in the French language and culture. The missionaries drew on a variety of learning strategies to get their message across. They taught Indian adults and children in their villages against the backdrop of the indigenous language and culture, and experimented with sending Indian boys and girls to France for a traditional Gallic education. Learning was also provided in Indian reserves, habitations established by the French to curb the roving instincts of the aboriginal populations, in order to make them easier targets for conversion. In addition, the Jesuits, the Recollets, the Sulpicians, the Ursulines, and the Congregation of Notre Dame established schools or seminaries in Quebec and Montreal for Indian boys and girls, in the hope that separation from their families and tribes would hasten and deepen their attachment to Christian and French ways.

Although the male and female orders could lay claim to numerous spiritual conquests, they failed in the overall goal of effecting mass conversion of the Indian peoples. They were even less successful in their civilizing attempts. The Hurons, Algonkins, Iroquois, and other tribes resisted the spiritual and cultural overtures of the Europeans, secure in the superiority of their own beliefs and way of life. In recognition of this cultural reality, European efforts to evangelize and civilize the Indian through the formal school were all but abandoned by the end of the seventeenth century.

The evolution of Canada into a French colony in the middle of the seventeenth century imposed a second and more permanent responsibility on religious authorities – that of educating the sons and daughters of colonists. Educational arrangements in the colony drew heavily upon the traditions and practices of the mother country. While clerics of every stripe, from the bishop to the parish priest, had a hand in learning, it was the male and female religious communities that were most directly involved in founding, staffing, and administering schools. At the same time, the educational role of the church was not exclusive. Civil authorities contributed financial aid to education, and the religious orders were seconded in the teaching function by a sizeable number of lay schoolmasters, most of whom performed as wandering teachers or family tutors.

In Canada, as in France, no organized system of education was in place. Instead, the colony numbered several types of schools, the majority of which were *petites écoles*, the forerunners of today's elementary schools. The aim of the "little schools" was moral, spiritual, and academic, as children were taught to be good Christians and to know their letters. In the girls' schools the basic curriculum was supplemented by instruction in domestic learning, in anticipation of the pupils' adult role as mothers and homemakers. Specialized schools such as the Jesuit college, the Seminary of Quebec, and several arts and crafts schools completed the institutional framework. For the most part, skilled workers were trained not in formal schools but via the apprenticeship system, which was successfully transplanted from Europe.

Most schools in seventeenth- and eighteenth-century Canada were urban institutions, catering to the educational needs of the population in and around Quebec, Montreal, and Trois-Rivières. The town in New France was the centre of social, political, and economic life in the colony, and as such required the services of lettered persons. As one left the urban centres, educational facilities fell off sharply, reflecting the rustic conditions of country life. Unlike France, where villages dotted the rural landscape, village development did not take hold in rural New France. As a result, learning suffered in the rural parishes because of a scattered population, a chronic shortage of parish clergy, and the absence of community life.

While the *petite école* was a fixture in the French colony, it did not evolve into a popular institution. Some children attended school, albeit for a limited time, but most did not, as evidenced by low literacy levels in the society. The marginal status of the school in early Canada is not steeped in mystery. Then, as now, education reflected the social and economic conditions of the period. Quite simply, for most people in the colony the knowledge of letters was not an indispensable possession. The principal activities of living and working, from farming, fishing, and fur trading to fighting, could be pursued without reference to literacy. The oral tradition held sway over the written tradition, as reflected in the absence of culturally reinforcing institutions such as printing presses, booksellers, and lending libraries. Moreover, schools themselves were fragile institutions, constantly threatened by a shortage of teachers, a lack of funds, and an indifferent public. That organized learning was sustained in some fashion throughout the period speaks well of civil and religious representatives.

It would be comforting to report that as the colony grew in size and population so too did learning, that educational facilities were more available and widespread in the middle of the eighteenth century than earlier. However, such was not the case. There were fewer schools on the eve of the fall of New France than thirty or forty years before. Furthermore, most of the schools in the 1750s were female establishments; in that decade, the Ursulines and the Congregation of Notre Dame had a combined total of eleven schools, seven of which were rural institutions. For their part, the Sulpicians and the Jesuits counted three, and possibly four, schools between them, all of which were urban institutions. The Charon Brothers, who had been active in both Montreal and rural education, were no longer a factor, having disappeared from the scene in 1747.

The educational decline in the eighteenth century may be traced, in the first instance, to diminishing resources. The religious orders, which provided the colony with the bulk of its schools and teachers, did not grow with the times. As a matter of fact, the religious communities had fewer members at the middle of the eighteenth century than at the beginning of the century, which reduced their ability to cope with the educational needs of an expanding population. The slowdown may also be ascribed to the changing character of the colonial population. What earlier had been a society peopled by Frenchmen born in France was increasingly a society of native-born

Canadians. The Canadianization of the colony gave rise to different values and behaviours, which impinged on education. In short, the written word held less attraction for Canadians. Reared in a frontier environment, they preferred the field and forest to the school as their place of learning; the axe and plough to books as their tools of instruction. Bougainville, Montcalm's aide-de-camp, said that the Canadians were little attracted to formal learning, which he attributed to their consuming passion for hunting and warfare. Evidence of this attitude is borne out by marriage-signature data, which show lower literacy rates in Canada in 1750–65 than in 1680–99.

This history of New France education reminds us that learning is not always marked by progress and development, that the passage of time is sometimes characterized by educational pauses, during which organized learning retreats rather than advances.

# *Notes*

ABBREVIATIONS

AAQ  Archives de l'Archevêché de Québec
ACND  Archives de la Congrégation de Notre-Dame de Montréal
ANP  Archives nationales Paris
ANQ  Archives Nationales du Québec
ASGM  Archives des Soeurs Grises de Montréal
ASQ  Archives du Séminaire de Québec
ASSM  Archives du Séminaire de Saint-Sulpice de Montréal
DCB  Dictionary of Canadian Biography
JR  Jesuit Relations and Allied Documents
NA  National Archives
RAPQ  Rapport de l'Archiviste de la Province de Québec

CHAPTER ONE

1 Ariès, *Centuries of Childhood,* 332.
2 Perrel, "Les écoles de filles dans la France d'ancien régime," 77.

CHAPTER TWO

1 The seventeenth-century Recollet Joseph Le Caron said, "It must be hoped that as the Colony is peopled we shall civilize the Indians ...

they will be regulated by French law and modes of living." Le Clercq, *The First Establishment of the Faith in New France*, 1:214.

2 Trigger, *The Children of Aataentsic: A History of the Huron People to 1660*, 1:378.

3 Ibid., 2:468–70.

4 Hennepin, *A Discovery of a Vast Country in America*, 63.

5 Parkman, *The Jesuits in North America*, 551.

6 Jaenen, "The Meeting of the French and Amerindians in the Seventeenth Century," 141.

7 Thwaites, *JR*, 51:17.

8 French traders always maintained that if they did not sell liquor to the Indians, they would buy it from the English and the Dutch.

9 Thwaites, *JR*, 5:195.

10 Ibid., 7:275.

11 One recalls the remarkable eighteenth-century British soldier and American pioneer Sir William Johnson. Thanks to his eloquence in the Mohawk language, he was able to shape Iroquois policy to the advantage of the British in their conflicts with the French.

12 Thwaites, *JR*, 2:9.

13 Ibid., 10:91.

14 Ibid., 7:31.

15 Talbot, *Saint among the Hurons*, 42.

16 Thwaites, *JR*, 12:61.

17 Trigger, *Natives and Newcomers*, 294.

18 Thwaites, *JR*, 17:15.

19 Ibid., 16:67.

20 Charlevoix, *Journal of a Voyage to North America*, 2:30.

21 Ibid., 106.

22 Lafitau, *Moeurs des sauvages amériquains*, 602.

23 Campeau, *La mission des Jésuites chez les Hurons 1634–1650*, 58, 61–3.

24 Thwaites, *JR*, 33:253.

25 Ibid., volumes 16 and 17.

26 Ibid., 15:167.

27 It cannot be said that Father Lalemant came to Canada with his eyes closed. Thirteen years earlier, his brother Charles, who was Jesuit superior at Quebec, had vividly described to him the hard life of the missionary. Thwaites, *JR*, 4:219.

28 Lalemant was not the only Jesuit to leave a depressing portrait of missionary life. Jean de Brébeuf spoke along similar lines, and Fran-

çois de Crespieul, who laboured among the Montagnais for thirty years, wrote that the "life of a missionary ... is a long, slow martyrdom ... Suffering and affliction are the lot of these holy and painful missions." Rochemonteix, *Les Jésuites et la Nouvelle-France au XVIIᵉ siècle*, 3:419–20.

29 Trigger, *The Children of Aataentsic*, 2:522.
30 Thwaites, *JR*, 10:19.
31 Trigger, *The Children of Aataentsic*, 2:557–8.
32 Thwaites, *JR*, 16:247.
33 Ibid., 10:15.
34 Ibid., 10:93.
35 Ibid., 19:3–4.
36 Ibid., 17:13–5.
37 Ibid., 5:33. Pierre Boucher, governor of Trois-Rivières in the seventeenth century, said, "Indians in general are quick witted, and dullness and boorishness, such as we see among our peasants in France, are very rarely to be seen among them." Boucher, *Canada in the Seventeenth Century*, 53.
38 Thwaites, *JR*, 8:145.
39 Teaching Indian children religious gestures served more than spiritual ends. Father Daniel was able to quiet a crying baby by teaching it to make the sign of the cross. Thwaites, *JR*, 10:21.
40 Ibid., 53:207–13.
41 Ibid., 56:133.
42 Oury, *Marie de l'Incarnation Correspondance*, 839–40.
43 Le Clercq, *New Relation of Gaspesia*, 126.
44 Battiste, "Micmac Literacy and Cognitive Assimilation," 31.
45 Thwaites, *JR*, 29:139–41.
46 Ibid., 18:167.

CHAPTER THREE

1 Thwaites, *JR*, 6:147.
2 Ibid., 14:205.
3 New France was not the only centre of reservation activity in seventeenth-century North America. Protestant clergymen of New England pioneered the development of "praying towns" for Indians, which aimed at combining spiritual commitment and Christian living. The most fully developed reserve system was in the American southwest, where Spanish missionaries maintained sophisticated habitations

which went further in their activities than the Canadian ones, providing religious and academic learning and teaching the Indians a trade so that they could earn a living. This was possible because the peoples of the southwest were generally peaceful and tractable, while those of New France were more independent and fiercer.

4 Groulx, "Missionnaires de l'est en Nouvelle-France," 56–7.

5 Dollier de Casson, *A History of Montreal, 1640–1672*, 19.

6 Rochemonteix, *Les Jésuites et la Nouvelle-France au XVIIᵉ siècle*, 3:375.

7 Thwaites, *JR*, 6:153–5.

8 Ibid.

9 Although there was only one Indian seminary, Le Jeune's report of 1639 refers to "séminaires." His use of the plural may have indicated the existence of separate classes for boys from different tribes. Thwaites, *JR*, 16:169.

10 Thwaites, *JR*, 52:47. Laval was not the first person to offer this interpretation. The Recollet Gabriel Sagard, who lived among the Hurons in the 1620s, made the same observation. Rioux, *Gabriel Sagard, Théodat*, 47.

11 The intendant Jean Talon attributed the small size of the Indian family to the inability of Indian women to bear many children, which he said was due to a life of heavy work and a tendency to nurse children too long. *RAPQ*, 1930–1931:31.

12 Thwaites, *JR*, 12:47.

13 Ibid., 16:181.

14 Ibid., 12:63.

15 Ibid., 24:103.

16 Ibid., 15:171.

17 Ibid., 24:121.

18 Ibid., 5:145.

19 Ibid., 7:259.

20 The arrival of the Ursulines in Quebec did not automatically relieve the Jesuits of all responsibility for female learning. A letter to Le Jeune from Marie de l'Incarnation in 1640 refers to Father Pijart's educational work at the Ursuline convent. Oury, *Marie de l'Incarnation Correspondance*, 93.

21 Ibid., 97.

22 *Glimpses of the Monastery*, 59.

23 Oury, *Marie*, 390.

24 Marshall, *Word from New France*, 71.
25 Oury, *Marie*, 104.
26 Mahoney, *Marie of the Incarnation*, 180.
27 Oury, *Marie*, 286.
28 Marshall, *Word from New France*, 336.
29 Oury, *Marie*, 144.
30 Ibid., 801.
31 *Les Ursulines de Québec depuis leur établissement*, 1:142.
32 De Meulles to minister, 12 November 1682, NA, Série C$^{11}$ A, 6:11–131.
33 The Sulpicians were also encouraged to promote French manners and dress among the Indians. Louis Tronson, superior of the Sulpician seminary in Paris, urged his Montreal counterpart to "introduce the use of skirts for the Indian women and underpants for Indian boys." Bertrand, *Correspondance de M. Louis Tronson*, 2:277.
34 Saint-Vallier, *Estat présent de l'église*, 66–7.
35 Seignelay to de Meulles, 10 April 1684, in O'Callaghan, *Documents Relative to the Colonial History of the State of New York*, 9:222.
36 Thwaites, *JR*, 8:237.
37 Saint-Ignace, *Les annales de l'Hôtel-Dieu de Québec, 1636–1716*, 89.
38 Ibid., 85.
39 Colbert to Talon, 5 April 1666, RAPQ, 1930–1931:46.
40 AAQ, Registre A, 77.
41 Colbert to Talon, 5 April 1667, RAPQ, 1930–1931:72.
42 Attempts by Recollet missionaries early in the century to teach the French language to the Hurons and other tribes ended in failure. Jouve, *Les Franciscains et le Canada aux Trois-Rivières*, 132–5.
43 Frontenac to Colbert, 2 November 1672, RAPQ, 1926–1927:20.
44 Oury, *Marie*, 828.
45 Talon to Colbert, 10 November 1670, RAPQ, 1930–1931:128.
46 Annales du Petit Séminaire, 1668–1771, ASQ.
47 Frontenac to Colbert, 14 October 1674, RAPQ, 1926–1927:66.
48 Duchesneau to Seignelay, 13 November 1681, in O'Callaghan, *Documents*, 9:150.
49 *Les Ursulines de Québec depuis leur établissement*, 1:209.
50 *Collection de manuscrits ... relatifs à la Nouvelle-France*, 1:337.
51 Denonville to minister, 13 September 1685, NA, Série C$^{11}$ A, 7:44–9.
52 Cadillac to minister, 31 August 1703, "Cadillac Papers," 167.

CHAPTER FOUR

1 Ouellet, "L'enseignement primaire," 171–87.
2 *Édits, ordonnances royaux ... concernant le Canada*, 2:465–66.
3 King to Beauharnois and Hocquart, 19 April 1729, NA, Série B, 53:518–19.
4 Garneau, *Histoire du Canada*, 233.
5 Concession d'un terrain à Trois-Rivières pour y établir les Soeurs de la Congrégation, 28 October 1688, ACND, Recueil-Documents 1, 1659–1698.
6 Minister to bishop, 27 May 1699, NA, MG 1, Série B, 20–2:215.
7 Minister to d'Auteuil, 31 May 1701, NA, Série B, 22:228.
8 Conventions entre Martin Boutet dit Saint-Martin, le curé et les marguilliers de la paroisse de Québec, 1 September 1651, ASQ, Documents Faribault.
9 *DCB*, 2:527.
10 Saint-Vallier, *Estat présent de l'église*.
11 In 1699, Bishop Saint-Vallier and the Seminary of Quebec signed an agreement to establish jointly a foundation for the support of a schoolmaster in the town "so that no person of any age shall fall into ignorance." ASQ, Paroisse de Québec, 126.
12 Saint-Vallier, *Rituel du diocèse de Québec*.
13 ASSM, Dossier 1, Section II, écoles primaires, 1657–1921, T. 46, no. 1a.
14 Têtu and Gagnon, *Mandements ... des évêques de Québec*, 169–74.
15 Roy, *Inventaire des ordonnances des intendants de la Nouvelle-France*, 2:11.
16 Ibid., 22.
17 Têtu and Gagnon, *Mandements*, 547–9.
18 ANQ, Greffe of Séverin Ameau, 4 November 1681.
19 Trudel, "Les élèves pensionnaires des Ursulines de Québec et les bourses d'étude, 1641–1662," 279.
20 Baillargeon, *Le Séminaire de Québec de 1685 à 1760*, 206.
21 ANP, États des Revenus des Communautés établies à la Nouvelle-France, Archives de la Marine, 3.
22 ASQ, Paroisse de Québec, 126.
23 ASSM, Dossier 1, Section II, écoles primaires, 1657–1921, T. 46, No. 5.
24 Annales du Petit Séminaire, 1668–1771, ASQ.

25 Archives de la paroisse Notre-Dame de Québec, Carton: anciens et précieux écrits, 1691.

26 Oury, *Marie de l'Incarnation Correspondance*, 507. Similar declarations can be found on pages 476 and 735.

27 Constitutions pour les frères hospitaliers de la Croix et de Saint Joseph, 1723, article 41, ASGM.

28 Règlement Particulier, ASQ, Séminaire 95, No. 23.

29 Règlement concernant la modestie dans les écoles des petites filles, 1692, ACND, Recueil-Documents I, 1659–1698.

30 Raudot to minister, 10 November 1717, NA, Série C¹¹ A, 26:150.

31 Denonville to minister, 13 November 1685, NA, Série C¹¹ A, 7:45.

32 In his study of eighteenth-century Lower Richelieu society, Allan Greer found no evidence of parental interference in the choice of marriage partners among the members of the *habitant* class. Greer, *Peasant, Lord, and Merchant*, 50.

33 Lemieux, *Les petits innocents: l'enfance en Nouvelle-France*, 170.

34 Boucher, *Histoire véritable et naturelle*, 139.

35 Têtu and Gagnon, *Mandements*, 282.

36 Ibid., 412.

37 Roy, *Inventaire des ordonnances des intendants*, 2:11.

38 Magnuson, "The Elusive Lay Schoolmasters of New France," 73–94.

39 ANQ, Greffe of Gilles Rageot, 18 April 1674.

40 ANQ, Greffe of Séverin Ameau, 4 November 1681.

41 Charbonneau and Légaré, *Répertoire des actes de baptême mariage sépulture*, volume 13.

42 Roy, *Inventaire des ordonnances des intendants*, 2:22.

43 Charbonneau and Légaré, *Répertoire*, volume 18.

44 Lay schoolmasters who became notaries were Claude Maugue, Nicolas Métru, Arnould-Balthazar Pollet, Jean-Baptiste Pottier, René Remy, Jacques-Barthélemy Richard, Pierre-François Rigault, and Jean-Baptiste Tétro. The long-time notary of Trois-Rivières, Séverin Ameau, doubled as a teacher, and Pierre-Georges Guelte, in a break with tradition, went from notary to schoolmaster.

45 Dechêne, *Habitants et marchands de Montréal au XVIIᵉ siècle*, 468.

46 Douville, *Les premiers seigneurs et colons*, 92.

47 Kellogg, *The British Régime in Wisconsin and the Northwest*, 226.

48 *Autrefois et aujourd'hui à Sainte-Anne de la Pérade*, 7.

49 "Correspondance de Madame Bégon 1748–1754," RAPQ, 1934–1935:103.

CHAPTER FIVE

1 Benson, *Peter Kalm's Travels in North America*, 2:415.
2 Gosselin, *L'instruction au Canada sous le régime français*, 475–7.
3 Moogk, "The Craftsmen of New France," 175.
4 Roy, *Les lettres, les sciences et les arts au Canada*, 55–56.
5 Furet and Ozouf, *Lire et écrire*, 1:27.
6 Gadoury, Landry, and Charbonneau, "Démographie différentielle en Nouvelle-France: villes et campagnes," 366.
7 Roy, Landry, and Charbonneau, "Quelques comportements des canadiens au XVIIᵉ siècle d'après les registres paroissiaux," 65.
8 Thanks to a massive project completed at the University of Montreal in the 1980s, the parish registers (including baptismal, marriage, and death acts) of Canada from the second half of the seventeenth century to 1765 have been brought to print. They are contained in the forty-five-volume work by Charbonneau and Légaré, *Répertoire des actes de baptême mariage sépulture et des recensements du Québec ancien*. The marriage data for 1750–65 are largely drawn from volumes 31–42. The data for 1680–99 have been adapted from Roy, Landry, and Charbonneau, "Quelques comportements des canadiens au XVIIᵉ siècle," 66. Additional information is taken from Lessard, "Nos ancêtres trifluviens savaient-ils écrire?," 18.
9 Cipolla, *Literacy and Development in the West*.
10 "Procès-verbaux sur la commodité et incommodité dressés dans chacune des paroisses de la Nouvelle-France par Mathieu-Benoît Collet," *RAPQ*, 1921–1922:264–362.
11 In 1727, Intendant Dupuy authorized Raymond Bertrand Junceria to teach school in Charlesbourg. It is not known how long Junceria taught. Roy, *Inventaire des ordonnances des intendants de la Nouvelle-France*, 2:22.
12 François Janelle is identified as *maître d'école* in Baie-du-Febvre in several notarial acts of the 1730s. See greffe of Pierre Petit of 18 May 1730, and that of Hyacinthe-Olivier Pressé of 4 June 1736. Olivier-François Nadeau is listed as *maître d'école* in Yamaska in a land sale of 1745. See greffe of Pressé of 25 July 1745. In a notarized contract prepared by Louis Pillard and dated 14 June 1762, Nadeau agrees to instruct the children of the Lauzière family of St-François-du-Lac. In 1747, Nadeau was appointed royal bailiff for the jurisdiction of Trois-Rivières. The two positions were not mutually exclusive, since

law officers sometimes doubled as schoolmasters in New France. Above documents ANQ.

13 Harris, *The Seigneurial System in Early Canada*, 176.

14 One historian suggests that the rural population of early Canada was not as independent as we have been led to believe, noting that the *habitant* was financially tied to the parish priest and the seigneur by a diverse array of ecclesiastical and feudal payments. In addition to the tithe, which paid the priest's salary, the inhabitants had to bear the burden of a range of collections, fees, and pew rents to meet the expenses of the parish. See Greer, *Peasant, Lord, and Merchant.*

15 Parkman, *The Old Régime in Canada*, 448–9.

16 Vaudreuil and Bégon to minister, 4 October 1718, NA, Série C¹¹ A, 39:8–9.

17 Denonville to Seignelay, 13 November 1685, RAPQ, 1939–1940:268–9.

18 Têtu and Gagnon, *Mandements, lettres pastorales et circulaires des évêques de Québec*, 543–5.

19 Bishop to minister, 8 April 1736, NA, Série C¹¹ A, 66:78–9.

20 Jaenen, *The Role of the Church in New France*, 57.

21 "Procès-verbaux ... par Mathieu-Benoît Collet," RAPQ, 1921–1922:264–362.

22 Jodoin and Vincent, *Histoire de Longueuil*, 264–5.

23 Cressy, *Literacy and the Social Order.*

24 Lockridge, *Literacy in Colonial New England*, 38–9.

25 Fleury and Valmary, "Les progrès de l'instruction élémentaire de Louis XIV à Napoléon III," 71–92.

26 Furet and Ozouf, *Lire et écrire*, 1:43.

27 Ibid., 238.

28 It is possible that the data are incorrect, and that the clergy were more careful to record the origins of males than of females. The argument against this possibility is that the seventeenth-century data show a similar ratio. Of the 2,170 couples listed in the marriage registers for 1680–99, 842 of the grooms but only 62 of the brides were born in France.

29 According to an Ursuline history, "under French domination the women were more educated than the men." See *Les Ursulines de Trois-Rivières depuis leur établissement*, 1:184.

30 Trudel, *L'église canadienne sous le régime militaire 1759–1764*, 2:222.

31 Thwaites, *JR*, 70:81–5.

32 Verrette, "L'alphabétisation de la population de la ville de Québec de 1750 à 1849," 74.

33 Lanctot, *Montreal under Maisonneuve 1642–1665*, 203.

34 Dechêne, *Habitants et marchands de Montréal au XVIIᵉ siècle*, 467.

35 Charbonneau and Légaré, *Répertoire des actes*, volumes 31–42.

36 Verrette, "L'alphabétisation de la population," 74.

37 Hardy and Ruddel, *Les apprentis à Québec 1660–1815*, 81.

38 Moogk, "The Craftsmen of New France," 175.

39 *DCB*, 2:467.

40 *DCB*, 1:663.

41 Charbonneau and Légaré, *Répertoire des actes*, volumes 31–42.

42 Shortt and Doughty, *Documents Relating to the Constitutional History of Canada 1759–1791*, 79.

43 Stevens et al., *Travels in New France by J.C.B.*, 22.

44 Proulx, "Les Québécois et le livre 1690–1760."

45 Roy, *Mémoires S.R. Canada Le Baron de Lahontan*, 97.

46 Proulx, "Les Québécois et le livre 1690–1760."

47 Roy, *Les lettres, les sciences et les arts au Canada*, 55–6. See also Drolet, *Les bibliothèques canadiennes 1604–1960*, 30.

48 Benson, *Peter Kalm's Travels*, 2:542.

49 Thwaites, *JR*, 49:167.

50 Fauteux, "Les débuts de l'imprimerie au Canada," 19.

51 Benson, *Peter Kalm's Travels*, 2:473.

52 Poutet, "Une institution franco-canadienne au XVIIIᵉ siècle," 82.

53 The written word sometimes appeared in strange guise. In 1673, the Sovereign Council found Charles Grosbon guilty of assault against Jean Milot and sentenced him to stand before the parish church in Montreal on Sundays, wearing a sign on his chest and back on which was written "Accessory in assault on Milot." *Jugements et délibérations du Conseil Souverain de la Nouvelle-France*, 1:840.

54 *Édits, ordonnances royaux ... concernant le Canada*, 2:336.

55 Benson, *Peter Kalm's Travels*, 2:422.

56 *Voyage de Pehr Kalm au Canada en 1749*, 438–9; 518.

57 "Mémoire sur l'état de la Nouvelle-France," *RAPQ*, 1923–1924:61.

58 Franquet, *Voyages et mémoires sur le Canada*, 57.

59 Têtu and Gagnon, *Mandements*, 543–5.

CHAPTER SIX

1 *DCB*, 1:436.

2 Rochemonteix, *Les Jésuites et la Nouvelle-France au XVIIᵉ siècle*, 3:559.
3 Gosselin, *L'instruction au Canada sous le régime français*, 43.
4 ASQ, Paroisse de Québec, 126.
5 Gosselin, *L'instruction*, 56.
6 ASQ, Paroisses diverses, 13 October 1689, 61.
7 Magnuson, "The Elusive Lay Schoolmasters of New France," 73–94.
8 ANQ, Greffe of Gilles Rageot, 18 April 1674.
9 Tronson to Dollier de Casson, 20 April 1684, in Bertrand, *Correspondance de M. Louis Tronson*, 2:270.
10 In addition to Rouillé, the foundation papers were signed by Nicolas Barbier, Michel-Philibert Boy, Pierre Gaulin, Jacob Thoumelet, and Benoist Basset. It is unlikely that Basset did any teaching, since his name does not appear on subsequent documents.
11 ASSM, Dossier I, section II, écoles primaires, 1657–1921, T. 46, No. 5.
12 Ibid., No. 12.
13 Minutes d'Adhémar, 9 October 1693, ASSM, ms. 1242.
14 Tronson to Dollier de Casson, 12 April–May 1695, in Bertrand, *Correspondance de M. Louis Tronson*, 2:350–1.
15 Gauthier, *Sulpitiana*.
16 It does not appear that Boësson and Donay did any teaching after 1702. See Poutet, "Une institution franco-canadienne au XVIIIᵉ siècle," 72–3.
17 *Édits, ordonnances royaux … concernant le Canada*, 1:278.
18 Félix-Paul, *Les lettres de S. Jean-Baptiste de La Salle*, 175.
19 Poutet, "Une institution franco-canadienne au XVIIIᵉ siècle," 449.
20 Magnien to de Belmont, 8 July 1718, ASGM.
21 Raudot to minister, 10 November 1707, NA, Série C¹¹ A, 26:150.
22 Raudot to minister, 18 October 1708, NA, Série C¹¹ A, 28:175–87.
23 Ramezay to minister, 12 November 1717, NA, Série C¹¹ A, 27:3–20.
24 Vaudreuil and Bégon to Council of Marine, 4 October 1718, RAPQ, 1941–1942:189.
25 *Édits, ordonnances royaux … concernant le Canada*, 2:390.
26 Ibid., 465–6.
27 Ibid., 390.
28 Ramezay to Council of Marine, 4 October 1721, RAPQ, 1941–1942:207.
29 Notice sur les frères, postulants, fondateurs et associés de la communauté des frères hospitaliers de la croix, RAPQ, 1923–1924:193–6.

30 Charbonneau and Légaré, *Répertoire des actes de baptême mariage sépulture et des recensements du Québec ancien.*

31 Letter of Ameau to Champigny, 28 May 1687. Cited in DCB, 2:16–17.

32 Charbonneau and Légaré, *Répertoire des actes*, volume 9.

33 Projet d'établissement à La Rochelle, 22 October 1724, RAPQ, 1923–1924:201.

34 Constitutions pour les frères hospitaliers de la Croix et de Saint Joseph, 1723, article 41, ASGM.

35 État des Bien-Fond de l'Hôpital Général de Montréal à la mort de Frère Charon, ASGM, Ancien Journal I, 1688–1857, 13.

36 Constitutions pour les frères, article 29, ASGM.

37 Ibid., article premier.

38 Ibid.

39 Ibid., article 32.

40 Charbonneau and Légaré, *Répertoire des actes*, volume 28.

41 King to Beauharnois and Hocquart, 11 April 1730, NA, Série B, 54:533–4.

42 Upon learning of the king's decision to cancel the Charon Brothers' subsidy, the Jesuits requested that one-half of the monies, or 1,500 *livres*, be diverted to them for the establishment of a college in Montreal. Beauharnois and Hocquart to minister, 6 October 1731, NA, Série C$^{11}$ A, 54:64–7.

43 Acte d'association entre les Frères de La Salle et les Frères hospitaliers, 11 September 1737, NA, Série C$^{11}$ A, 13:202–5.

44 Pétition en faveur des Frères et contre le projet des soeurs, 2 November 1738. Cited in Poutet, "Une institution franco-canadienne au XVIIIᵉ siècle," 473–4.

45 Ministry of Marine to Beauharnois and Hocquart, 21 April 1739, NA, Série B, 68:n.p.

46 The Recollet missionary and historian Chrestien Le Clercq, whose *Premier établissement de la foy dans la Nouvelle-France*, first published in 1691, was, among other things, an indictment of the Jesuit missions in Canada.

47 Not a few historians, including Pierre-Joseph Chauveau in the nineteenth century and Amédée Gosselin and Odoric-Marie Jouve in this century, have spoken of Recollet teachers and schools in New France. More recently, Gérard Filteau, in *La Naissance d'une Nation, Tableau de la Nouvelle-France en 1755*, 134, mentioned Recollet schools in Quebec, Montreal, and Trois-Rivières. Similarly, Cornelius J. Jaenen

wrote that the Recollets had schools in Montreal, in Trois-Rivières, and on Île Royale, as well as in the forts of the upper country. See Jaenen, *The Role of the Church in New France*, 102.

48 *DCB*, 4:752.

49 *DCB*, 3:552.

50 Belisle, "Le mythe Récollet: l'ensemble de Montréal."

51 In his article on educational provision in the Trois-Rivières region in the seventeenth century, Raymond Douville found no evidence of Recollet participation. See Douville, "L'instruction primaire dans la région trifluvienne au début de la colonie," 39–60.

52 Odoric-Marie Jouve offers no evidence for his assertion that Recollet teachers succeeded the lay schoolmaster Rigault in Trois-Rivières after he quit the town in 1739. See Jouve, *Les Franciscains et le Canada aux Trois-Rivières*, 283.

53 Several writers, including Louis-Philippe Audet and the Recollet historian Odoric-Marie Jouve, cite the 1821 document. See also Sulte, *Mélanges historiques*, 21.

54 Quoted in Lemay, "Les Récollets de la Province de Saint-Denis et ceux de la Province de Bretagne à l'Île Royale, de 1713 à 1731," 103.

55 Benson, *Peter Kalm's Travels in North America*, 2:453.

CHAPTER SEVEN

1 Raudot to minister, 10 November 1707, NA, Série C[11] A, 26:150.

2 Ramezay to minister, 12 November 1707, NA, Série C[11] A, 27:3–20.

3 *Les écrits de mère Bourgeoys*, 284.

4 Donation de M. Lamy, 9 November 1685, ACND, Recueil-Documents 1, 1659–1698.

5 Gosselin, *L'instruction au Canada sous le régime français*, 199.

6 Testament de M. Rémy, 20 October 1705, ASSM.

7 Reglemens communs pour les soeurs seculières de la Congrégation de Notre-Dame de Montréal, 1698, chapter 7, ACND.

8 Saint-Vallier, *Estat présent de l'église*, 66.

9 Ibid.

10 Acceptation de la donation faite par Mgr de Québec aux Soeurs de la Congrégation de Montréal, 12 March 1689, ACND, Recueil-Documents 1, 1659–1698.

11 Ibid.

12 Quelques Règlements pour les filles de la Congrégation de Québec, 15 March 1689, ACND, Recueil-Documents 4, 1678–1853.

13 Archives de la paroisse Notre-Dame de Québec, Carton: Anciens et précieux écrits.
14 Ibid.
15 Mandement de St Vallier, 26 January 1714, ACND, Recueil-Documents 4, 1678–1853.
16 Charbonneau and Légaré, *Répertoire des actes de baptême mariage sépulture*, 8:557.
17 Ibid., volumes 25, 32, 36, and 38.
18 Franquet, *Voyages et mémoires sur le Canada*, 31–2.
19 Reglemens communs pour les soeurs, 1698, chapter 27, ACND.
20 *Histoire de la Congrégation de Notre-Dame de Montréal*, 2:23.
21 Johnston, *Religion in Life at Louisbourg, 1713–1758*.
22 Ibid.
23 Cadillac to minister, 31 August 1703, in "Cadillac Papers," 167.
24 Letter of M. de Pontbriand, 10 November 1746, Archives de la marine, ANP.
25 Ibid., 4 November 1749.
26 Farmer, *History of Detroit ... and Early Michigan*, 333.
27 Liénard to Duquesne, 13 February 1755. Cited in *Histoire de la Congrégation de Notre-Dame de Montréal*, 4:237–9.
28 Vaudreuil to minister, 30 October 1755, NA, CG, C¹¹, 100, folio 132.
29 Hamilton to the Earl of Dartmouth, 29 August to 2 September 1776, "Haldimand Papers," 266.
30 Reglemens communs pour les soeurs, 1698, chapter 7, ACND.
31 Inventaires de la communauté 1723–1793, III, 9, ACND.
32 Ibid.
33 Bourgeoys said that it was imperative that pupils keep busy, since "idleness is the means of rendering them libertine." *Les écrits de mère Bourgeoys*, 249.
34 Cited in *The Pearl of Troyes*, 209–10.
35 Reglemens communs pour les soeurs, 1698, chapter 28, ACND.
36 Ibid., chapter 7.
37 *Les écrits de mère Bourgeoys*, 284.
38 Oury, *Marie de l'Incarnation Correspondance*, 852.
39 Gosselin, *L'instruction au Canada sous le régime français*, 160.
40 Oury, *Marie*, 852.
41 *Les Ursulines de Québec depuis leur établissement*, 2:169–70.
42 Oury, *Marie*, 852.
43 Trudel, "Les élèves pensionnaires des Ursulines de Québec," 280.
44 Oury, *Marie*, 802.

45 An account from the year 1646 reveals that a boarder paid her *pension* in kind in five instalments: 3½ cords of firewood on 13 January; 4 cords of firewood on 6 March; 1 pot of butter weighing 12 pounds on 13 March; 1 fat pig and 1 barrel of peas on 13 November; and 1 barrel of salted eels at an unknown date. *Les Ursulines de Québec depuis leur établissement*, 1:141–2.

46 Oury, *Marie*, 637.

47 Trudel, "Les élèves pensionnaires," 289.

48 Oury, *Marie*, 802.

49 Benson, *Peter Kalm's Travels in North America*, 2:470–1.

50 Marie Raisin was one of Marguerite Bourgeoys's first recruits from France, arriving in Canada in 1659. Her stay with the Ursulines in 1666 lasted only three months, as she was unable to adapt to the cloistered life of the nunnery. She returned to Montreal, and in the succeeding years held a number of responsible positions with the congregation.

51 Governor Bienville was less successful in his efforts to promote boys' education. He asked the Jesuits to establish a college in New Orleans, but the order declined on the grounds of insufficient resources. Apparently the town had a boys' elementary school in the 1720s run by a Capuchin schoolmaster.

52 D'Allaire, *l'Hôpital Général de Québec 1692–1764*, 120–1.

53 Ferland-Angers, *Mère d'Youville*, 104–5.

54 ASGM, Ancien Journal, 1, 1668–1857, 55.

55 État des Rentes et Argent que l'Hôpital Général de Montréal a en France, 29 July 1763, ASGM.

### CHAPTER EIGHT

1 Campeau, *Les commencements du Collège de Québec*, 69.

2 Têtu and Gagnon, *Mandements ... des évêques de Québec*, 36.

3 Gosselin, *L'instruction au Canada sous le régime français*, 264.

4 Benson, *Peter Kalm's Travels in North America*, 2:428.

5 Thwaites, JR, 66:209–11.

6 Rochemonteix, *Les Jésuites et la Nouvelle-France au XVIIᵉ siècle*, 1:218.

7 Gosselin, *L'instruction*, 293.

8 Thwaites, JR, 60:143.

9 Ibid., 64:149.

10 Benson, *Peter Kalm's Travels*, 1:375–6.

11  Boucher, *Histoire véritable et naturelle.*
12  Gosselin, "Les Jésuites au Canada – Le P. de Bonnécamps, dernier professeur d'hydrographie au collège de Québec, avant la conquête," 27.
13  Têtu and Gagnon, *Mandements*, 302–4.
14  Rochemonteix, *Les Jésuites ... au XVIIᵉ siècle*, 3:366–7.
15  Thwaites, *JR*, 64:149.
16  Requête des habitants du pays à M. de Beauharnois pour l'établissement d'un collège de Montréal, NA, Série C¹¹ A, 49(1):76–9.
17  Council of Marine to Beauharnois, 14 May 1728, NA, Série B, 52:495.
18  Beauharnois and Hocquart to minister, 6 October 1731, NA, Série C¹¹ A, 54:64–7.
19  *Édits, ordonnances royaux ... concernant le Canada*, 1:33–5.
20  Annales du Petit Séminaire, 1668–1771, ASQ.
21  Règlement Particulier, ASQ, Séminaire 95, No. 23.
22  ASQ, carton Séminaire 95, 49–49a.
23  Fabre-Surveyer, "Louis-Guillaume Verrier (1690–1758)," 169.
24  Vachon, *Histoire du notariat canadien 1621–1960*, 47.
25  ANQ, Greffes of Louis Pillard, 14 April 1736 and 1 June 1737.
26  Abbott, *History of Medicine in the Province of Quebec*, 28.
27  *Jugements et délibérations du Conseil supérieur de Québec*, 6:1160.
28  Oury, *Marie de l'Incarnation Correspondance*, 219.
29  Ordinance of Hocquart, 20 April 1734.
30  ANQ, Greffe of Louis Chambalon, 15 July 1705.
31  Between 1648 and 1759, fewer than 10 per cent of all apprentices in the town of Quebec had to pay for their training. Hardy and Ruddel, *Les apprentis à Québec 1660–1815*, 51.
32  Almost half of the apprentices in Quebec were paid a salary. Ibid.
33  About one-third of Quebec apprentices signed the contract of apprenticeship. Ibid., 34.
34  Moogk, "The Craftsmen of New France," 283.
35  Ibid., 161.
36  Peter Moogk, who has written widely on apprenticeship training in New France, challenges the traditional view that an arts and crafts school was established in Saint-Joachim, arguing that no document of the period makes reference to an *école des arts et métiers* there. His contention is more semantic than substantive, since he admits that the trades were taught there in some form. See his "Réexamen de l'école des arts et Saint-Joachim," 3–29. A rejoinder to Moogk's thesis is

Campeau, "À propos de l'école des arts et métiers de Saint-Joachim," 567–70.

37 Annales du Petit Séminaire, 1668–1771, ASQ.

38 ASQ, Manuscrit 2, 6.

39 Saint-Vallier, *Estat présent de l'église*, 53.

40 États des Revenus des Communautés à la Nouvelle-France, Archives de la Marine, 3.

41 Denonville to minister, 13 November 1685, NA, Série C$^{11}$ A, 7:53.

42 Annales du Petit Séminaire, 1668–1771, ASQ.

43 Inventaire des documents et des imprimés concernant la communauté des Frères Charon, *RAPQ*, 1923–1924:170.

44 Roy, *Inventaire des insinuations du Conseil souverain*, 107.

45 ANQ, Greffe of Antoine Adhémar, 3 February 1695.

46 ANQ, Greffe of Michel Lepailleur, 15 November 1719.

47 Charlevoix, *Journal of a Voyage to North America*, 1:248.

# Bibliography

PRIMARY SOURCES

Archives de la Congrégation de Notre-Dame de Montréal. Recueil-Documents, 1–4, 1659–1853.
Archives des Soeurs Grises de Montréal. Ancien Journal 1, 1668–1857.
Archives du Séminaire de Québec.
Archives du Séminaire de Saint-Sulpice de Montréal. Dossier 1, Section II, écoles primaires, 1657–1921.
Archives nationales du Québec. Montreal and Quebec City branches.
National Archives. Série B, official correspondence from France to Canada; Série C$^{11}$ A, official correspondence from Canada to France.

SECONDARY SOURCES

Abbott, Maude E. *History of Medicine in the Province of Quebec.* Montreal: McGill University 1931.
Ariès, Philippe. *Centuries of Childhood: A Social History of Family Life.* Translated by Robert Baldick. New York: Knopf 1962.
Audet, Louis-Philippe. *Histoire de l'enseignement au Québec 1608–1971.* Vol. 1. Montreal: Holt, Rinehart & Winston 1971.
– "Programmes et professeurs du Collège de Québec (1635–1763)." *Les Cahiers des Dix* 34 (1969), 13–38.
– *Le système scolaire de la Province de Québec: l'instruction publique de 1635 à 1800.* Vol. 2. Quebec City: Les Presses universitaires Laval 1951.
*Autrefois et aujourd'hui à Sainte-Anne de la Pérade.* Trois-Rivières: E.S. de Carufel 1895.

Baillargeon, Noël. *Le Séminaire de Québec de 1685 à 1760*. Quebec City: Les Presses de l'Université Laval 1977.

Battiste, Marie. "Micmac Literacy and Cognitive Assimilation." In *Indian Education in Canada: The Legacy*, edited by Jean Barman, Yvonne Hébert, and Don McCaskill, Vol. 1, 23–44. Vancouver: University of British Columbia Press 1986.

Belisle, Jean. "Le mythe Récollet: l'ensemble de Montréal." Master's thesis, University of Montreal 1974.

Benson, Adolph B., ed. and trans. *Peter Kalm's Travels in North America*, 2 vols. New York: Wilson-Erickson 1937.

Bertrand, L., ed. *Correspondance de M. Louis Tronson*. 2 vols. Paris 1904.

Biggar, H.P., ed. *The Works of Samuel de Champlain*. 6 vols. Toronto: Champlain Society 1922–35.

Boucher, Pierre. *Canada in the Seventeenth Century*. Translated by Edward Louis Montozambert. Montreal: George E. Desbarats 1883.

– *Histoire véritable et naturelle des moeurs et productions du pays de la Nouvelle-France*. Paris: Florentin Lambert 1664.

"Cadillac Papers." *Michigan Historical Collections* 33 (1904): 36–715.

Campeau, Lucien. "À propos de l'école des arts et métiers de Saint-Joachim." *Revue d'histoire de l'Amérique française* 29 (March 1976): 567–70.

– *Les commencements du Collège de Québec 1626–1670*. Montreal: Les Éditions Bellarmin 1972.

– *La mission des Jésuites chez les Hurons, 1634–1650*. Montreal: Les Éditions Bellarmin 1987.

Charbonneau, Hubert, and Jacques Légaré. *Répertoire des actes de baptême mariage sépulture et des recensements du Québec ancien*. 45 vols. Montreal: Les Presses de l'Université de Montréal 1980–88.

Charlevoix, Pierre-François-Xavier. *History and General Description of New France*. Edited and translated by John Gilmary Shea. 6 vols. New York: J.G. Shea 1866–72.

– *Journal of a Voyage to North America*. Edited and translated by Joan Phelps Kellogg. 2 vols. Chicago: The Caxton Club 1923.

Cipolla, Carlo M. *Literacy and Development in the West*. Harmondsworth: Penguin 1969.

*Collection de manuscrits contenant lettres, mémoires, et autres documents historiques relatifs à la Nouvelle-France*. 4 vols. Quebec City 1883–85.

Cressy, David. *Literacy and the Social Order: Reading and Writing in Tudor and Stuart England*. Cambridge: Cambridge University Press 1980.

D'Allaire, Micheline. *L'Hôpital-général de Québec 1692–1764*. Montreal: Fides 1971.

Dechêne, Louise. *Habitants et marchands de Montréal au XVII<sup>e</sup> siècle*. Paris: Plon 1974.

Delanglez, Jean. *Frontenac and the Jesuits*. Chicago: Institute of Jesuit History 1939.

*Dictionary of Canadian Biography*. Vols. 1–4. Toronto: University of Toronto Press 1966–74.

Dionne, N.E. "Le Séminaire de Notre-Dame-des-Anges." *Revue Canadienne* 26 (1890): 65–81, 148–66.

Dollier de Casson, François. *A History of Montreal 1640–1672*. Edited and translated by Ralph Flenley. Toronto: J.M. Dent 1928.

Douville, Raymond. "L'instruction primaire dans la région trifluvienne au début de la colonie." *Les Cahiers des Dix* 34 (1969): 39–59.

– *Les premiers seigneurs et colons de Sainte-Anne de la Pérade 1667–1681*. Trois-Rivières: Éditions du Bien Public 1946.

Drolet, Antonio. *Les bibliothèques canadiennes 1604–1960*. Ottawa: Le Cercle du Livre de France 1965.

Eccles, W.J. *Essays on New France*. Toronto: Oxford University Press 1987.

*Édits, ordonnances royaux, déclarations et arrêts du Conseil d'état du roi concernant le Canada*. 3 vols. Quebec City 1854–56.

Fabre-Surveyer, Edouard. "Louis-Guillaume Verrier (1690–1758)." *Revue d'histoire de l'Amérique française* 6 (1952–53): 157–76.

Fahmy-Eid, Nadia. "L'éducation des filles chez les Ursulines de Québec sous le Régime français." In *Maîtresses de maison, maîtresses d'école. Femmes, famille et éducation dans l'histoire du Québec*, edited by Nadia Fahmy-Eid and Micheline Dumont, 49–75. Montreal: Boréal Express 1983.

Farmer, Silas. *History of Detroit and Wayne County and Early Michigan*. Detroit: Gale Research 1969.

Fauteux, Aegedius. "Les débuts de l'imprimerie au Canada." *Les Cahiers des Dix* 16 (1951): 17–37.

Félix-Paul, Fr. *Les lettres de S. Jean-Baptiste de La Salle, Édition critique*. Paris: Institut des Frères des écoles chrétiennes 1954.

Ferland-Angers, Albertine. *Mère d'Youville*. Montreal: Beauchemin 1945.

Filteau, Gérard. *La naissance d'une nation, tableau de la Nouvelle-France en 1755*. Montreal: Les Éditions de l'Aurore 1978.

Fleury, Michel, and Pierre Valmary. "Les progrès de l'instruction élémentaire de Louis XIV à Napoléon III." *Population* 12 (January–March 1957): 71–92.

Fortier, Alcée. *A History of Louisiana*. Vol. 1. Baton Rouge: Claitor's 1966.

Franquet, Louis. *Voyages et mémoires sur le Canada*. Quebec City: A. Côté 1889.

Furet, François, and Jacques Ozouf. *Lire et écrire: l'alphabétisation des français de Calvin à Jules Ferry*. 2 vols. Paris: Les Éditions de Minuit 1977.

Gadoury, Lorraine, Yves Landry, and Hubert Charbonneau. "Démographie différentielle en Nouvelle-France: villes et campagnes." *Revue d'histoire de l'Amérique française* 38 (Winter 1985): 357–78.

Garneau, François-Xavier. *Histoire du Canada*. Vol. 1. Paris: Librairie Félix Alcan 1920.

Gauthier, Henri. *Sulpitiana*. Montreal: Bureau des oeuvres paroissiales de St-Jacques 1926.

Gibson, George D. "Jesuit Education of the Indians in New France, 1611–1658." Ph.D. thesis, University of California at Berkeley, 1940.

Gilbert-Léveillé, Pierrette. *Répertoire des greffes des notaires*. 2 vols. Quebec City 1985–86.

*Glimpses of the Monastery: A Brief Sketch of the History of the Ursulines of Quebec during Two Hundred Years*. Quebec City 1875.

Gosselin, Amédée. *L'instruction au Canada sous le régime français*. Quebec City: Laflamme & Proulx 1911.

Gosselin, Auguste. "Les Jésuites au Canada – Le P. de Bonnécamps, dernier professeur d'hydrographie au collège de Québec, avant la conquête." *Mémoires et comptes rendus de la société royale du Canada*, Second Series, 1 (1895): 25–61.

Greer, Allan. "The Pattern of Literacy in Quebec, 1745–1899." *Histoire sociale/Social History* 11 (November 1978): 295–335.

– *Peasant, Lord, and Merchant: Rural Society in Three Quebec Parishes 1740–1840*. Toronto: University of Toronto Press 1985.

Groulx, Lionel. *L'enseignement français au Canada*. Vol. 1. Montreal: Librairie d'Action canadienne-française 1931.

– "Missionnaires de l'est en Nouvelle-France: Réductions et séminaires indiens." *Revue d'histoire de l'Amérique française* 3 (1949): 45–72.

"Haldimand Papers." *Michigan Historical Collections* 10 (1888): 210–672.

Hamelin, Pierre. "L'alphabétisation de la Côte-du-Sud, 1680–1869." Master's thesis, Laval University, 1982.

Hardy, Jean-Pierre, and David-Thiery Ruddel. *Les apprentis à Québec 1660–1815*. Montreal: Les Presses de l'Université du Québec 1977.

Harris, Richard Colebrook. *The Seigneurial System in Early Canada*. Madison: University of Wisconsin Press 1966.

Hennepin, Louis. *A Discovery of a Vast Country in America*. Vol. 2. London: M. Bentley 1698.

*Histoire de la Congrégation de Notre-Dame de Montréal*. Vols. 1–4. Montreal: Congrégation de Notre-Dame 1913–41.

Jaenen, Cornelius J. "Education for Francization: The Case of New France in the Seventeenth Century." In *Indian Education in Canada: The Legacy*, edited by Jean Barman, Yvonne Hébert, and Don McCaskill, Vol. 1, 45–63. Vancouver: University of British Columbia Press 1986.

– *Friend and Foe, Aspects of French-Amerindian Cultural Contact in the Sixteenth and Seventeenth Centuries*. Toronto: McClelland and Stewart 1976.

– "The Meeting of the French and Amerindians in the Seventeenth Century." *Revue de l'Université d'Ottawa* 43 (January–March 1973): 128–44.

– *The Role of the Church in New France*. Toronto: McGraw-Hill Ryerson 1976.

Jamet, Dom Albert. *Marguerite Bourgeoys 1620–1700*. 2 vols. Montreal: La Presse Catholique Panaméricaine 1942.

Jetté, René. *Dictionnaire généalogique des familles du Québec: Des origines à 1730*. Montreal: Les Presses de l'Université de Montréal 1983.

Jodoin, Alex, and J.L. Vincent. *Histoire de Longueuil*. Montreal: Gebhardt-Berthiaume 1889.

Johnston, A.J.B. *Religion in Life at Louisbourg, 1713–1758*. Montreal: McGill-Queen's University Press 1984.

Jouve, Odoric-Marie. *Les Franciscains et le Canada aux Trois-Rivières*. Paris: Procure des Missions franciscaines 1934.

– *Les Franciscains et le Canada: l'établissement de la foi 1615–1629*. 3 vols. Quebec City: Couvent des SS. Stimates 1915.

*Jugements et déliberations du Conseil Souverain de la Nouvelle-France 1663–1716*. 6 vols. Quebec City 1885–1891.

Kellogg, Louise Phelps. *The British Régime in Wisconsin and the Northwest*. Madison: State Historical Society of Wisconsin 1935.

Lafitau, Joseph-François. *Moeurs des sauvages amériquains, comparées aux moeurs des premiers temps*. Vol. 1. Paris: Chez Saugrain 1724.

Lanctot, Gustave. *Montreal under Maisonneuve 1642–1665*. Translated by Alta Lind Cook. Toronto: Clarke, Irwin 1969.

Le Clercq, Chrestien. *The First Establishment of the Faith in New France*. Edited by John Gilmary Shea. 2 vols. New York: J.G. Shea 1881.

– *New Relation of Gaspesia with the Customs and Religion of the Gaspesian Indians*. Edited and translated by W.F. Ganong. Toronto: The Champlain Society 1910.

Lemay, R.R. Hugolin. "Les Récollets de la Province de Saint-Denis et ceux de la Province de Bretagne à l'Île Royale, de 1713 à 1731." *Mémoires et comptes rendus de la société royale du Canada* 24, Third Series (1930): 77–113.

Lemieux, Denise. *Les petits innocents: l'enfance en Nouvelle-France.* Quebec: Institut québécois de recherche sur la culture 1985.

*Les écrits de mère Bourgeoys.* Montreal: Congrégation de Notre-Dame 1964.

Lessard, Claude. "Nos ancêtres trifluviens savaient-ils écrire?" *Le Coteillage* 1 (December 1981): 18.

*Les Ursulines de Québec depuis leur établissement jusqu'à nos jours.* 4 vols. Quebec City 1863–66.

*Les Ursulines de Trois-Rivières depuis leur établissement jusqu'à nos jours.* Vol. 1. Trois-Rivières: P.V. Ayotte 1888.

Lockridge, Kenneth A. *Literacy in Colonial New England.* New York: W.W. Norton 1974.

Magnuson, Roger. *A Brief History of Quebec Education: From New France to Parti Québécois.* Montreal: Harvest House 1980.

– "The Elusive Lay Schoolmasters of New France." *Historical Studies in Education/Revue d'histoire de l'éducation* 2 (Spring 1990): 73–94.

– "Jesuit Pedagogy and the Wilderness Classroom in 17th-Century Canada." *Canadian Journal of Native Education* 17 (1990): 68–75.

Mahoney, Mother Denis. *Marie of the Incarnation.* Garden City, NJ: Doubleday 1964.

Marshall, Joyce., ed. and trans. *Word from New France: The Selected Letters of Marie de l'Incarnation.* Toronto: Oxford University Press 1967.

Martel, Jules. "Index des actes notariés du Régime français à 1634–1740." Mimeographed, n.d.

Massicotte, E.Z. "Fondation d'une communauté de frères instituteurs à Montréal en 1686." *Bulletin des recherches historiques* 28 (1922): 37–42.

– "Les Frères Charon et les Frères de la Salle." *Bulletin des recherches historiques* 23 (August 1917): 252–4.

Maurault, Olivier. "Les origines de l'enseignement secondaire à Montréal." *Les Cahiers des Dix* 1 (1936): 95–104.

Moogk, Peter N. "The Craftsmen of New France." Ph.D. thesis, University of Toronto, 1973.

– "Manual Education and Economic Life in New France." In *Studies on Voltaire and the Eighteenth Century.* Vol. 167, edited by James A. Leith, Oxford: Oxford University Press, 1977.

– "Réexamen de l'école des arts et métiers de Saint-Joachim." *Revue d'histoire de l'Amérique française* 29 (June 1975): 3–29.

Morin, Marie. *Annales de l'Hôtel-Dieu de Montréal.* Edited by A. Fauteux et al. Montreal: Société historique de Montréal 1921.

Morrisset, Gérard. "L'école des arts et métiers de Saint-Joachin." *Mémoires de la Société généalogique canadienne-française* 16 (April–May–June 1965): 67–73.

O'Callaghan, E.B., ed. *Documents Relating to the Colonial History of the State of New York.* 15 vols. Albany: Weed, Parsons and Co. 1856–83.

Ouellet, Fernand. "L'enseignement primaire: responsabilité des églises ou de l'État? (1801–1836)." *Recherches sociographiques* 2 (April–June 1961): 171–87.

Oury, Dom Guy., ed. *Marie de l'Incarnation Correspondance.* Solesmes: Abbaye Saint-Pierre 1971.

Parkman, Francis. *The Jesuits in North America.* Boston: Little, Brown 1963.

– *The Old Régime in Canada.* Boston: Little, Brown 1895.

Perrel, Jean. "Les écoles de filles dans la France d'ancien régime." In *The Making of Frenchmen: Current Directions in the History of Education in France, 1679–1979*, edited by Donald N. Baker and Patrick J. Harrigan, 75–83. Waterloo, Ontario: Historical Reflections Press 1980.

Perrot, Nicolas. *Mémoire sur les moeurs, coustumes et relligion des sauvages de l'Amérique septentrionale.* Paris: A. Franck 1864.

Poutet, Yves. "La compagnie de Saint-Sulpice et les petites écoles de Montréal au XVIIᵉ siècle (1657–1700)." *Bulletin du Comité des Études de la compagnie de Saint-Sulpice* 5 (April–June 1961): 166–82.

– "Une institution franco-canadienne au XVIIIᵉ siècle: les écoles populaires de garçons de Montréal." *Revue d'histoire ecclésiastique* 59, Nos. 1, 2 (1964): 52–88; 437–84.

– "Les voeux des Frères Charon, hospitaliers-enseignants." *Revue d'histoire de l'église de France* 49 (1963): 19–45.

Proulx, Gilles. "Les Québécois et le livre 1690–1760." Paper presented at the annual conference of the Canadian Historical Association, Montreal, May 1985.

*Rapport de l'Archiviste de la Province de Québec.* 1920–62.

Rioux, Jean-de-la-Croix. *Gabriel Sagard, Théodat.* Ottawa: Fides 1964.

Rochemonteix, Camille de. *Les Jésuites et la Nouvelle-France au XVIIᵉ siècle.* 3 vols. Paris: Letouzey 1895–96.

– *Les Jésuites et la Nouvelle-France au XVIIIᵉ siècle.* 2 vols. Paris 1906.

Roy, Antoine. *Les lettres, les sciences et les arts au Canada sous le régime français*. Paris: Jouve 1930.

Roy, J. Edmond., ed. *Mémoires S.R. Canada Le Baron de Lahontan*. Montreal: Éditions Élysée 1974.

Roy, Pierre-Georges. *Inventaire des concessions en fief et seigneurie*. 6 vols. Beauceville, Quebec, 1927–1929.

– *Inventaire des insinuations du Conseil souverain de la Nouvelle-France*. Beauceville, Quebec, 1921.

– *Inventaire des insinuations de la Prévôté de Québec*. 3 vols. Beauceville, Quebec, 1936–1939.

– *Inventaire des jugements et déliberations du conseil supérieur de la Nouvelle-France de 1717 à 1760*. 7 vols. Beauceville, Quebec, 1885–1940.

– *Inventaire des ordonnances des intendants de la Nouvelle-France*. 4 vols. Beauceville, Quebec, 1919.

– *Ordonnances, commissions, etc., des gouverneurs et intendants de la Nouvelle-France, 1639–1706*. 2 vols. Beauceville, Quebec, 1924.

Roy, Pierre-Georges, and Antoine Roy. *Inventaire des greffes des notaires du régime français*. 27 vols. Quebec City 1943–76.

Roy, Raymond, Yves Landry, and Hubert Charbonneau. "Quelques comportements des canadiens au XVIIᵉ siècle d'après les registres paroissiaux." *Revue d'histoire de l'Amérique française* 31 (June 1977): 49–73.

Sagard, Gabriel. *Histoire du Canada et voyages que les Fréres Mineurs Recollects y ont faicts pour la conversion des Infidelles*. Paris: Tross 1866.

– *The Long Journey to the Country of the Hurons*. Edited by George M. Wrong. Toronto: The Champlain Society 1939.

Saint-George, Luce. "L'enseignement catéchétique des Jésuites au XVIIᵉ siècle: l'exemple Montagnais." Master's thesis, University of Montreal, 1982.

Saint-Ignace, Juchereau de la Ferté. *Les annales de l'Hôtel-Dieu de Québec, 1636–1716*. Edited by Albert Jamet. Quebec City: L'Hôtel-Dieu 1939.

Saint-Vallier, Jean Baptiste de la Croix Chevrières. *Estat présent de l'église et de la colonie francoise dans la Nouvelle France*. Paris, 1688.

– *Rituel du diocèse de Québec*. Paris, 1703.

Shortt, Adam, and Arthur G. Doughty., eds. *Documents Relating to the Constitutional History of Canada 1759–1791*. Ottawa: King's Printer 1918.

Steven, Sylvester K., et al., eds. *Travels in New France by J.C.B.* Harrisburg: Pennsylvania Historical Commission 1941.

Sulte, Benjamin. *Mélanges historiques*. Vol. 19. Montreal: Éditions Edouard Garand 1932.

Talbot, Francis X. *Saint among Savages – the Life of Isaac Jogues*. New York: Harper 1935.

– *Saint among the Hurons – the Life of Jean de Brébeuf*. New York: Harper 1949.

Tanguay, Cyrien. *Dictionnaire généalogique des familles canadiennes depuis la fondation de la colonie jusqu'à nos jours*. 7 vols. Montreal: E. Senécal & Fils 1871–90.

Têtu, H., and C.O. Gagnon, eds. *Mandements, lettres pastorales et circulaires des évêques de Québec*. Vol. 1. Quebec City, 1887.

*The Pearl of Troyes*. Montreal: Canada Print 1878.

Thwaites, Reuben G., ed. *The Jesuit Relations and Allied Documents*. 73 vols. Cleveland: Burrows 1896–1901.

Trigger, Bruce. *The Children of Aataentsic: A History of the Huron People to 1660*. 2 vols. Montreal: McGill-Queen's University Press 1976.

– *The Huron: Farmers of the North*. Toronto: Holt, Rinehart & Winston 1969.

– *Natives and Newcomers: Canada's "Heroic Age" Reconsidered*. Montreal: McGill-Queen's University Press 1985.

Trudel, Marcel. *L'église canadienne sous le régime militaire 1759–1764*. 2 vols. Quebec City: Les Presses universitaires Laval 1957.

– "Les élèves pensionnaires des Ursulines de Québec et les bourses d'étude, 1641–1662." In *Mélanges de civilisation canadienne-française offerts au professeur Paul Wycznski*, 275–91. Ottawa: l'Université d'Ottawa 1977.

Vachon, André. *Histoire du notariat canadien 1621–1960*. Quebec City: Les Presses de l'Université Laval 1962.

Veilleux, Christine. "L'évolution de l'alphabétisation dans le comté de Portneuf, 1690–1849." Master's thesis, Laval University, 1981.

Verrette, Michel. "L'alphabétisation de la population de la ville de Québec de 1750 à 1849." *Revue d'histoire de l'Amérique française* 39 (1985): 51–76.

*Voyage de Pehr Kalm au Canada en 1749*. Edited and translated by Jacques Rousseau and Guy Béthune. Montreal: Pierre Tisseyre 1977.

# Index